# THE WAR TRILOGY

# Roberto Rossellini

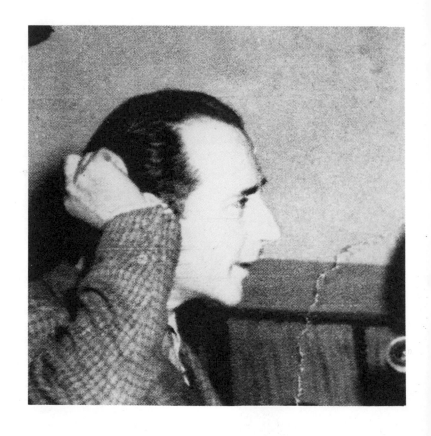

# The War Trilogy

## Open City
## Paisan
## Germany–Year Zero

*Edited and with an introduction by Stefano Roncoroni*

*Translated from the Italian by Judith Green*

*Grossman Publishers    New York    1973*

# Acknowledgments

The editor wishes to thank for their collaboration in this work:

Fernando Di Giammatteo, Leonardo Fioravanti, and Fausto Montesanti of the Experimental Film Center, where the National Film Library is located.

Giacomo Gambetti for permission to compare the prints in the Film Library of Italian State Television.

Tecnostampa for the print of *Germany—Year Zero*.

Leonardo Pescarolo for the moviolas.

Otello Savi for having provided a frame counter. Maria Michi, Jone Tuzi, Renzo Avanzo, and Carlo Lizzani for photographs.

Ken Belton for transcription of the English dialogue. Almuth Brandes Pizzo and Giorgio Manacorda for transcription of the German dialogue.

Giuseppe Ferrara and Ceko Zamurovič for permission to consult and to reprint in part herein their screenplay of *Open City*.

The publishers extend their thanks not only to Roberto Rossellini, but also to Sergio Amidei, Federico Fellini, and Carlo Lizzani for permission to publish the three screenplays in this book, of which they are the joint authors.

# Introduction
# Stefano Roncoroni

Publication of Rossellini has to begin with *Open City,
Paisan* and *Germany—Year Zero (Città Aperta, Paisà,* and
*Germania—Anno Zero)*, which are considered classics of film
history. I enthusiastically accepted the proposal to edit this
volume and to write a brief introduction to these films, for
while I realize that this is an exceptional opportunity to
contribute to a critical discussion of Rossellini, I have no intention of lapsing, as have most critics, into consecration of "this"
Rossellini. I do not believe that Rossellini is the author of
only these three films, and I hope that this book will lead
to the publication of further Rossellini volumes. I feel that
their publication, along with an analysis of Rossellini before
and after these three films, will give a better perspective on
the value of this trilogy.

Basically, the greatest wrong Rossellini has suffered has
been precisely the false perspective in which he has always
been viewed. Film criticism has not ignored Rossellini, but it
has not understood him. The prime culprits responsible for
misleading the critics have been precisely these three films,
which have greatly conditioned the understanding of his subsequent works and have impeded the construction of a correct
overall view.

What the original reviews of the individual films did not
perceive, or expressed only in very general terms, was later reflected in general critiques and monographs, where Rossellini's
development was characterized as a series of twists and turns,

contradictions, capitulations, spiritual involutions, returns to better times, hack work, incompetent narrative, and so forth. The critics gave only token signs of understanding that they ought to have been examining Rossellini's development, instead of remaining anchored to the obviousness and crudity of the works and to the continual, distorting perspective of the search for a masterpiece. This is, in substance, why I believe that all Rossellini criticism that underestimates his work after *Germany—Year Zero* ought not to be taken into consideration.

Rossellini's failure to be published earlier and his substantial unpopularity, particularly among the critics, can be attributed to the failure to recognize his real stylistic and ideological identity, thanks to the continual exploitative tactics of both Marxist and Catholic critics, who have alternately eulogized and repudiated him, from *Open City* to *The Acts of the Apostles*.

*Open City* was an immediate reflection of those dangerous days, made while their impression was still vivid. It was in its very essence traditional cinema, and as an examination of conscience it was wanting in sincerity, insofar as Rossellini was still encumbered with dated, warmed-over ideas and rhetoric left over from his previous work. But the sense of urgency that informed the making of the film resulted in patriotic and populist tones of great sincerity and validity. Those who today find *Open City* inconsistent and confused ought to be aware that this was not due to Rossellini's own inconsistency and confusion, for the film was conditioned by the period in which it was made. The common sense of Amidei and of the other collaborators on the film contributed to the final result no less than did Togliatti's speech at Salerno. Rossellini's search for authenticity was continually impeded, achieved, and contradicted in his drive to make the film at all costs, against everyone and everything.

The most vital critiques, hatred, friendship, judgments, and artistic collaborations of the Italian cinema converged on this film, a key one for Rossellini. It was a real point of departure. Its lack of success in Italy, its subsequent sale to the Americans, and its success in New York led Rossellini to shift his goals and their formulation in his next film, *Paisan*.

The overall unity of *Paisan* demonstrates the validity of the choice of episodes among those proposed during the writing of the script (see, for example, the episode rejected in favor of the present sixth one, cited by Baldelli), and Rossellini's practical sense and artistic intuition. *Paisan* also confirms the idea that the ideological dimension must be reached through analysis of style, not simply of content. Rossellini accentuates his artistic egotism, tries to be himself, realizes himself in his films, tries to film his states of mind, and utilizes ideologies, power, dollars, religion, without selling his soul to any of these. His redemption occurs at the level of the work.

*Germany—Year Zero* is the last act of the confession: it is acceptance in full of the drama, which therefore occurs later, when things have already changed, when the politics of "washing dirty linen" has already begun. The tragedy is therefore set in Germany but inspired by a possible Italian experience of Rossellini's son Romano, who died prematurely. Far from being a surrender, *Germany—Year Zero* is one of the high points of Rossellini's art and anticipates in its style a religious spirituality. It is at once a point of arrival and of departure; it is the story of Marcello in *Open City*, with the sequence of Joe and Carmela in the first episode of *Paisan*. The later films—*Francesco, Giullare di Dio; Europe 1951; Voyage in Italy; Fear*— are born of the premises laid in this trilogy of war.

I might have begun this introduction with the fact that Rossellini is the only director of value whose career covers a very long period in the history of Italian cinema, throughout which he has contributed fundamental works. He is also the only one who has managed to link the Fascist period to the Republican. These films automatically break Rossellini's work into three parts, in a schematic and empirically rough way. An understanding of his work during the Fascist period is necessary for an understanding of his subsequent activity, not only from a stylistic point of view, but also for a comparison between the two ideologies—between the results of that formalistic type of cinema, with its pretty exterior and its lack of content, and those of the neorealistic cinema.

The films presented here, which are far from being Rossellini's only positive results, can also take on new value if compared and related to his subsequent films. If publication of these screenplays is followed by that of his other fine films, it will be easier to see how Rossellini clearly represents the highest artistic emanation of the Italian bourgeoisie, how its political and ideological progress is represented in his work, even at the biographical level, at least from the time the cinema, and now television, was chosen as its medium of expression. Symbolically, psychoanalytically, and sociologically, his films mirror the myths, problems, illusions, and contradictions of a respectable, bourgeois Italy, which never really found itself understood and explained in official manifestations—films, novels, social, or political structures.

Only with this suggestive working hypothesis, I believe, can we explain more coherently those continual contradictions and involutions for which the critics have always reproached Rossellini. More than the other great directors, he veered with all the deepest oscillations of Italian society, from *The White Ship* to *Open City*, from *Paisan* to *Francesco, Giullare di Dio*, to instructional cinema and the consequent transition to government television, "where the margins of liberty are wider." But while he has always been sensitive to what the power choices of his class would be, he always viewed these problematically, always redeemed them in his conception of the cinema, and remained always firmly anchored in a "cinéma d'auteur," of ideas, of demonstration.

A geometrical metaphor for Rossellini's progress may be found without difficulty: not a straight line but a parallel. By this I mean that Rossellini has had a linear development, consequential and not causal, with some curves and tortuous windings, but always parallel to its subject-object, the other parallel, though with some degree of autonomy in determining the distance between them. While I do not claim to illuminate anything with this working hypothesis, I am increasingly convinced that it is the means by which Rossellini criticism can be freed from the shallows in which it is presently stranded. It may also help to improve our capacity to theorize on an operative level and to introduce into film criticism the extremely banal working principle that, while a film must be analyzed concretely for a correct "reading," its author's intentions and the historical situation in which he conceived and realized it must also be evaluated. I shall go no further than this simple hypothesis, for fear of falling into pseudohistoricism, but it could serve as a guide, especially for deciphering the dialogues of these three films.

The screenplays should be considered as a whole, and the progression from one to the next seen as continuous. A screenplay, however, is only partial and tendentious description, and in the last analysis it is an ineffective working instrument if read apart from constant comparison with the film. I would hope that as a result of reading this book, the reader would be moved not so much to see these three films again, but rather to see or see again Rossellini's other films, and that he would feel the need for the fullest possible knowledge of all the phases, high and low, of Rossellini's work, so as to comprehend the continuity and significance of his thought.

# The Intelligence of the Present
# Roberto Rossellini

In all honesty, I must say that my recollection of these three films is very dim. I know that I made them, of course, but I could not, if asked, reconstruct them—explain how they begin, develop, and end—because I have always tended to free myself of all that I have done. When I make a film, I can see it fifteen, twenty, or a hundred times (though this is not so for all of them). Then, suddenly, I cannot bear to see it again. Now, when invited to a showing of one of my films, I wait out in the lobby until it is over. I do not have the strength to watch it. It has been many years now since I have seen *Open City*, *Paisan*, and *Germany—Year Zero*, which explains why I have no very clear memory of them. At most I may have some sentimental memories; and yet even this is not quite so, for basically it is everyday feelings that mostly occupy me.

However, while I may not remember these films, I am fully convinced that there is a logical connection between them and all my subsequent work. The things that have always interested me are closely interlinked; and, after all, I am still the same person acting, dreaming, becoming concerned and impassioned. So, appearances to the contrary, I believe there is no substantial difference between these films and the didactic television documentaries such as *The Rise of Louis XIV* or *Man's Struggle for Survival*. *Open City* and *Paisan* were also didactic, and even *Germany—Year Zero* was didactic, because

I was making an effort—I am quite sure of this—to under-stand events that had involved me personally, and that had overwhelmed me. They were explorations of historical facts, but more particularly of attitudes, of types of behavior deter-mined by a particular historical climate or situation.

Even at that time I felt a need to orient myself properly in order to understand things, and this is just what moves me even today: taking the phenomenon as my point of departure and exploring it, to discover all its consequences, including the political ones. I have never taken the consequences themselves as the point of departure, and I have never wished to demon-strate anything, but simply to observe, to contemplate reality objectively and morally, trying to explore it in such a way as to discover a number of facts from which one could draw certain conclusions.

I firmly believe that all the misunderstanding that arose, during that period of Italian cinema in which realism (or neo-realism, as it was called) was identified with social realism, had its origin in precisely this difference in points of de-parture. Some people shared my own attitude, while others set off from the opposite position, from an ideology that they accepted freely enough, and that then constituted the filter through which they viewed everything.

*Open City* and *Paisan* were films intended to represent a sort of balance sheet of that period of history, of those twenty years of Fascism that ended with the great drama of the war, fruit of something that had been much stronger than us and had overwhelmed, crushed, and implicated us. Once the balance sheet had been drawn up, perhaps we could start with a fresh page.

My desire to study this phenomenon led me to an interest in many others, for the world does not consist only of the phenomenon of the Resistance. And for better or worse, the things I looked at and explored afterward were linked to what was happening after the Resistance, to what was born of the Resistance. What happened after the Resistance? Reconstruc-tion: the reconstruction of the state, the republic. There were men who now had to deal with life on completely new terms. My interest turned to them, but it was the same interest as I had had in these two films. Thus *Germany—Year Zero* was born, and all my other films.

Today the crisis of the cinema may not be fatal, for the simple reason that we are living in an era characterized by the image, and the cinema is image par excellence. I feel that this crisis is not due, as many think, to the bicycle, the motorcycle, the car, the motorboat, or television. These are all superficial excuses. The fact is that the cinema has lost vitality because it has become confused. Experimentation, which ought to be the most precious thing for a new art form like the cinema, is stifled at birth by critics and by those who make films. This I know from forty years of personal experience in the cinema world. The critics have always been against the young and the experimenters—an attitude substantially the same today as in the past. When every reflection turns to insult, into cries of outrage because the established patterns have not been followed, because the timetable has not been respected, confusion is bound to ensue, and with it immense damage to the cinema.

In a world where it is increasingly difficult to orient oneself, this continual, almost maniacal attack on novelty—this process of destruction, which chips away at experimentation, demolishes and drags it into the mud—begins to limit subject matter, language, and eventually everything. This attitude is totally inconsistent, for where has it been said, where is there a rule, that a person must make a masterpiece every day, and what does it mean to make a masterpiece? The important thing is that a person try to make something, that he try to broaden his consciousness and strengthen his adherence to reality, that he try to understand and comprehend reality. And when I say "reality"—one can adhere even to the imagination, for the imagination is part of reality too.

The result today is that the cinema treats three or four subjects, because dramatically there are no more than three or four, though from time to time there are variations arising from contingent political facts. However, these concern the political fact, not the overall phenomenon of the world. There is the war in Vietnam, so we have the Vietnam war seen through Freud, sex, violence. Everything is always explained with those three or four formulas because today the modes of discussion have been reduced to just a few. What we have not yet achieved is a vision of the phenomenon in itself; nor a sense of the value that the image could have for orienting ourselves in a world in which it is increasingly difficult to do so. I believe that this paucity of cinematic themes today—this empty virtuosity, this schematization and oversimplification of problems—all this is a truly anguishing situation.

It was precisely to escape this anguish that I gradually set out to study certain particular things. But not through the books that treat them: they've been worn out by continual use and have themselves contributed handsomely to mythicizing these themes. Thus by chance, as soon as I began to explore, I realized that things were infinitely more complex, and that to "know" meant to know infinitely more than this.

With this, I do not mean to say that I "know," because I have an extremely clear idea of what should be known and what is not known. If we examine the general phenomenon of the world, we must realize that the war in Vietnam is the result, not the phenomenon; it is an incident of the phenomenon in the overall structure. If we look at it in political terms, it is clear what kind of reasoning must follow. But if we look at it in terms of the phenomenon, obviously the perspective becomes altogether different. As the years pass, I realize more and more that I want to deepen my exploration, taking the overall phenomenon, not its results, as my point of departure.

It is very clear that we live in a complicated period, one that becomes more complicated every day. If we want to follow it as conscientious men, as normally intelligent men, we must at least be informed of what is happening, and we must seek its significance, albeit imperfectly. But if one undertakes to understand the phenomenon, if one makes the effort to delineate it, even very sketchily, then judgment clearly becomes more precise; it is based upon intelligence, and no longer simply upon moods and sentiments.

This is the spirit that informs the type of cinema I am doing now, but the point of departure is the same as in the past; the exploration is just infinitely more vast. I have been asked what these three films bring back to me, what they represent for me. The fact that I have not spoken of them in this introduction is symptomatic. They were experiences, of course; all of them were experiences I had to go through. But I do not have a real memory of them because it has been pulverized by events. This is why these films set me to talking about what I am doing today. And while I am pleased to know that the screenplays of *Open City, Paisan,* and *Germany—Year Zero* are being published, I do not think it a worldly or superficial pleasure, for I have always fought for the things I have done and thought, and consequently have sometimes had to bear the burden of hasty incomprehension. But this has not made me give up my ideals and my struggle. Quite the contrary.

# A Note on the Screenplays

Since the working scripts of these three films are no longer in existence, and since the various prints in circulation are in a rather poor state, I have tried to reconstruct the original by comparing a series of prints. These have all turned out to be incomplete, lacking groups of scenes or single shots at the beginning and end of reels, or with frames missing due to rips and tears. Particularly to further the critical purposes outlined here, the greatest effort was made to decipher and faithfully transcribe the dialogue. Partly because of the state of the prints, and partly because many changes were made in the dialogue during editing (more than are normally made for other films), the soundtrack is sometimes not perfectly synchronized and becomes incomprehensible.

In transcribing the "action track" of the screenplays, I felt it critically correct to integrate the action of the characters as much as possible with the movements of the camera. As a result, the description is somewhat awkward and arid, but those not interested in the technical description may skip it.

The illustrations are all taken from the original shots of the films, though I was not always free to choose, and not all the sequences I should have liked to document could be illustrated. My choices were greatly restricted by the state of the prints at my disposition, and by technical requirements. Despite variations in the choice of photographs, they do convey what I wanted to illustrate in terms of the costumes and settings.

For *Open City* and *Paisan*—these prints were the most

damaged and incomplete—I have calculated the number of frames in each shot and its duration.

The difficulties were greatest for *Open City*. In mid-April of 1968, the Italian newspapers reported that the original copy had been sold to West Germany. It seemed that only the mutilated prints in circulation remained in Italy, and that the only way to reconstruct the original screenplay was to compare several prints. For the screenplay given here, the following were used: a print conserved in the Film Library of Italian State Television; two prints conserved in the National Film Library; a print normally in circulation; a screenplay published in *L'Avant-Scène*; and the unpublished screenplay edited some years ago, from a print different from mine, by Ceko Zamurovič and Giuseppe Ferrara. One negative of the original—saved with difficulty from the German sale—does exist in the National Film Library, but owing to lack of funds a copy was not yet printed.

For *Paisan*, one print in the Film Library of the Italian State Television, two in the National Film Library, and another normally in circulation were compared.

For *Germany—Year Zero*, I used one print in the National Film Library and another owned by Tecnostampa. Since the prints were identical, I have not given the figures for the number of frames and duration.

S.R.

# Abbreviations Used in the Text

ECU      Extreme close-up
CU      Close-up
MCU      Medium close-up
MS      Medium shot
MLS      Medium long shot
LS      Long shot
ELS      Extreme long shot
FS      Full shot
WF      Whole figure
TQ      Three-quarter view
HF      Half figure
RA      Reverse angle of previous shot, unless otherwise noted

Note: The figures at the right margin of *Open City* and *Paisan* indicate: the shot sequence number; the number of frames in the shot; and the number of minutes (where applicable), seconds, and twenty-fourths of seconds (film speed being twenty-four frames per second). For *Germany—Year Zero* only the shot sequence number is given.

# Open City (1945)

# Contents

# Credits

Presented by Minerva Films

Production by Excelsa Films

Scenario and script by Sergio Amidei, in collaboration with
    Federico Fellini
Directed by Roberto Rossellini
Photography by Ubaldo Arata
Music by Renzo Rossellini, conducted by L. Ricci

*Cast:*

| | |
|---|---|
| *Marcello* | Vito Annichiarico |
| *Sexton* | Nando Bruno |
| *Don Pietro* | Aldo Fabrizi |
| *Bergmann* | Harry Feist |
| *Francesco* | F. Grand-Jacquet |
| *Pina* | Anna Magnani |
| *Marina* | Maria Michi |
| *Manfredi* | Marcello Pagliero |
| *Police Sergeant* | Eduardo Passanelli |
| *Commissioner of Police* | Carlo Sindaci |
| *The Austrian* | Akos Tolnay |
| *Hartmann* | Joop Van Hulzen |

The facts and characters of this film, while based on the tragic and heroic events during nine months of Nazi occupation, are imaginary, and any resemblance to actual facts and characters is purely coincidental.

*(Camera pans left from the Pincian Hill over the rooftops of Rome. A German military song fades in over the background music.)*

Freunde-Bergischer Wald
mit den Berger Fräulein ist
Dein Heimatland
Heimatland
Sei gelobt Du roter Adler . . .

Under
Credits:
13″18

*(The Piazza di Spagna at night, FS; the Spanish Steps and the church of Santa Trinità dei Monti seen from Via Condotti.)* 1:163-6″19

*A German patrol marches across the piazza from the left to right. Music begins.*

GERMAN PATROL, *singing*:
Hoch über Sturmbaudland
Hoch über dunklen Wäldern
Heil dir mein Bergeburger Land . . .
*(Dissolve to . . .*

*(Patrol crossing the piazza, LS; camera pans right.)* 2:326-13″14

GERMAN PATROL:
Hoch über dunklen Wäldern
Heil dir mein Bergeburger Land . . .
*(Dissolve to . . .*

*(German Red Cross truck driving across the piazza, early dawn, LS; camera pans right after it.)* 3:474-19″18

*The truck stops. Five soldiers jump out, run over to a building, and knock violently on the door. Music ends.*

*(The balcony of an apartment, MLS)* 4:292-12″4

*After a moment, a shutter opens and an elderly servant, Nannina, looks out. The knocking on the door merges with the voice of the Radio London announcer, which can be dimly heard from inside the apartment. Music begins.*

RADIO *(off screen)*: London calling Italy. The voice of
London.

*(Camera subjective from Nannina's viewpoint, LS; the*    5:38-1"14
*soldiers climbing out of the ambulance.)*

*(The balcony, MLS)*    6:101-4"5

NANNINA, *closing the shutter*: Oh, dear God!

*(Wipe to right)*

*(Terrace of the apartment, where Manfredi lives.)*    7:83-3"11

*Manfredi pulls on his jacket as he opens the terrace door.*
*He runs off screen to right (camera pans slightly right*
*after him).*

*(RA)*    8:126-5"6
*Manfredi runs across the terrace (camera pans right after*
*him) and stops at the skylight over the stairway. (FS)*

*Crouching down, Manfredi peers through the skylight.*    9:26-1"2
*(HF)*

*(Stairway, WF; Insert: German soldiers)*    10:77-3"5

*A German soldier rings the doorbell.*

*Manfredi (HF) straightens up and*    11:66-2"18

*runs across the terrace (camera pans left after him). He*    12:254-10"4
*clambers over a parapet and disappears. The church of*
*Santa Trinità dei Monti is in the background.*

*In the corridor of the apartment (FS), Nannina runs to-*    13:749-31"5
*ward the door on which the soldiers are knocking. Before*
*opening the door, she turns on the light and crosses*
*herself (camera adjusts slightly to right).*

NANNINA: I'm coming, I'm coming! Oh, dear God!

*She opens the door as the landlady hurries down the hall. The three German soldiers enter. The first has his submachine gun at the ready.*

NANNINA: Oh!

GERMAN OFFICER: Where's Giorgio Manfredi?

NANNINA: He's not here.

GERMAN OFFICER: Where is he?

LANDLADY: We don't know. He doesn't always sleep here.

GERMAN OFFICER: Where does he go?

LANDLADY: I don't know. You know these young bachelors . . .

GERMAN OFFICER: Which way is his room?

LANDLADY: Over that way.

GERMAN OFFICER, *to soldiers*: Wir wollen noch durchsuchen. [Let's have a look.]

*The landlady and the officer go off screen to right, and as the other two soldiers start down the other side of the hall, Nannina closes the door.*

*(Manfredi's room, WF)*                    14:775-32"7

*The officer enters the room from the left, followed by the landlady, who turns on the light.*

GERMAN OFFICER: Does he have many visitors?

LANDLADY: He used to, but . . . no one's come for a long time now.

GERMAN OFFICER: Mm, of course not.

*The officer (HF) goes over to the dresser and searches through the top drawer. Finding nothing, he goes to the*

LANDLADY, *softly, to Nannina:* Remember, keep calm.

NANNINA: Dear God. . . .

*(Terrace of Manfredi's building, WF)*          25:323-13″11

*Submachine guns at the ready, the Germans come forward (to HF) and go off screen. The two women can be seen behind them.*

*The officer is leaning against the parapet, looking out*    26:63-2″15
*over it. (HF)*

*(Camera, subjective from officer's viewpoint, pans down-*    27:66-2″18
*ward from the roof to a courtyard, LS)*

*The officer turns. (HF)*                  28:31-1″7

*(WF; resume on officer's turn; a soldier is behind the*    29:143-5″23
*two women.)*

GERMAN OFFICER: Who lives there?

LANDLADY: That's the Spanish Embassy.

GERMAN OFFICER, *turning back to the other building*:
     Ah. . . .

*(Dissolve to . . .*

*(Gestapo Headquarters at night; insert of a map of Rome,*    30:376-15″16
*on which an officer's hand indicates various points;
camera pulls back.)*

*Major Bergmann (HF) is talking to the Italian Police
Commissioner. (TQ)*

BERGMANN *(off screen)*: The city will be divided into
     fourteen sectors. The Schröder plan *(on screen)*,
     which we have already applied in several European
     cities, allows us to comb through large masses of
     people scientifically, using the minimum effort.

POLICE COMMISSIONER *(listening deferentially)*: Aah!

*The two men turn as they hear someone knocking at the door.*

*The door opens and Krammer, Bergmann's aide, enters and salutes. (TQ)*  31:136-5"16·

BERGMANN *(off screen)*: Herein. [Come in.]

KRAMMER: Herr Sturmbannführer, Offizier Bauer hat telefonisch mitgeteilt . . . [Major, Sergeant Bauer's telephoned . . .]

*The major and the Police Commissioner are in front of the map.*  32:95-3"23

KRAMMER *(off screen)*: . . . die betreffenden Personen nicht gefunden zu haben. [. . . the persons they were looking for have not been found.]

BERGMANN: Nein! . . . Seltsam! [No! Strange!]

KRAMMER: Es wohnen dort zwei Frauen, die Wirtin und das Dienstmädchen. Sollen sie herbeigeführt werden, Herr Sturmbannführer? [There are two women living there, the landlady and a servant. Do you want us to bring them in, major?]  33:105-4"9

BERGMANN *(waving Krammer out)*: Nein, nicht nötig. Danke. [No, that's not necessary. Thanks.]  34:65-2"17

*Krammer salutes and goes out, walking backward. (TQ)*  35:60-2"12

*Bergmann comes over to the desk (camera pans right). The Police Commissioner follows him, comes on screen, and stops on the other side of the desk (camera pulls back briefly).*  36:483-20"3

POLICE COMMISSIONER *(off screen)* : Bad news?

BERGMANN: Someone who didn't show up for an appointment.

POLICE COMMISSIONER: Someone important?

BERGMANN: Hm. I hope so. *He takes some photographs from a drawer and shows them to the Police Commissioner.* You know them?

*(Insert: a photograph of Manfredi and Marina on the Spanish Steps; part of the Police Commissioner's left hand is included in the framing.)*   37:44-1"20

BERGMANN: Please sit down.

*The two men sit down.*   38:79-3"7

POLICE COMMISSIONER: No. Who are they?

*(Resume on Bergmann sitting down, HF)*   39:67-2"19

BERGMANN: He calls himself Manfredi, an engineer.

POLICE COMMISSIONER *(off screen)*: Manfredi?

BERGMANN: Precisely.

POLICE COMMISSIONER, *obsequiously (HF)*: We have some- 40:142-5″22
thing on that name. He seems to be one of the
military leaders of the National Liberation Committee.

BERGMANN, *confidently (HF)*: I have good reason to 41:78-3″6
believe it's the same man.

POLICE COMMISSIONER: But how did you people catch up 42:58-2″10
with him?

BERGMANN: I met him right here, on this desk. Every 43:365-15″5
afternoon I take a long walk through the streets of
Rome, but without stepping out of my office. . . .
*Pleased with himself, he fiddles with the photographs.*
I'm extremely fond of this type of photograph,
which takes people almost by surprise.

*The Police Commissioner is listening attentively. (HF)* 44:70-2″22

BERGMANN *(off screen)*: One meets such interesting people.

*He opens a drawer on his left and takes out more photo-* 45:348-14″12
*graphs. (HF)*

BERGMANN: Not very long ago, for example, I met this
Mr. Manfredi and his little girl friend. I said to myself, "I've seen this face somewhere before."

*The major stands up and hands the Police Commissioner* 46:171-7″3
*a photograph and a magnifying glass, then sits on the*
*edge of the desk. (TQ)*

BERGMANN: Take a look at this group, for example—the
second from the left. I've received these photographs
from Berlin.

*(Insert of two photographs, with part of the Commis-* 47:86-3″14
*sioner's hand showing; as the lens moves slowly, an*
*enlarged detail from the first photograph is shown, then*
*one from the second, which is of a group of soldiers.)*

BERGMANN *(off screen)*: I believe I'm not mistaken. You agree?

*The Commissioner continues to peer through the lens, while Bergmann, still perched on the desk, smiles with satisfaction. (TQ)*     48:240-10″

POLICE COMMISSIONER: Of course you're not! It's him! It's the same person!

*A tortured prisoner screams off screen. The two men turn toward the sound. The major rings the bell on his desk.*

BERGMANN: Oh, how annoying! Excuse me a moment . . .

POLICE COMMISSIONER: Go right ahead.

*The door opens and a soldier enters, salutes, and awaits orders. (TQ)*     49:106-4″10

BERGMANN: Was soll dieser Lärm bedeuten, Müller? [What's all this noise, Müller?]     50:37-1″13

MÜLLER, *at attention (TQ)*: Ich bitte um Verzeihung, Herr Sturmbannführer, die verhören jenen Professor, aber— [I'm sorry, sir, we're questioning that professor, but—]     51:92-3″20

BERGMANN, *interrupting him*: Schon gut, er soll aber endlich schweigen. [All right, but keep him quiet!]     52:41-1″17

*Bergmann starts to stand up, facing the Commissioner (HF; camera tilts up).*     53:48-2″

BERGMANN, *scornfully*: How much screaming these . . .

*The Commissioner, still seated, tries to change the subject. (HF from above)*     54:96-4″

BERGMANN *(off screen)*: . . . Italians do.

POLICE COMMISSIONER: Mm . . . and who's the girl?

BERGMANN, *standing (HF)*: She's called Marina Mari, a music-hall girl.     55:86-3″14

POLICE COMMISSIONER: Ah, yes, I know her. I've seen her.　56:109-4″13
A pretty girl.

BERGMANN: Very pretty.　57:35-1″11

*(Dissolve to . . .*

*(Street, FS)*　58:151-6″7

*Several dozen women and children are converging on and raiding a bakery. In the confusion a police sergeant gives up trying to defend the store, steps to one side, and, lifting up his cap, wipes his forehead. Agostino, the sexton, comes up to him.*

SERGEANT: Take it easy, hold it there! Ugh! I can't stand it.

*The sergeant and Agostino chat against the background*　59:227-9″11
*of the store. (MS)*

AGOSTINO: What's going on here?

SERGEANT: You can see for yourself. They've raided the bakery.

AGOSTINO: What're you doing about it?

SERGEANT: Unfortunately I'm in uniform.

BAKER *(off screen)*: Sergeant, sergeant!

SERGEANT, *turning toward the crowd*: What do they want?

*Shouting, the crowd masses under the windows of the*　60:78-3″6
*baker's house, where the baker and his wife are trying to calm them down. (FS)*

*The sergeant and the sexton (backs to camera) watch the*　61:471-19″15
*raid, then turn away. (WF)*

SERGEANT, *to baker*: I can't do a thing, this is a riot. *To Agostino*: I'm helpless!

AGOSTINO: I know, I know—*The noise of the crowd covers their words.*—but a hundred grams a day!

*A woman comes on screen from right with her shopping bag full.*

FIRST WOMAN, *to sergeant*: The dirty skunk, he even had pastry! Look here!

SERGEANT: Oh, this is serious.

ANOTHER WOMAN: And he said he had no flour!

*Agostino takes a pastry from the first woman's bag and takes a bite.*

AGOSTINO: Yum. . . .

FIRST WOMAN: Hey, Agostino, why don't you go get some yourself?

AGOSTINO: I can't, I'm a sexton. I'd end up in Hell!

FIRST WOMAN, *snatching the pastry from the sexton's mouth*: Then you'll eat your cake in Paradise!

*The other woman laughs (FS). Both go off screen to right (camera adjusts left to the others).*

*(Camera pans slightly left, continuing the previous shot, HF)*    62:338-14″2

*A pregnant young woman, Pina, makes her way out of the noisy crowd raiding the bakery. She picks up a small loaf of bread she has lost in the shuffle. The sergeant comes on screen heading toward her (WF), and helps her out of the crowd. Her shopping bag is full of bread, which she protects from the eager hands of the other women.*

PINA: Leave it alone!

SERGEANT: But, Miss Pina, this is a crazy thing to be doing in your condition!

PINA: I'm supposed to die of hunger?

*Someone, probably the baker's wife, shouts for help through the noise of the crowd.*

BAKER'S WIFE *(off screen)*: Sergeant, help!

PINA, *to baker's wife*: Go hang yourself!

SERGEANT, *to Pina*: I'll see you home.

*They go off screen to right. (HF)*

*Agostino casts his eyes up to the heavens, crosses himself, and makes ready to enter the bakery (HF). The raiders are already drawing off (camera pans to right, following him).*   63:136-5″16

VOICES SHOUTING: Bread, bread, bread, we want bread! *(Wipe to right)*

*(Street in front of Pina's building, FS)*   64:578-24″2

*Pina walks beside the sergeant, who is carrying her bag.*

*They stop (TQ) and he hands it back to her.*

SERGEANT: Here we are!

PINA: Thanks a lot.

SERGEANT: My duty! Shall I take it up for you?

PINA: No.

SERGEANT: It's heavy. . . .

*Pina glances at him, then takes out two rolls, which she gives to him.*

PINA: This'll make it lighter.

SERGEANT: I really shouldn't, but I've been starving!

*They move on together toward Pina's building (camera*

*pans to right after them).*

SERGEANT: Miss Pina, what do you think, do these Americans really exist?

*Pina stops to look at the bombed-out building behind her.*

*(The bombed-out building, FS; camera subjective from Pina's viewpoint.)*     65:52-2"4

PINA *(off screen)*: It looks that way.

SERGEANT *(off screen)*: Right!

*As they approach the entrance of Pina's building a man*     66:52-2"4 *comes toward them.*

MAN, *stopping them (HF):* Hey, Miss Pina, you want some    67:298-12″10
eggs at sixteen?

PINA: Forget it!

SERGEANT: How dare you! In my presence! This is the
black market!

PINA, *laughing:* Don't worry about it, sergeant, save your
breath. So long!

MAN: So long.
*(Wipe to left)*

*(Stairway of Pina's building, WF)*    68:157-6″13

*Pina (seen from above) is climbing the stairs as two little
boys run down. Pina (TQ) looks up and sees a man standing on the landing.*

PINA: Who're you looking for?

*The man is Manfredi. (TQ from below)*    69:61-2″13

MANFREDI: Excuse me, does Francesco, the printer, live
here?

*Pina continues up the stairs. (TQ from above)*    70:40-1″16

PINA: Yes, but he's away now.

MANFREDI, *approaching Pina (TQ):* You don't happen to    71:30-1″6
know where he went?

PINA, *continuing up the stairs (TQ):* How should I know?    72:40-1″16
That's his business!

MANFREDI: Excuse me, but who are you?    73:35-1″11

PINA: Excuse me, what's it to you?

*Pina (WF from above) comes toward Manfredi (up to    74:891-37″3
TQ), stopping on the next-to-last step. Manfredi comes*

*over to her (camera adjusts slightly to right).*

MANFREDI: Ah, I see. You're Miss Pina!

PINA, *going up the last step*: How do you know?

MANFREDI: Francesco's always talking about you.

PINA: Oh, then you—

MANFREDI, *interrupting her*: A friend.

PINA: Oh, what a goose I am! I thought you were a cop!

MANFREDI: I noticed.

PINA: What can I do for you?

MANFREDI: I'd like to get into Francesco's place.

PINA: I'll open up right away. I'll get my key. Here it is.

*Pina goes to her door. Manfredi remains alone. Two girls pass by him as they go up the stairs, carrying a demijohn of wine. Pina comes out of her doorway without her coat. She closes the door behind her and goes toward Francesco's door (camera pans left with her, TQ).*

PINA, *walking*: I'm sorry, I couldn't find the key. Go right in.

*Pina unlocks the door. Manfredi enters first, removing his hat.*

PINA: After you . . .

MANFREDI: Thanks.

*(Room in Francesco's apartment, TQ)*      75:424-17″16

*Manfredi waits while Pina closes the door.*

PINA: It's a mess in here, but it's really impossible—

MANFREDI, *interrupting*: No, no, don't bother, it doesn't matter. Look, do you know Don Pietro?

PINA: Of course.

MANFREDI: The priest of San Clemente. I'd like to talk to him.

PINA: I'll go get him.

MANFREDI: No, no, no. Not you!

PINA: I'll send my boy, all right?

MANFREDI: Yes, that would be better.

PINA: Then wait for me in there.

*Manfredi goes into the room Pina indicates as she starts to go out the door.*

*(Stairway of Pina's building, TQ)*      76:123-5″3

*Pina goes to the banister (camera pans slightly right) and calls upstairs.*

PINA: Marcello, Marcello!

*(Top flight of stairs, WF)*      77:97-4″1

*Pina's son, Marcello, wearing a soldier's cap, opens the*

roof door and comes down a few steps (camera pans left). He leans over the banister. (TQ)

PINA (off screen): Marcello!

MARCELLO: What d'you want?

PINA: Come down here a minute!                                  78:29-1″5

(Camera subjective from Pina's viewpoint, looking up,     79:113-4″17
FS)

MARCELLO: I can't.

PINA (off screen): You've got to go to Don Pietro. Hurry
up!

MARCELLO: I'm busy.

PINA, angrily (TQ): Come right down here, I said!          80:44-1″20

MARCELLO, starting down stairs reluctantly: Darn it!      81:67-2″19

Pina awaits Marcello, who appears on screen as he comes     82:318-13″6
down the stairs. (WF)

PINA: I told you a thousand times not to go up to Romoletto's. It's dangerous. You've got to go to Don Pietro.
Hurry up!

MARCELLO: What am I supposed to tell him?

PINA, straightening his cap: Tell him to come here right
away. And make it snappy. And don't fool around on
the way either.

Marcello goes on down with a long face while Pina goes
back into Francesco's apartment (camera pans left after
her).

(Francesco's apartment, TQ)                                     83:68-2″20

Pina crosses the room (camera pans right) and enters the
next room.

*Pina goes over to the bed (TQ; camera pans right) and*   84:292-12″4
*begins to straighten it. Manfredi follows her, coming on*
*screen from right, crossing in front of the camera, and*
*going off screen to left.*

PINA: He's left. Don Pietro'll be here soon.

MANFREDI *(off screen)*: Oh, thanks.

PINA: This morning we raided a bakery.

MANFREDI: Really?

PINA: It's the second one this week.

MANFREDI *(off screen)*: How are the women?

*Pina turns toward Manfredi.*

*Manfredi listens to Pina, his back to a window. (HF)*   85:66-2″16

PINA *(off screen)*: Well, some of them do know why
 they're doing it . . .

PINA, *looking toward Manfredi (HF)*: . . . but most of   86:184-7″16
 them just grab as much bread as they can. And this
 morning somebody filched a pair of shoes and a scale.

*The angry voice of Pina's sister, Laura, is heard from*
*Pina's apartment.*

LAURA *(off screen)*: I'd like to know who filched . . .

*Manfredi turns to see who is talking (TQ). Behind him is*   87:28-1″4
*a map of the Rome region.*

LAURA: . . . my stockings!

PINA, *going off screen to left (HF)*: Excuse me . . .   88:44-1″20

*Laura (WF), in dishabille, enters the room (camera pulls*   89:451-18″19
*back to reveal Pina and Manfredi, HF). Laura comes for-*
*ward and stops beside Pina. (HF)*

LAURA, *to Pina*: It must have been you. . . . *She stops in surprise as she notices Manfredi.* Oh, Mr. Manfredi!

MANFREDI *(off screen)*: Hello, Laura.

LAURA, *embarrassed*: Hello! How come you're here? You came to look for me?

MANFREDI: Yes, yes. Actually—

PINA: I met this gentleman on the stairs. I let him in here. I thought that—

LAURA: You could have told me right away!

PINA: Well, I was just about to come back. Take it easy!

MANFREDI: It doesn't matter. I just wanted to ask a favor.

LAURA, *embarrassed, trying to straighten her clothes*: I'll go put something on. . . .

MANFREDI: No, you're perfectly all right that way. *To Pina*: Excuse us a moment, Pina.

PINA: Of course.

*Manfredi takes Laura's arm and goes off screen to left.*

MANFREDI *(off screen)*: Listen, Lauretta, you see Marina, don't you?

*Pina remains alone.*

*Laura and Manfredi are near the window. (HF)*  90:228-9"12

LAURA: Yes, in the afternoon, at the cabaret.

MANFREDI: Well, would you please tell her that I won't be able to see her for a few days? I'll phone her if I can.

LAURA: All right. Anything else?

MANFREDI: No, nothing else.

LAURA, *taking Manfredi's hand*: Good-bye, Mr. Manfredi.

I have to go.

*Laura and Manfredi shake hands (WF). As Laura goes*    91:578-24″2
*off screen to right, Manfredi comes forward (camera pans*
*slightly to left, to include Pina, TQ).*

MANFREDI: She lives with you?

PINA: She's my sister.

MANFREDI: Oh, your sister?

PINA, *picking up a jacket and a towel from a chair*: That
   surprises you, doesn't it? Who knows what kind of
   lies she's told you, that she lives goodness knows
   where, eh? She's ashamed of us because she says she's
   an artist while we're just poor working women. But
   I wouldn't change places with her!

MANFREDI: Ah, I understand you.

PINA: Not because she's bad. She's stupid!

*Pina goes off screen with the clothes as Manfredi watches*
*her (camera pans slightly right). Manfredi remains alone.*

PINA, *putting the jacket in a wardrobe (TQ)*: But how do    92:179-7″11
   you know Lauretta? Oh, I'm sorry, I shouldn't ask.

MANFREDI *(HF)*: No . . . Lauretta's a good friend of a    93:66-2″18
   girl I know.

PINA, *closing the wardrobe (HF)*: Who, Marina?    94:18-0″18

MANFREDI, *interested (HF)*: Oh, you know her?    95:25-1″1

PINA, *still holding the towel (HF)*: Oh, heavens, since she    96:295-12″7
   was born! Her mother was a concierge in Via Tibur-
   tina, where my father had a tinsmith's shop. She and
   Lauretta grew up together, you might say. Oh, but
   please don't tell Marina that. . . . *She hangs the towel*
   *over a screen and goes off screen to left.*

*Pina comes on screen from right. Manfredi is seen in*    97:911-37"23
*profile. (HF)*

PINA: . . . I told you. Please, really.

MANFREDI: No, of course not. And anyway, I'm not going
to see her anymore.

PINA: Why not?

*Pina goes off screen. Manfredi takes out a cigarette.*

MANFREDI: I don't know why, but I have the feeling it's
all over. Anyway, it's already gone on too long.

PINA *(off screen)*: You've known her for a long time?

*She comes back on screen with an ashtray. Manfredi sits
down near the table. She brings the ashtray over to him
(camera pans slightly after her).*

MANFREDI: Yes, it's four months now. I'd just come to
Rome. She used to eat in a little restaurant near the
Piazza di Spagna. One day the air-raid alarm went
off. Everybody else ran for it, but we two stayed
there by ourselves. She was laughing—she wasn't
scared at all.

PINA: So you fell in love with her!

MANFREDI: Happens all the time.

PINA: All the time.

*Manfredi lights the cigarette, then goes over to the
window (TQ; camera pans left after him). He looks out
as he talks.*

MANFREDI: But she's not the right kind of woman for me.
Maybe if I'd known her before, when she lived in
Via Tiburtina.

PINA *(MCU)*: Well, a woman can always change, espe-    98:40-1"16
cially . . .

*Manfredi turns toward Pina and goes up to her (camera*     99:334-13"22
*pans right after him until Pina is included in TQ).*

PINA *(off screen):* . . . when she's in love.

MANFREDI: But what makes you think she's in love?

PINA: Why shouldn't she be? *She changes her tone of*
*voice.* Oh, heavens! I didn't even offer you coffee!
You want some?

MANFREDI: No, don't bother.

PINA: Not at all! Just one minute! I'll put it right on.

*She goes toward the door (camera pans right after her),*
*then stops for a moment.*

PINA: That is, so-called coffee.

*(Courtyard of Don Pietro's church, FS)*                    100:263-
                                                                 10"23
*A group of boys is playing a noisy game of soccer with*
*Don Pietro (the camera pans after them, first left and*
*then right). The boys are shouting. Don Pietro's whistle*
*blows.*

*A group of boys (seen from above) charges the ball. (WF)*   101:38-1"14

*Don Pietro is refereeing the game (FS; camera pans left*    102:99-4"3
*and then right, following the ball's path).*

*Some boys try to hit the ball with their heads. (WF)*       103:47-1"23

DON PIETRO, *shouting:* Cut this business out!

*(Camera pans right and left, following the ball, WF.)*      104:302-
                                                                    12"14
*The boys chase the ball, Don Pietro with them. (FS)*        105:107-4"11

DON PIETRO, *blowing his whistle:* I told you before, no
rough stuff!

*A boy kicks the ball into the air. (WF)*                    106:17-0"17

*Two boys watch the ball (CU); one covers his head with*   107:18-0″18
*his hands, warning Don Pietro.*

BOY: Look out, Don Pietro!

*Don Pietro, surrounded by the boys, waits with closed*   108:50-2″2
*eyes for the ball to land, which it does, right on his head.*
*The boys laugh. (HF)*

*Marcello makes his way through the crowd of boys. (FS)*   109:78-3″6

*Marcello comes on screen from right (TQ), heading for*   110:942-39″6
*Don Pietro, who continues to referee the game. Finally*
*he notices Marcello. They both remove their hats.*

DON PIETRO: Oh, it's you! What a miracle, to see you at
   the oratory!

MARCELLO: I came because my mother sent me.

DON PIETRO: She's right. It'll do you some good too.

MARCELLO: Don Pie', let me finish. She says you should
   come to our place right away. It's important. *(The
   camera follows their movements, panning slightly.)*

DON PIETRO: What is?

MARCELLO: I don't know. She wouldn't tell me. But I
   think there's somebody in Francesco's apartment.

DON PIETRO: Hm, all right. Let's go!

*Don Pietro starts toward the rectory (camera pans left).*
*He turns toward the boys and whistles long and loud,*
*halting the game. Then he hands his whistle to the biggest*
*boy. Marcello runs off screen.*

DON PIETRO: Gilberto. . . . Look—*Turning to another
   boy*—get out of here! *To Gilberto*: Agostino will be
   here soon. You referee. And be good kids, will you?

MARCELLO (off screen): Here, get this one!

DON PIETRO, to Marcello: Come here! Do you always have
   to disappear?

Don Pietro and Marcello go off (camera pans left with
them).

(Dissolve to . . .

(Church of San Clemente)                                  111:378-
                                                             15"18
Music begins. Marcello and Don Pietro pass by the altar
and genuflect briefly. Then they head for the entrance,
going off screen to left.

They stop (backs to camera, WF) at the holy-water font,   112:256-
dip their fingers, and cross themselves. A woman passes      10"16
by in the background. Don Pietro and Marcello go out
of the church (camera pans with them).

(Street in front of Don Pietro's church, LS)              113:189-7"21

Marcello and Don Pietro cross the street, where a few
cars and passersby are seen. A streetcar hides them from
view. The music is covered by the noise of the streetcar.

(Wipe to right)

Marcello and Don Pietro walk along (TQ; camera tracks     114:326-
to right with them).                                         13"14

DON PIETRO: How come you never come to the oratory
   anymore?

MARCELLO: How can a guy go waste time at the oratory,
   the way things are?

DON PIETRO, shocked: What are you saying?

MARCELLO: You're a priest; you can't understand. But we
   have to close ranks against the common enemy.

DON PIETRO, *stopping*: Who's been telling you that kind of stuff?

MARCELLO, *worried (ECU)*: Romoletto.  115:123-5″3

DON PIETRO *(off screen)*: Ah! Romoletto!

MARCELLO: Don Pie', please! Don't tell anybody!

*They start walking again. Marcello indicates the sexton,*  116:54-2″6
*who is coming up to them.*

MARCELLO: Here comes Purgatory!

*The sexton approaches. (WF)*  117:45-1″21

*Don Pietro and Marcello have stopped to wait for the*  118:90-3″18
*sexton. Agostino comes on screen from left, carrying*
*several loaves of bread under his cape.*

AGOSTINO: Oh, Don Pie'!

DON PIETRO, *suspiciously (HF)*: What've you got there?  119:62-2″14

AGOSTINO: I've been shopping.

*(TQ of all three)*  120:206-8″14

MARCELLO: Wow, what a load of bread! Is that your whole ration book?

AGOSTINO: Not even one coupon!

DON PIETRO, *seriously*: How come so much bread?

AGOSTINO: Ah, don't ask me. They were celebrating this morning.

DON PIETRO: What?

*Don Pietro (in profile) scrutinizes the sexton in front of*  121:86-3″14
*him (Marcello's back is to the camera).*

AGOSTINO: I don't know what holiday it was. Not even the

baker knew. Excuse me, Don Pietro, I have to go.

*Agostino hurries off screen to right. Don Pietro, per-* 122:181-7"13
*plexed, starts off again (camera tracks left with him).*
*Marcello follows.*

MARCELLO: I wonder what holiday it was.

DON PIETRO: I don't understand. . . .

MARCELLO: Let's hope my mother heard about it.

*(Francesco's apartment)* 123:700-29"4

*Pina enters with the coffee. She comes toward the table*
*(camera pans left and tracks back to reveal Manfredi*
*sitting there). She pours the coffee into a cup.*

PINA: Here you are. Not very good, but at least it's hot.
Drink it right up.

MANFREDI: Oh, thanks. Francesco told me you two are
getting married.

*Pina places her hands on her belly. Manfredi begins to*
*drink his coffee.*

PINA: A little late, this wedding—in this condition. We'd
settled the date a long time ago, but then for one
reason or another we've always had to postpone it.
But this time it's really settled.

MANFREDI: When'll it be?

PINA: Tomorrow.

MANFREDI: Ah, then I'll have to get you a gift!

*Pina sits down (HF; camera pans down and left to*
*Manfredi).*

PINA: Oh, heavens! This is a wartime wedding. We'll just
run over to Don Pietro's, and it'll be all over in a
minute.

MANFREDI, *drinking his coffee (MCU)*: So you're having a church wedding. . . .                    124:26-1″2

PINA *(MCU)*: Yes. Actually, Francesco didn't want to, but I told him: better for Don Pietro to marry us, at least he's on the right side, rather than go to City Hall and be married by a Fascist. Don't you think so?                    125:240-10″

MANFREDI: In a way, you're right.                    126:33-1″9

PINA: Yes; the truth is that I . . . really believe in God.                    127:116-4″20

MANFREDI: Oh. And what do you do now? You work?                    128:66-2″18

PINA: I did. At the Breda textile machinery plant, but they threw us out. The Germans are taking everything away. . . .                    129:181-7″13

*The doorbell rings.*

*Manfredi starts to get up.*                    130:27-1″3

PINA, *standing up*: It must be Don Pietro.                    131:55-2″7

*Manfredi stands up. (MCU)*                    132:55-2″7

*Pina opens the door, and Don Pietro enters. (TQ)*                    133:290-12″2

PINA: Hello, Don Pietro!

DON PIETRO: Hello!

PINA: Well, excuse me. I'll go to my place

*As Pina goes out, Manfredi comes forward, coming on screen from right, and shakes Don Pietro's hand.*

MANFREDI: Thank you for coming.

DON PIETRO: Don't mention it.

*(Stairway outside Pina's apartment, TQ)*                    134:392-16″8
*Marcello is eavesdropping. Pina surprises him in the act as she opens the door.*

PINA: What're you up to there, boy?

MARCELLO: Who's in there?

PINA: None of your business. Move! Go get some water!
    Hurry up! Move!

*Marcello starts slowly and reluctantly down the stairs
(camera pans to right after him). As soon as Pina goes
into her apartment Marcello turns back (camera pans
left with him) and runs on tiptoe up to the next floor.*

*(Wipe to left)*

*Marcello approaches the attic door (WF; camera pans to*    135:158-6″14
*right after him). He whistles a signal.*

MARCELLO: I have to tell you something.

*The door is opened by Romoletto, a one-legged boy with a crutch.*

ROMOLETTO: Come in!

*Marcello enters and closes the door behind him.*

*(Francesco's apartment, HF)*  136:1210-
50"10

*Manfredi, standing, looks at Don Pietro, who is sitting at the table, wiping his glasses.*

MANFREDI: There are more than five hundred in the mountains above Tagliacozzo. They're a band of boys really on the ball, they can't be abandoned. The appointment is for six this evening at the Tiburtina Bridge. One of them will come. It's better that I don't go, because now . . . I'm a marked man, and also the curfew's been switched to five o'clock.

DON PIETRO, *getting up, putting on his glasses*: Yes. I'll go.

MANFREDI: I was sure you would.

DON PIETRO: What's the message?

MANFREDI: No message. It's money from the military committee.

DON PIETRO: Ah!

MANFREDI: I've asked too much?

DON PIETRO: No. For those who are sacrificing themselves, it's even too little. How am I to recognize him?

MANFREDI: He'll stop on the bridge and whistle that song, "Mattinata Fiorentina." But wait, you don't know it!

DON PIETRO: I don't know. What song?

MANFREDI: It goes like this. *He whistles the tune.*

DON PIETRO: Oh! *He whistles it too, letting himself go,*

*then stops short.* Of course, everybody's singing it.

*(Dissolve to . . .*

*(Street near printer's shop, FS from below)*  137:129-5"9

*Don Pietro crosses the street.*

*(Antique shop, FS)*  138:842-35"2

*Don Pietro, seen from inside the shop, looks through the window, then enters the store from the left (camera pans to right after him until the antique dealer, in coat and hat, is included in TQ).*

ANTIQUE DEALER: Hello, Father.

DON PIETRO: Hello.

ANTIQUE DEALER: May I help you?

DON PIETRO, *looking around*: You wouldn't have a Saint Anthony Abbot, by any chance?

ANTIQUE DEALER: Sorry. We used to have some, but nobody much wanted them. But I've got a Saint Roch.

DON PIETRO: Thanks, but I'm not interested.

ANTIQUE DEALER: What? You're not interested in a saint like Saint Roch? *Don Pietro is perplexed.* Come over here.

*Don Pietro and the dealer move toward the left (FS;*  139:578-24"2
*camera pans after them). Two statues—a nude woman on the right and the Saint Roch on the left—are in the foreground.*

ANTIQUE DEALER: Come, come over here. It's a beauty too, you know.

DON PIETRO: Well, let's have a look.

*Don Pietro and the dealer are behind the statues. The*

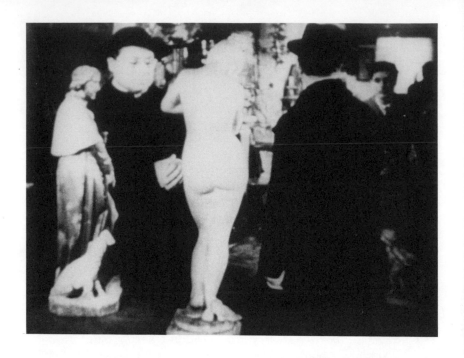

*shop assistant, seen in the background, stops cleaning and
gestures to the dealer.*

ASSISTANT: Well, I'll be going now.

ANTIQUE DEALER, *to assistant*: All right. Remember to stop
at Chiurazzi's!

ASSISTANT: All right.

ANTIQUE DEALER, *to Don Pietro*: You can have it for
almost nothing.

DON PIETRO, *in a guarded voice*: I have to talk to Francesco. The man with tight shoes sent me.

ANTIQUE DEALER: Wait one minute. *He goes off screen
to left (toward the camera).*

*Don Pietro looks around; his eyes linger on the nude
statue, then on the Saint Roch (HF). The contrast makes*    140:460-19″4

*him uncomfortable, and he turns the nude so that its back is to the saint. Then he realizes that the saint's eyes are staring at the nude's bare back. Comically shocked, he hesitates, then turns the saint's face away. He goes off screen to right.*

ANTIQUE DEALER *(off screen)*: This way, Father. They're waiting for you.

*As Don Pietro comes on screen from left, the dealer points out the way to the print shop and leads the way. (Wide WF)*　141:107-0 23

*(Stairway leading down to the print shop and the print shop itself, wide TQ)*　142:155-6"11

DON PIETRO: Where is it?

ANTIQUE DEALER, *opening a door*: Right down these stairs.

*He points to a corridor on the right, and they go down the stairs.*

*As Don Pietro goes down the stairs he meets a man in coveralls, Francesco, who comes on screen from left (WF; camera shoots straight up the stairs).*　143:496-20"16

FRANCESCO: Oh, it's you, Don Pietro!

DON PIETRO: Hello.

FRANCESCO: But what's happened?

*The antique dealer closes the door at the head of the stairs as Francesco and Don Pietro go down the remaining steps together (camera adjusts slightly downward).*

DON PIETRO: Nothing serious, thank heaven, but it might have been. Last night the SS were at Manfredi's—

FRANCESCO: We heard that, but where is he now?

DON PIETRO, *taking a note from his right pocket*: At your place.

FRANCESCO: Mine?

DON PIETRO: Yes. Pina let him in. He'll stay for a few days. . . . *They go off screen together to left. (HF)*

*They approach a table with printing machinery, from the right. (TQ)*          144:264-11″

DON PIETRO: He gave me this note. I wanted to send him to the Passionist monks at San Giovanni e Paolo. He'd have been safer—*He hands Francesco the note.* —but he didn't want to. He says he'd be cut off.

FRANCESCO: Sure.

*The master printer, a man of about forty, wearing glasses,*          145:802-
*joins the conversation from the middle of the shop (HF).*          33″10
*A man is working in the background. Don Pietro and Francesco come on screen from left. Francesco hands the note to the master printer.*

PRINTER: He's right.

DON PIETRO *(off screen)*: Yes, but it's more dangerous *(on screen)* for him to work now that they've caught on to him.

PRINTER: I know, Father, but there are only a few of us, and if everybody goes into the monasteries. . . .

DON PIETRO: I understand.

*Francesco introduces the printer to Don Pietro. They shake hands.*

FRANCESCO: Excuse me, Don Pietro, our editor.

DON PIETRO: Very pleased to meet you.

PRINTER: The same. I've heard a lot about you.

DON PIETRO: That's not good for my modesty—or my health.

PRINTER: You've done and are doing a lot for all of us. Thank you.

DON PIETRO: It's my duty to help those who need it.

PRINTER: Will you come into the office?

*They go off (WF) toward the rear of the shop. Francesco goes off screen to right. Three men can be seen working in the background.*

*The printer opens the glass-paned door of the office (TQ). A clerk comes out as the printer and Don Pietro go in. Don Pietro goes over to the desk. The printer glances at the note and goes off screen to right, leaving Don Pietro alone (camera adjusts slightly to left). The printer (HF) comes back on screen with three books, old octavo volumes, which he places on the desk.*

146:974-
40"14

PRINTER: Here you are, Father.

DON PIETRO: But Manfredi told me it was a sum of money.

PRINTER: They're books, but there's not much to read in them.

LAURA: No, I said. And I didn't ask him anything. I was in my robe—imagine—with curlers. Aren't you going to change? *Marina does not answer.* You're on soon.

MARINA, *standing up*: How'd he know where you live?

LAURA: How did he? You must have told him.

*Marina undresses (camera pans right). Laura is off screen.*

MARINA: I never told him.

LAURA *(off screen)*: Well, I don't know. I certainly . . .

*(Laura in the armchair, HF)*                      152:267-11″3

LAURA: . . . didn't tell him. I really don't care to go around telling people where I live. And while we're on the subject, Marina, I can't stand that place anymore. If you wouldn't mind, I'd come stay with you until I find another room.

*Buttoning up her plaid blouse, Marina goes over to the*      153:1367-
*mirror, to the left (TQ; camera pans after her until it*         56″23
*includes Laura, TQ). Laura stands up.*

MARINA: Come whenever you want. I told you so many times.

LAURA: Oh, you're an angel!

*Laura kisses Marina, adjusts her dress in the mirror, and then picks up Marina's handbag. Marina, vexed, stops her by taking her hand.*

MARINA: What're you looking for?

LAURA: A cigarette.

MARINA, *taking the handbag*: I'll get it for you.

LAURA: Oh, all right. *She takes the cigarette Marina hands her, without having understood Marina's gesture, and lights it.* Thanks.

MARINA: When did he come?

LAURA: Who?

MARINA: Giorgio!

LAURA: Oh, this morning. I wasn't even dressed.

*(The camera remains immobile while both the women move.) Someone knocks on the door.*

VOICE *(off screen)*: Miss Marina, you're on!

*Marina sighs.*

LAURA: I don't understand you. Are you in love with him or not? He's a nice guy, I don't deny that—

MARINA: Would you please keep out of it?

LAURA: Oh, it's none of my business! As long as you like him. . . .

*Marina leans exhaustedly on the armchair, holding her head with her hand. Laura sees her in the mirror and worriedly approaches her (camera adjusts to right).*

LAURA: Don't you feel well?

MARINA, *lifting her head*: No, no, it's nothing.

LAURA: Marina, again? You know it's bad for you!

MARINA, *sitting on the arm of the chair*: That's silly! Lots of things are bad for us, but we do them all the same. *Someone knocks at the door again.* I'm coming!

*Laura goes to open the door; she is concealed behind it as it opens.*

*Ingrid enters (HF). Elegant and self-assured, she smiles ambiguously as she greets Marina. She speaks with a strong foreign accent.*

154:281-
11″17

INGRID: Hello, how are you?

MARINA *(off screen)*: All right, and you?

*Ingrid goes over to Marina (camera pans left after her until it includes Marina) and embraces her.*

MARINA: Oh, how lovely you look tonight! But then, you're always so chic.

LAURA *(off screen)*: Well, I'll be going now.

INGRID, *turning*: Lauretta. . . .

*Laura hesitates at the door, then goes out (HF; camera adjusts slightly to right).*    155:76-3"4

LAURA: Try to hurry up, otherwise the manager'll be after you.

*Marina and Ingrid are standing. The music of the band is heard again.*    156:535-22"7

MARINA: Excuse me, I have to go.

INGRID: Yes, dear.

MARINA: You found some?

INGRID: Uh-huh.

MARINA: Oh, you're a darling!

*Marina embraces Ingrid and goes off screen. Ingrid looks about and goes over to the mirror (camera pans left and tracks forward with her). A copy of the photograph of Marina and Manfredi in Piazza di Spagna, seen earlier in the Gestapo office, has been stuck in a corner of the mirror. In the distance is the sound of a door being closed. Ingrid smiles contentedly as she gazes at her image in the mirror (MCU). Music ends.*

*(Wipe to right)*

*(Don Pietro's rectory)*    157:208-8"16

*Agostino is down on his knees, poking at the fire in the wood-burning heater, on which a pot is boiling. He stands up and stirs the pot with a wooden spoon.*

AGOSTINO: His schedule's gone to pot. He comes and goes, goes and comes, and in times like these, when a person shouldn't even put their nose out the window! Not him—he's always out!

*Pina, in her coat, is sitting on a sofa in a corner of the room, with her shopping bag at her feet. (WF)*          158:422-17″14

PINA: He must have his reasons.

AGOSTINO *(off screen)*: Let's hope they're good ones.

PINA, *standing up*: Agostino! I'm surprised at you!

*Pina approaches Agostino (camera pans and tracks left after her). He comes on screen (TQ). Pina sits down again.*

AGOSTINO *(off screen)*: Don't kid me! You think I don't know you're at the bottom of all these goings-on at the bakery today?

PINA: Me?

AGOSTINO: Yes, you. You think I'm stupid? I see everything, I understand everything, and I also know that if . . .

*Agostino (back to camera, CU, his head out of the frame)          159:559-23″7
continues to talk to Pina, who is sitting opposite him.
(MS)*

AGOSTINO: . . . you people keep on this way, you're heading for trouble.

PINA: Let's hope not.

AGOSTINO: Let's hope not. *He lifts the cover of the pot to stir the contents.*

PINA, *grimacing in disgust*: Mmmm. . . .

AGOSTINO: Cabbage soup.

PINA: You can tell by the smell! What time is it? Because

the curfew starts at five.

AGOSTINO, *taking his watch from his pocket*: Let's see—
four-thirty.

*Pina stands up (camera adjusts slightly upward).*

PINA: Well, I have to go.

AGOSTINO: If you want to leave a message. . . .

PINA: No, I wanted to talk to Don Pietro, but it doesn't
matter. I'll see him tomorrow morning before my
wedding.

*They hear a door opening.*

AGOSTINO: Oh, here he is, at last!

*Don Pietro enters with the package of books (TQ). Pina's*   160:871-36"7
*back is to the camera.*

PINA: Hello, Don Pietro.

DON PIETRO: Hello, Pina, hello.

*He goes over to the heater (camera pulls back and adjusts). Pina (HF) follows him. He lifts the cover off the pot and turns to Agostino.*

DON PIETRO: I told you time and again not to cook on the heater—and it's cabbage, no less!

AGOSTINO, *muttering*: If I want to, I can even cook a chicken on it.

DON PIETRO: Agostino, don't answer back!

AGOSTINO: Well, make up your mind, we use the heater or we use the stove!

*All three move toward Don Pietro's desk (camera tracks after them and pans right, to HF).*

DON PIETRO: Carry on, carry on.

*Agostino tries to take the books from Don Pietro, but the priest quickly stops him.*

AGOSTINO: Always books! We don't have enough money for food, and you keep on buying books!

DON PIETRO: Leave them be! I have to take them to the priest at San Lorenzo.

AGOSTINO: You're going out again? The curfew starts in twenty minutes!

DON PIETRO, *wrapping the books in an old newspaper*: It doesn't matter. Doctors and priests can go out.

AGOSTINO: Sure, and midwives too!

DON PIETRO (*HF; front view*): Well?     161:30-1″6

AGOSTINO: I read it on the posters, but in the dark it     162:227-9″11
wouldn't be hard to stop a bullet, with these darned
Jerries around!

*Don Pietro turns to Pina.*

PINA: Don Pietro, I came for—yes, for confession.

*Don Pietro (HF; head-on) talks with Pina (back to the*     163:83-3″11
*camera).*

DON PIETRO: How can I, now? I've got to go out. Maybe
tomorrow morning.

PINA, *approaching Don Pietro*: All right, then I'll come     164:145-6″1
with you. We can go a little way together, all right?

DON PIETRO, *embarrassed*: Well. . . .

*Pina tries to take his package of books, but Don Pietro
fends her off.*

PINA: Give it to me, I'll carry your package.

DON PIETRO: No, no, no.

PINA: Are you crazy, a priest carrying a package?     165:38-1″14

DON PIETRO: Please!

PINA, *seizing the package*: Don't make me laugh! And     166:303-
anyway, I won't even feel the weight. I've already got     12″15
so much stuff!

*Pina goes back to the sofa (camera pans left), picks up
her shopping bag, and starts out. Don Pietro follows her.*

DON PIETRO, *anxiously*: But look here, Pina—

PINA: Let's go, or we'll be late! Come on, come with me!
'Bye, Agostino.

*They both go toward the door (WF; camera pans left*

*after them).*

DON PIETRO, *to Agostino in TQ*: Don't worry, will you?

AGOSTINO: If they don't end this war fast I'll go crazy!

*(Don Pietro's church, FS)*

167:1161-
48"9

*Music begins. Don Pietro and Pina come out of the rectory, genuflect before the altar, then come forward. As Don Pietro raises his eyes he is suddenly taken aback to see a German Army officer (an Austrian) waiting for him (camera pulls back to reveal the officer, back to camera and at left margin of frame).*

AUSTRIAN: You are the priest here?

DON PIETRO: Yes.

AUSTRIAN: Don Pietro Pellegrini?

DON PIETRO: That's right.

AUSTRIAN: I'd like to speak to you.

DON PIETRO: Over that way, please. *He gestures toward the rectory (TQ), then turns to Pina.*

PINA, *embarrassed*: Well, I'll go then. Here's your package.

DON PIETRO: Yes, yes. . . .

PINA: What do you suppose he wants?

DON PIETRO: Who knows? Then it'd be better. . . .

*Uncertain, Don Pietro turns to look at the officer, who in the meantime has reached the altar and waits there (back to camera). Don Pietro resolutely hands the package back to Pina and gestures for her to wait for him in a corner of the church.*

DON PIETRO: Wait over there for me.

PINA: All right, all right!

*Don Pietro (HF) joins the officer and takes him toward the rectory. Pina goes in the opposite direction (camera tracks back in front of her).*

*(Don Pietro's rectory, WF)*                    168:459-19″3

*Agostino removes the pot from the heater and takes it to the table (camera pans right after him). In the meantime the door opens and the officer enters, followed by Don Pietro, who throws the sexton a significant glance. The officer goes off screen to left.*

DON PIETRO, *to officer*: Go right in. *To Agostino*: Wait outside a minute.

*Agostino goes out, and Don Pietro (camera pans left after him) comes up to the officer (back to camera). Don Pietro (TQ), standing by the desk, invites the officer to be seated.*

DON PIETRO: Please be seated. *They both sit down.* What is it?

*The officer looks down and removes his pistol from its*        169:59-2″11
*holster. (HF)*

*Don Pietro (HF), startled by this gesture, instantly places*    170:20-0″20
*both hands on the desk and stares at the officer in dismay and fright.*

*The officer starts to remove the magazine from the pistol.*     171:28-1″4

*Don Pietro closes his eyes and sighs in relief.*                172:50-2″2

*The officer removes a cartridge from the magazine, opens*       173:367-15″7
*it with his teeth, and extracts from it a note, which he hands to Don Pietro.*

AUSTRIAN: From Don Saverio Derisi . . .

*Don Pietro unrolls the note, then removes his glasses.*         174:155-6″11

AUSTRIAN *(off screen)*: . . . the Minturno priest.

*The officer observes the priest.* 175:37-1″13

*Don Pietro turns on the desk lamp, reads the note, gazes* 176:185-7″17
*at the officer, and then thoughtfully refolds the note.*

*The officer bows his head and clenches his fists.* 177:149-6″5

AUSTRIAN: You must not think me a coward. I can't stand
it anymore!

*Don Pietro stands up and goes off screen to left.* 178:85-3″13

*The officer (HF), dejected and lost in thought, is ap-* 179:334-
*proached by Don Pietro, who comes on screen from right.* 13″22

DON PIETRO: Keep your spirits up. I'll try to help you.
Where are you coming from?

AUSTRIAN: From Cassino. It's a hell!

*(Wipe to left)*

*(Don Pietro's church, MS)* 180:414-17″6

*Pina is kneeling at a prie-dieu. She rises with a question-*
*ing look as Don Pietro returns. He insists on having his*
*package back.*

PINA: What'd he want? . . . Leave it be! . . . Who is he?

DON PIETRO: He wanted some information.

PINA: Hm. When I see them, ugh!

*They go toward the exit. Music ends, covered by the*
*sounds from the following scene.*

*(Wipe to left)*

*(A Roman street, Via Casilina, TQ)* 181:2038-
1′24″22

*Pina and Don Pietro walk along (camera tracks left after*
*them).*

PINA: It's been so long since I was at confession, I'm almost ashamed.

DON PIETRO: No—

PINA: No, let me talk, Don Pietro. I realize that I've been living wrong . . .

*Pina stops (camera stops tracking). A train is seen passing behind her.*

PINA: . . . I've done so many things I shouldn't have! But what d'you think, that I'm not ashamed to go to the altar in this condition?

*Pina starts walking again, followed by Don Pietro (camera continues tracking left in front of them).*

PINA: But you can't understand me, Don Pietro. A person does these things without thinking, without feeling they're doing wrong. I was so much in love! And he's so good, such a fine guy! *She stops (HF; camera stops tracking).* I've thought so many times he could really have found somebody better'n me—yes, a younger

girl, not a widow with a child, and without a cent. Because I've had to sell everything to keep going— *She walks on (HF; camera tracks left)*—and things keep getting worse. How'll we ever forget all this suffering, all these anxieties, all this fear? *She stops.* Doesn't Christ see us?

DON PIETRO: A lot of people ask me that, Pina. *They resume their walk (HF).* Doesn't Christ see us? But are we sure we didn't deserve this plague? Are we sure we've always lived according to the Lord's laws? And nobody thinks of changing their lives, of examining their lives. Then, when the piper has to be paid *(sound of train)* everybody despairs, everybody asks: Doesn't the Lord see us? Doesn't the Lord pity us? *He stops, takes another few steps, stops again (HF; camera stops tracking).* Yes, the Lord will take pity on us. But we have so much to be forgiven, and so we must pray, and forgive much.

PINA: You're right, Don Pietro, but how can we do it? When you see those guys . . .

*Three Italian soldiers, from the Fascist militia, are check-*    182:60-2″12
*ing a coachman's papers. (MLS)*

PINA *(off screen)*: . . . you get the urge to at least smash
     your pocketbook in their faces! You understand? . . .

DON PIETRO: You're right there. Oh, what're you making    183:265-11″1
     me say?

PINA: Yes.

DON PIETRO: Give me the package. It's getting late. Good-
     bye, Pina, good-bye.

*Don Pietro shakes Pina's hand and goes off screen to left.*

*Pina remains standing there.*

*The soldiers hand the coachman back his papers. Don*    184:176-7″8
*Pietro passes by in the background.*

*(Dissolve to . . .*

*(Area near the railroad, FS, in the afternoon)*    185:252-
                                                     10″12
*Don Pietro (TQ) strolls circumspectly on the embank-*
*ment overlooking the railroad at a point where the tracks*
*twist in a maze of switches. He looks around, then goes*
*off (WF). Off screen, a railwayman is whistling "Mattinata*
*Fiorentina."*

*Whistling, the railwayman climbs up the embankment.*    186:123-5″3
*(WF)*

*The railwayman comes on screen from left and passes*    187:295-12″7
*in front of Don Pietro, who begins to whistle in turn*
*(TQ). The man goes off screen to right and then returns.*
*Both are whistling the tune. Don Pietro hands his package*
*to the railwayman.*

*(Dissolve to . . .*

*(Street near Francesco's building, WF)*    188:698-29″2

*Three Fascist soldiers pass along a wall on which is written "Viva Lenin" (camera pans and tracks left after them).*

FIRST SOLDIER: She came to ask for help. The Germans had taken her boy friend to the Gestapo. "Don't worry, I'll take care of it," I told her. You should've seen her legs!

*The soldiers laugh. Francesco turns a corner and appears in front of the soldiers.*

SECOND SOLDIER: Halt! Hands up!

*Francesco stops (back to camera) with his hands up.*

FRANCESCO: I've got a permit. Printer!

SECOND SOLDIER: Ah, a printer!

FRANCESCO: Yes, look at my permit. *He takes out his permit and hands it to the soldiers.*

SECOND SOLDIER, *checking the document*: All right, go on home! And be quick about it!

FRANCESCO: Thanks!

*He goes off screen without looking back, while the soldiers watch him.*

*Francesco hurries along the wall (WF; camera pans left after him). He stops at his building, unlocks the door, and enters.*                189:171-7"3

*(RA; entranceway of Francesco's building, WF)*                190:317-13"5

*Francesco enters, closes the door behind him, and starts toward the stairs. Outside, a car is heard braking to a stop. Francesco hides under the stairs (camera pans slightly left).*

*Laura appears in the doorway, laughing. A German officer follows her. (WF)*                191:689-
28"17

LAURA: Auf wiedersehen, captain, and thanks.

CAPTAIN: Guten nacht. Auf Morgen, nicht vergessen. [Good night. See you tomorrow, don't forget.]

LAURA: Yes.

*The car is heard departing. Laura closes the door and slips the money the officer has given her into her garter.*

*At the corner of the stairs she is startled to notice Francesco.*

LAURA: Oh, Francesco! You scared me! I'm a little late, but they insisted on bringing me home. Nothing wrong in that, is there?

*Without answering, Francesco turns his back on her and starts up the stairs. The embarrassed Laura (TQ) follows.*

*(Dissolve to . . .*

*(Francesco's apartment, HF)*

192:1172-
44″1€

*Manfredi, seated at the table, rises as Francesco enters and shakes his hand warmly.*

MANFREDI: Oh, hello, Francesco!

FRANCESCO: Hello! You had a close call there!

MANFREDI, *sitting down again*: I made it this time. The landlady and Nannina were terrific.

FRANCESCO, *taking off his raincoat*: You know they went back this morning and turned the whole place upside down?

MANFREDI: They were wasting their time. There wasn't anything there!

FRANCESCO: Don Pietro said Pina let you in.

MANFREDI: Yes, she was very kind.

FRANCESCO: What do you think of her?

*He walks through the room (camera pans right after him up to TQ). He puts his pipe down on the dresser.*

MANFREDI: She'll be good for you.

*Francesco crosses the room (camera pans left to exclude Manfredi) and starts to wash up in a basin behind the screen.*

MANFREDI *(off screen)*: She thought I was a cop at first. She gave me a really rough time.

FRANCESCO: I can imagine!

*Manfredi comes on screen from left.*

FRANCESCO: You know that Don Pietro met Gino?

MANFREDI: He did? I'm glad. What did Gino say about my business?

*Sound of water being poured out.*

FRANCESCO: He's worried. You were supposed to meet the old man today.

MANFREDI: When did he get here?

*Francesco, after drying his hands, takes a plate and sets it on the table in front of Manfredi, then sits down opposite him.*

FRANCESCO: Last night. But you can't see him. Gino says you have to break all contact with the Center for a while.

MANFREDI: He's right. But to have to stop short after months of work! Ah, I can't figure out how they caught on to me. We ought to try to find out what they know about me.

*(RA)*
*Francesco ladles the soup into the plates (HF; Manfredi is at left margin of frame).*    193:336-14″

FRANCESCO: Well, we'll try, but it's hard to get information about the Gestapo. If it were the Italian police. . . .

MANFREDI: Let's hope Don Pietro made contact with our friend from Tagliacezzo.

FRANCESCO: Let's hope so.

*Francesco and Manfredi are eating. Francesco takes a copy of* Unità, *the clandestine newspaper, from his pocket and hands it to Manfredi. (HF)*    194:410-17"2

FRANCESCO: Ah, I brought you the paper. Came out well, didn't it?

MANFREDI, *glancing through the paper*: How many copies?

FRANCESCO: Twelve thousand. *They hear a door opening. Francesco get up and goes to the door.* Here's Pina.

*Francesco is at the door as Pina enters, a worried look on her face. She caresses Francesco's face. He puts his hand on her shoulder. They come back to the table together (WF; camera pulls back with them until it includes Manfredi, TQ). Manfredi is standing.*    195:656-27"8

PINA: Hi, how are you? I've been so worried about Marcello.

FRANCESCO: What's he done?

PINA: He's disappeared.

FRANCESCO: What d'you mean, disappeared?

PINA: I looked all over the building for him. He's not here.

FRANCESCO: He must be at Romoletto's.

PINA: No, he's not. And Otello, and Adele the Sicilian's

boy, are gone too.

FRANCESCO: Where d'you think they've gone?

PINA: I'm scared they've gone out.

MANFREDI: At this hour? With the curfew?

*Suddenly there is a loud explosion outside, which makes the windowpanes rattle. Music begins. The three turn automatically toward the windows, which are crossed with strips of paper, glued on, for protection. Pina goes to close the door (camera pans left after her). She turns out the light and returns to the others, who are now at the window looking outside, where a fire lights up the black sky.*

*(Railway, FS; camera subjective from Pina, Francesco, and Manfredi's viewpoint.)*                196:30-1″6

*Flames can be seen in the night.*

*Francesco's apartment (HF), Pina, Francesco, and Man-*   197:48-2″
*fredi, clearly worried, continue to look out the window, on which the light from the flames is reflected.*

*Near the railway (LS), a group of boys emerges from the*   198:236-9″20
*dark background, partly lit up by the flames. They come forward (WF). Among them is Romoletto, leaning on his crutch (camera pans left). Music grows louder.*

*(Passageway in cellar of Francesco's building, WF)*       199:157-6″13

*In single file, the boys reach a window and begin to clamber in through it.*

*The boys, including Romoletto, climb in through the*       200:130-5″10
*window. (TQ)*

*Romoletto and the boys wait in the cellar until the last*   201:93-3″21
*ones have entered. (HF)*

*Romoletto is surrounded by his friends. (MCU)*    202:197-8"5

ROMOLETTO: Good boys! I'm proud of you! *He turns and goes off screen.*

MARCELLO, *taking his place*: Let's step on it, boys!

*(Stairway of Francesco's building, WF)*    203:250-
10"10

*Marcello and two other boys have stopped at the doorway between the cellar and the main stairway. They watch their friends pass by on their way out the front door.*

FIRST BOY: Let's wait for Otello.

SECOND BOY: Yes.

*Otello appears, and the four boys start up the stairs. Music ends.*

*Two boys (backs to camera) go up the stairs (TQ; camera pans up after them). Marcello and the fourth boy come on screen after them. The first boy stops at his own door.*    204:387-16"3

FIRST BOY: Good night.

SECOND BOY: Good night.

THIRD BOY: See you.

*The first boy rings his doorbell as the others continue up the stairs (camera pans left after them). The door opens.*

*Off screen, shouts, slaps, and the boy's wailing can be heard. Frightened, the other three turn (CU) and begin to run up the stairs.*

VOICE *(off screen)*: Oh, you're still alive? I'll murder you! *Shouts and crying off screen.*

*Outwardly calm, one of the three boys stops in front of his own door and rings the bell. (TQ)*    205:210-8"18

SECOND BOY: Oh, if my father was like that I'd show him!

Good night!

*Marcello and Otello continue on (camera pans after them). They hear the door opening and turn to watch. (HF)*

*Looking down from the stairway (WF; camera subjective from Marcello and Otello's viewpoint), they see the father beating the boy, who screams and tries to shield himself.*   206:42-1"18

FATHER: You good-for-nothing devil! You come home at this hour!

SECOND BOY: Help! *Shouts and crying off screen.*

*Increasingly worried, Marcello and Otello continue up the stairs. Otello touches his face. (TQ)*   207:61-2"13

*Marcello and Otello, whose families share the apartment with others, have reached their door. (WF)*   208:317-13"5

OTELLO: We'd better go in one at a time.

MARCELLO: Right. You go first.

PINA *(off screen)*: Ah, you're back? You good-for-nothings!

*Hearing Pina's voice as she comes out of Francesco's apartment, the boys rush inside.*

*(Pina outside Francesco's apartment, TQ)*   209:159-6"15

PINA, *to Francesco*: They're back!

OTELLO'S FATHER *(off screen)*: You devils!

*Pina comes on screen (WF) and slaps both boys violently. They try to avoid the blows.*   210:126-5"6

PINA: I'll get hold of you! I'll skin you alive, you devils, giving me heart failure! Stand still, you!

FRANCESCO, *from his doorway (HF), to Manfredi*: I'm   211:98-4"2

going over there a minute or there'll be bloody
murder!

*(Pina's apartment, FS)*                                    212:40-1″16

*In the dining room are two couples—one couple sitting
at the table—and the two boys (TQ; backs to camera).*

PINA, *appealing to the adults*: Look how they look!

OTELLO'S MOTHER: Where've you been?

*(RA)*                                                      213:59-2″11
*Behind the two boys is the grandfather, who is in bed.
(TQ)*

OTELLO: At Romoletto's.

OTELLO'S MOTHER *(off screen)*: That's a lie! Nobody was
up there!

MARCELLO: We were downstairs.                              214:323-
                                                               13″11
OTELLO'S MOTHER: Where downstairs?

PINA: Why bother to ask them? You can see they're trying
to make fools out of us!

*Furious, Otello's father gets up to hit his son.*

OTELLO'S FATHER: I'll murder him! He's not going to get
away with. . . .

PINA: Me, I'll murder them, these good-for-nothings, these
devils! Trying to give me heart failure!

*Francesco comes on screen (WF) and prevents Pina from
hitting the boys.*

FRANCESCO, *to boys*: Go on, go on, right to bed, you two,
move! *To Pina*: Take it easy!

PINA: These kids are just too much!

FRANCESCO: They're just kids!

GRANDFATHER, *chuckling (HF)*: Heh, heh, heh.                    215:40-1"16

*(Pina and Francesco, TQ)*                                       216:220-9"4
*Laura, in her bathrobe, enters from the open door leading*
*to the next room. Otello's father sits down again.*

LAURA: How long's this going to go on? You can't have a
    moment's peace in this place. I work all day long!

OTELLO'S FATHER: Some kind of work!

*Obviously stung by this remark, Laura comes over to*
*the table and bangs her fist on it.*

LAURA: What did you say? Let's hear it! Say that again!

OTELLO'S MOTHER, *stepping in (TQ)*: You better go back       217:31-1"17
    to bed.

LAURA: Why? What if I don't? I can't talk in my own           218:91-3"19
    house?

OTELLO'S MOTHER, *standing up*: This is my house! If you      219:50-2"2
    want to talk, talk in your own room!

LAURA: We pay for kitchen privileges too here.                220:136-5"16

PINA: Oh, Laura, forget it!

LAURA: What d'you mean, forget it? I'm sick and tired of
    living in this zoo!

OTELLO'S MOTHER: So get out! Who's stopping you?              221:41-1"17

FRANCESCO: Do you people have to fight every night?          222:120-5"

LAURA: This is the last time, I tell you! I'm getting out
    of here tomorrow! *Still shouting, she goes into the*
    *other room.*

OTELLO'S MOTHER, *sitting down*: If she doesn't leave, one    223:103-4"7
    of these days I'll. . . .

GRANDFATHER, *in bed*: Tilde, isn't it ready?                 224:72-3"

OTELLO'S MOTHER: Oh, Mother of God, it'll be burned to a crisp! *She runs out of the room, followed by Pina.* 225:110-4"14

PINA: That wretch!

GRANDFATHER, *to Francesco*: Come here! It's a surprise! Tilde's baking a cake for tomorrow, for the wedding! 226:539-22"11

FRANCESCO: Ah!

GRANDFATHER: Sure, because . . .

FRANCESCO: Take it easy.

GRANDFATHER: . . . because we're going to have a feast, hee hee!

*Francesco laughs, nods to the grandfather, and goes off screen.*

*Otello's father is sitting at the table (TQ). Francesco comes on screen.* 227:78-3"6

OTELLO'S FATHER: Lucky you, you've got nothing else to worry about!

FRANCESCO: Well, let's go to bed. Good night!

*The couple who did not participate in the argument are ready for bed. The husband, in his shorts, gets into bed with his wife. (TQ)* 228:59-2"11

HUSBAND: What's-your-name, would you turn out the light?

*Francesco turns out the light (TQ) and goes out of the room.* 229:72-3"

*(Marcello's room, MCU)* 230:47-1"23

*Marcello is lying on the bed, talking to a girl with braids, Andreina, who is about his age. She is taking care of a two-year-old sister.*

MARCELLO: We sure fixed them good, eh?

ANDREINA *(MCU)*: You never take me with you!  231:42-1″18

MARCELLO: You? You're a woman!  232:37-1″13

ANDREINA: So what? Women can't be . . .  233:42-1″18

*The two-year-old is sitting on a potty. (WF)*  234:94-3″22

ANDREINA *(off screen)*. . . . heroes?

MARCELLO *(off screen)*: Sure they can, but Romoletto . . .

. . . says that women always . . .  235:60-2″12

*Francesco appears in the doorway. (TQ)*  236:51-2″3

MARCELLO *(off screen)*: . . . mean trouble.

FRANCESCO: Aren't you asleep?

*Smiling, Marcello quickly hides under the bedclothes.*  237:39-1″15

MARCELLO, *whispering*: Under we go!

*Andreina takes the child off the potty. He begins to cry. (WF)*  238:60-2″12

*Andreina puts the baby to bed with another little girl. (HF)*  239:95-3″23

FRANCESCO, *putting his finger to his lips*: Ssssh! To sleep!  240:299

12″11

*The baby stops crying. Francesco comes forward (into MF) and sits down beside Marcello (camera adjusts slightly down). He caresses the boy's head. Marcello pulls his face out from under the covers.*

FRANCESCO: You're not asleep?

*(Francesco and Marcello talk, MCU)*  241:707-

29″11

MARCELLO: I'm not sleepy.

FRANCESCO: Where'd you go with Romoletto?

MARCELLO: I can't tell you.

FRANCESCO, *pointing to himself*: Not even me? *He caresses Marcello's cheek.*

MARCELLO: No, it's a secret.

FRANCESCO: Well, then, you're right! You can't tell anybody.

*Music begins.*

FRANCESCO: Well, good night!

*Francesco stands up (camera adjusts slightly up). He pulls up the boy's covers, caresses him again, and goes off screen to left. He turns out the light as Marcello sits halfway up in bed and calls him (camera adjusts slightly down).*

MARCELLO: Hey!

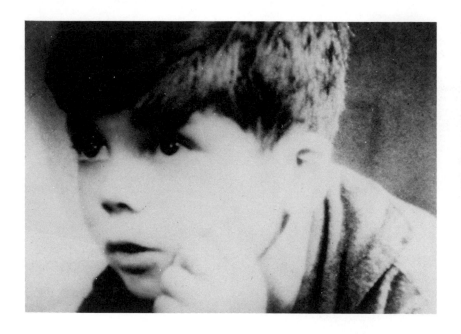

*Francesco, in the doorway, turns, then comes back
(camera pans downward after him) and sits down beside
the boy. (MCU)*

242:466-
19"10

FRANCESCO: What is it?

MARCELLO: Is it true that from tomorrow on I have to
call you "Papa"?

FRANCESCO: If you want to.

MARCELLO, *embracing Francesco*: Yes. I love you!

*Again Francesco pulls the covers up around Marcello and
caresses him. Then he stands up and goes off screen.*

*(The landing in front of Francesco's apartment, HF)*

243:825-34"9

*Pina opens the door and steps out onto the landing with
a sigh (camera pans left after her and includes Francesco
as he comes up to her). Dejected, she covers her face
with her hand.*

FRANCESCO: What's the matter?

PINA: I had a fight with my sister.

FRANCESCO: Again?

PINA, *her voice broken with tears*: She wants to leave! She
says she won't even come to the wedding!

FRANCESCO: Well, that's just talk. *He leans his hand
against the wall and comes nearer to her.*

PINA: No, no, she meant it. She's packing. *She sobs.*

FRANCESCO: Tomorrow morning she'll change her mind.
Take it easy!

*Pina lays her head on Francesco's chest. He holds her
tight, moving to the left (camera pans slightly with him).*

PINA: I'm so tired!

FRANCESCO: Take it easy!

PINA: I'm so tired! *She is still weeping.*

FRANCESCO: You're crying? Come on in for a little while.
*(Dissolve to . . .*

*Francesco leading Pina toward his room (HF; camera pans left with them).*    244:546-
22"18

PINA: But he's in there, I don't want to.

FRANCESCO: What difference does it make? He's a friend.

PINA: I know, but it's been so long I wanted to talk to you alone!

FRANCESCO: All right.

*They stop, then turn back (camera pans right after them up to TQ). Pina leads Francesco gently over to the top step.*

PINA: Come over here. Let's sit down here, like when we talked to each other for the first time. You remember? *They sit down (camera pans down on them).*

FRANCESCO: You came knocking on my door, mad as a wet hen!

*(Francesco and Pina in MCU)*    245:2407-
1'40"7

PINA *(MCU)*: I sure was! You were hammering a nail in the wall, and you made my mirror fall down. But it didn't break.

FRANCESCO, *jokingly mimicking Pina*: Who do you think you are, anyway, the king of the world? *He laughs.*

PINA: I thought you were so nasty! You'd been living here for two months, and when you passed by on your way downstairs you'd never say hello. Two years ago—it seems so long ago, doesn't it? And things are so different now! But the war was already on.

FRANCESCO: And everybody thought it'd be over soon, and that we'd only get to see it in the movies. But. . . .

PINA: But when'll it end? Sometimes I just can't go on. This winter it seems like it'll never end!

FRANCESCO: It'll end, Pina, it'll end, and spring will come back, and it'll be more beautiful than ever, because we'll be free. We have to believe it, we have to want it! See, I know these things, I feel them, but I can't explain it. Manfredi'd be able to, he's an educated man, he's been to college, he's traveled. He can talk so well. But I think that's the way it is, that we shouldn't be afraid now or in the future. Because

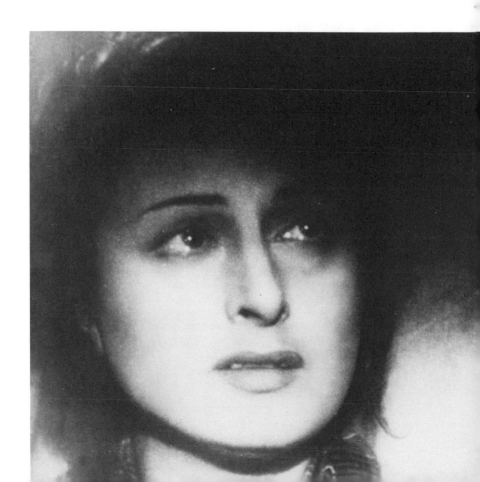

we're in the right, the right's on our side. Understand, Pina?

PINA: Yes, Francesco.

FRANCESCO: We're fighting for something that has to be, that can't help coming! Maybe the way is hard, it may take a long time, but we'll get there, and we'll see a better world! And our kids'll see it! Marcello and—and him, the baby that's coming . . .

. . . *(CU)* So you shouldn't ever be afraid, Pina . . .   246:120-5″
whatever happens.

*(Francesco and Pina, CU. Pina, deeply moved, has tears*   247:193-8″1
*in her eyes.)*

FRANCESCO: Understand?

PINA: Yes, Francesco. But I'm never afraid . . . ever!

*Music ends.*

*(The corridor in Manfredi's pension, HF)*   248:260-
10″20

*The telephone rings. Nannina opens the door and goes to*
*answer it. The landlady can be seen through the open*
*door, knitting.*

NANNINA: Yes? Oh, yes, miss! . . . No, he hasn't been back!

*(Bedroom of Marina's apartment, WF)*   249:235-9″19

*Marina, in dressing gown, is stretched out on her unmade*
*bed, telephoning.*

MARINA: He hasn't even phoned? He hasn't sent anybody?
Nannina, tell me the truth—you know something.
You know where he is!

NANNINA: I don't know, miss, I swear to you! If I knew   250:309-
I'd tell you! . . . Let's hope not! . . . Good-bye. *She*   12″21
*puts down the receiver and returns to the room*
*where the landlady is sitting.* What a dope! Asking

for information over the phone! It's enough to bring the Gestapo down on all of us! *She closes the door behind her.*

*Marina leans back on the pillow, thinking.*                    251:52-2″4

*(Gestapo office, HF)*                                          252:39-1″15

*Bergmann (seen from the front) is glancing through a batch of clandestine newspapers.*

*Bergmann (HF; seen in profile) continues to look through*     253:901-
*the newspapers, whose titles can be seen:* Il Popolo, Unità,            37″13
Avanti!, Voce Operaia, Italia Libera, Risorgimento
Liberale. *Someone knocks at the door. He folds the newspapers, then stands up (camera pans with him up to CU,
which includes, in WF in the background, his aide). The
aide, Krammer, opens the door and comes to attention.*

BERGMANN: Herein! [Come in!]

KRAMMER: Der römische Polizeipräsident, Herr Sturm-
    bannführer. [The Rome Police Commissioner, sir.]

BERGMANN: Lassen Sie hereinkommen. [Let him in.]

*The aide salutes and goes out, then shows the Police
Commissioner in. Bergmann comes toward him (up to
WF) and stretches out his arm in the Fascist salute.
They shake hands.*

BERGMANN: My dear friend, you've picked just the right
    time to come! There's something very interesting.
    Our Manfredi was seen this morning in the Prenes-
    tine area. . . . Please. . . .

*He takes the Commissioner's arm and leads him over to
a pair of armchairs on one side of the office (camera pans
after him into TQ).*

POLICE COMMISSIONER: Thanks.

*He sets the voluminous file he has been carrying down on a small table between the two armchairs and removes his coat.*

*Bergmann and the Commissioner sit down opposite each other. (HF)*

254:577-24″1

BERGMANN: And a short while ago a bomb blew up a tank car of gasoline at the railroad yards in the same area.

*The Commissioner picks up his file, takes a paper out of it, and hands the paper to Bergmann.*

POLICE COMMISSIONER: Excuse me, my dear major, but my news is much more sensational than yours. I spent the afternoon at our file center, and I too have had a very interesting meeting.

BERGMANN: Fantastic! Luigi Ferraris, born in Turin . . .

*(Insert: the major's hands are seen holding the paper, which contains two photographs of Manfredi, full-face and profile, five fingerprints, and a written record.)*

255:117-4″21

BERGMANN *(off screen):* . . . on October 3, 1906, arrested in Bologna on February 4, 1928 . . .

256:979-
40″19

. . . sentenced to twelve years for conspiring against the state. Escaped during transport to prison . . . seen in Paris and Marseilles . . . *He raises his eyes, though he does not look at the obviously self-satisfied Commissioner. He places the paper on the table.* Luigi Ferraris . . . You've beaten me!

*Bergmann stands up, hands in his pockets. The Commissioner stands too (camera pans up with them). They come forward (camera pulls slightly back, into HF).*

POLICE COMMISSIONER: I wouldn't dream of it. At any rate, the most difficult part is still to be done: catch him.

BERGMANN: Don't worry, he won't escape me.

POLICE COMMISSIONER: Do you want me to take care of it?

BERGMANN, *turning quickly toward him*: No, I forbid it!
*He corrects himself, smiling.* That is, I mean—not
because I don't trust your methods, but I prefer to
do it myself. Excuse me.

*The Commissioner bows deferentially. Bergmann opens
a padded double door and goes out (camera pans right
after him).*

*(Drawing room of Gestapo Headquarters, HF)*　　　　257:97-4"1

*Bergman opens a second double door, leading to the
drawing room, and closes it behind him, going off screen
to right. Piano music is heard off screen.*

*Bergmann (FS; back to camera) goes forward into the*　258:266-11"2
*drawing room. There are paintings on the walls, carpets
on the floors, and flowers. Several German officers are
drinking and playing cards at the tables; one plays the
piano in the background. Ingrid is leaning against the
piano, listening.*

BERGMANN: Ingrid!

*Ingrid turns and comes to him in the center of the room.
He whispers something in her ear. She immediately starts
out of the room, with Bergmann following (camera pans
left).*

*They come on screen from right. Bergmann opens the*　259:80-3"8
*door for her. Piano music ends.*

*(Bergmann's office, HF)*　　　　　　　　　　　　260:469-
　　　　　　　　　　　　　　　　　　　　　　　　　　19"13

*Ingrid, smiling, enters and offers her hand to the
Commissioner.*

INGRID: Oh, good evening! How are you? *(Camera pans*

*left after her.)*

POLICE COMMISSIONER, *kissing her hand*: Ah!

BERGMANN, *stepping between them*: Commissioner, you're corrupting my employees, but you are forgiven. *To Ingrid*: He has made a most interesting discovery.

INGRID: Really?

*Bergmann goes to the table. He picks up the paper, glances over it, then hands it to Ingrid, who has followed him. The Commissioner follows her (camera tracks briefly and adjusts).*

*Ingrid takes the paper and examines it (MCU). The Commissioner and Bergmann await her reaction.* 261:339-14"3

INGRID: Phantastisch! [Fantastic!]

BERGMANN: The time for talk is over, Ingrid. We must act now, and right away! *He takes back the paper,*

*checking it once more.*

INGRID, *staring straight ahead, as if enraptured*: Yes!
Leave it to me.

*(Fade-out)*

*(Don Pietro's rectory, TQ)* 262:634-
26"10

*Don Pietro (back to camera) opens the door and greets a
group of children who have come for their morning
catechism lesson. The sun shines brightly in the courtyard.*

CHILDREN: Hello!

DON PIETRO: Hello, children!

CHILDREN: Praised be Jesus Christ!

DON PIETRO: Forever and ever!

*The priest steps aside to let the children in. He is about
to close the door when Marcello runs in, panting.*

DON PIETRO, *grumpily*: Well?

MARCELLO: Praised be Jesus Christ!

DON PIETRO, *mollified*: Ah . . . Forever and ever! But
you're always the last one to praise Him!

*Marcello goes off screen to right. Don Pietro closes the
door.*

*(Fade-out)*

*(Francesco's apartment, TQ)* 263:172-7"4

*One foot up on a chair, Francesco whistles as he polishes
his shoes. Manfredi is lathering his face with a shaving
brush. Someone knocks on the door. Manfredi turns in
alarm. Francesco reassures him with a gesture.*

FRANCESCO: Who is it?

SERGEANT *(off screen)*: Police!

FRANCESCO: Hello, Sergeant!

*(Landing outside Francesco's apartment, TQ)* 264:311-
12″23

*The black-marketeer and the sergeant are waiting outside Francesco's door with a bouquet of flowers.*

FRANCESCO *(off screen)*: Wait a minute, I'm getting dressed!

SERGEANT: Then, with your permission, we'll go pay our respects to your future. . . .

*The sergeant gestures eloquently and starts toward Pina's door (camera pans slightly right). Suddenly Pina comes out, in great agitation, and runs toward Francesco's apartment.*

PINA: Francesco!

*(Francesco's apartment, TQ)* 265:103-4″7

*Pina enters the room (camera pans left after her). Music begins.*

PINA: The Germans and the Fascists are surrounding the building!

*Manfredi and Francesco go to the window with Pina and open it.*

*On the street in front of Francesco's building (LS from above), passersby are fleeing. A German motorcycle drives up from the background.* 266:71-2″23

*The motorcycle swings around in a half-circle in front of the building and stops (LS from below). Two German trucks drive up from the background.* 267:153-6″4

*A crowd of men, women, and children (seen head-on) throngs the entrance of the building. (MLS)* 268:56-2″8

*(The crowd, seen from the right, LS)* 269:49-2″1

*Two trucks stop at the corner (MLS). The car accom-*     270:100-4″4
*panying them continues on (camera pans left after it).*

*(LS from above; resume on the movement of the vehicles.)*     271:229-9″13
*The street is deserted except for the soldiers jumping out*
*of the trucks. The car stops, and several people get out.*

*The car is surrounded by Fascist and German officers, to*     272:136-5″16
*whom a German officer is giving orders. (MLS)*

OFFICER *(off screen)*: Los, schnell, schnell raus aus dem
     Kastell! Schnell, macht, das ihr da rauskommt.
     [Hurry up, everybody out of the building! Hurry up,
     everybody out!]

*In Francesco's apartment (HF), Pina continues to look*     273:125-5″5
*out the window. Francesco and Manfredi step back to*
*avoid being seen.*

PINA: Look, they're surrounding the building! Get back!

*(Street, FS)*     274:181-7″13

*A squad of soldiers marches down the street (camera pans*
*right) and divides into two files to surround the area.*

*(Courtyard of Francesco's building, MLS)*     275:385-16″1

*A group of soldiers, led by a corporal and accompanied*
*by a woman in uniform, the interpreter, is waiting for*
*orders. A tenant who was about to enter flees as he*
*sees them.*

CORPORAL: Los, ihr geht da rauf, ja, bis auf die Treppe,
     bis oben rauf die Treppe. Alle runterholen hier auf
     den Hof. [Go on upstairs, yes, all the way to the top.
     Get them all down to the courtyard.]

*The soldiers go off singly to the right and the left. Music*
*ends.*

CORPORAL: Ja halt! Drüben auf der anderen Seite genau dasselbe. Ja, all runter. [Yes, one minute! Do the same thing on the other side. Yes, everybody down here.]

*The corporal stops a group of Fascists who are just coming up. (LS)*    276:159-6″15

CORPORAL: Hier auf den Hof. *To Fascists*: Halt! *To interpreter*: Hören Sie zu, übersetzen Sie: Die Leute sollen raufgehen, alle Leute hierunter auf den Hof bringen. . . . [Here in the courtyard. Halt. Look, translate that they have to go upstairs and bring everybody down to the courtyard. . . .]

*The interpreter listens to the corporal (back to camera), then translates for the Fascist soldiers who have stopped in front of them. (TQ)*    277:793-33″1

CORPORAL: Sofort, verstanden? [Right now, understand?]

INTERPRETER: You three go there and make everybody come down. And you do the same on the other side.

*Three go to the left, three to the right.*

CORPORAL: Also, fühlen Sie die Leute mal ordentlich auf den Zahn! [And be strict with these tenants!]

*The corporal and the interpreter remain alone. The Italian police sergeant has come down the stairs and is about to leave when the German corporal notices him and calls him over. The sergeant comes toward him, giving him the Fascist salute.*

CORPORAL: Hä, Sie! Was machen Sie denn hier? Kommen Sie mal her! [Hey, you! What're you doing here? Come here!]

SERGEANT: Who, me?

CORPORAL: Kommen Sie her! *To interpreter*: Fragen Sie ihn was er hier sucht! [Come here! Ask him what he's looking for here!]

INTERPRETER: What are you doing here?

SERGEANT: I'm here on duty. I have to go now. I'm a sergeant. Sergeant! *He points to his chevrons. (WF)*

INTERPRETER: Er sagt er ist dienstlich beauftragt, er ist ein Wachtmeister. [He says he's on duty, that he's a sergeant.]

CORPORAL: Ach, Quatsch! Der soll hier bleiben! [Oh, nonsense! He has to stay here!]

*The sergeant again raises his arm to salute. The corporal gestures sharply with his hand.*

INTERPRETER: You must stay here!

*(Wipe to right)*

*(Street in front of Don Pietro's church, MLS)*      278:103-4"7

*A donkey-drawn cart comes down the street from left to right. The sound of a child's crying is heard along with the noise of the cart. Andreina, holding two children by the hand, is about to enter the church.*

*(Church, MLS)*      279:77-3"5

*Four boys are moving a prie-dieu. The child's crying is heard off screen.*

*(RA)*      280:74-3"2
*Andreina runs into the church with one of the children in her arms (WF). The other, about four years old, follows. Andreina puts the baby down and goes off screen to left.*

ANDREINA: Marcello, Marcello, Marcello!

*The boys carrying the prie-dieu turn toward Andreina,*      281:236-9"20
*who appears on screen (back to camera). Marcello ap-*

*pears from behind the altar and comes toward her with the other boys. Don Pietro steps down from the altar dais and approaches her too.*

MARCELLO: What's up, Andreina?

ANDREINA: The Germans, the Fascists!

MARCELLO: Where?

ANDREINA: At our place!

MARCELLO: Let's go, boys!

DON PIETRO: Hold it! Wait a minute!

*Don Pietro (back to camera) faces the boys. (HF)*　　　282:42-1"18

MARCELLO, *to Don Pietro*: Can't you understand? It's the Germans.

*(RA)*　　　283:128-5"8
*Don Pietro (seen head-on) tries to calm the boys, especially Marcello, who is evidently very upset. (TQ)*

DON PIETRO: Don't leave here! I'll go see what's happening!

MARCELLO: But we have to go!

DON PIETRO, *firmly*: I said stay here, understand?

MARCELLO, *pulling Don Pietro's sleeve*: But, Don Pietro,　　　284:61-2"13
there are bombs in Romoletto's attic!

*Don Pietro is astounded.*　　　285:53-2"5

*(Courtyard of Francesco's building, MLS)*　　　286:46-1"22

*In the foreground are two German soldiers (backs to camera); farther back, a crowd of people is massed at the sides and in front of the doorway.*

*(Laundry room of Francesco's building, MS)*　　　287:287-
　　　11"23

*Some men are escaping through a window that leads to a passageway. Off screen the noise of the crowd outside is heard.*

*(Courtyard, WF)* 288:54-2″6

*Closer view of shot 286; the interpreter, German soldiers, and the crowd of tenants around the doorway.*

*From the laundry room (LS), the men continue to escape.* 289:129-5″9
*Manfredi waits his turn beside a man in workman's coveralls. A woman stands nearby.*

WOMAN: Quick, to the railroad! Hurry up!

WORKMAN: Hurry up! The Germans are in the courtyard!

MANFREDI: What about Francesco?

WORKMAN: He didn't make it in time. He's gone to Duilio's to get rid of all that stuff!

MANFREDI: But how will he get away?

*Manfredi finally clambers over the windowsill. (TQ)* 290:71-2″23

WORKMAN: Don't worry! The building's so big they'll never find him!

MANFREDI: Don't tell Pina.

*(Cellar passageway, TQ)* 291:73-3″1

*Manfredi jumps down from the window and goes off to the rear. The workman jumps down after him.*

WOMAN *(off screen)*: Go on, go on, don't worry!

*The woman approaches the laundry tub (FS; camera* 292:283-
*pans left after her). She has barely resumed her washing* 11″19
*when two Italian soldiers and an officer enter.*

LIEUTENANT, *in Tuscan accent*: What are you doing here?

WOMAN: I'm getting my stuff.

LIEUTENANT: Get outside! No one's going to touch your stuff. We're here!

*The lieutenant and the two soldiers pass around the tub (camera adjusts slightly to right) and go over to the window (TQ) through which the fugitives have just escaped. The woman, muttering to herself, goes toward the door.*

WOMAN: Oh, of course, how stupid of me! I didn't think of that!

*(Cellar passageway, HF)* 293:109-4"13

*Rifle at the ready, a soldier leans through the window, looking to his right (at the camera). Manfredi and the workman are escaping down the passageway, to his left. The soldier then looks upward and grins broadly.*

*(Stairway, MS; camera subjective from soldier's view-point. The legs of the women standing on the stairway are seen from below.)* 294:46-1"22

*(Courtyard, WF)* 295:70-2"22

*Carrying her basin of laundry, the woman who had been in the laundry room passes by the German corporal, the interpreter, and the Italian sergeant (camera pans left after her). The sergeant pushes her toward a group of women.*

SERGEANT: Hurry up, get a move on! Over here!

*(RA)* 296:61-2"13
*The woman with the tub passes by the group of women standing against the wall (camera pans left after her). She stops beside Pina, who looks questioningly at her. The woman puts down her basin.*

*The woman moves closer to Pina (HF). A German soldier*     297:160-6"16
*—only his arm is seen—pushes her closer to the other*
*women.*

PINA: Where's Francesco?

WOMAN: Don't worry, he's safe.

*Off screen, voices of German soldiers are heard.*

CORPORAL *(off screen)*: Raus! [Out!]

SECOND WOMAN: These bastards! They're even pulling
     sick folks out of the building!

*Escorted by two soldiers, two women come out of the*     298:53-2"5
*crowded doorway, supporting a man wrapped up in*
*blankets. (FS)*

*At the doorway, Otello's mother worriedly questions the*     299:114-4"18
*sergeant. (TQ)*

OTELLO'S MOTHER: Grandpa refuses to be carried down!
     What'll they do to him?

SERGEANT: Nothing, nothing! Don't worry! Go over there.

*The residents of the building are all lined up against the*     300:68-2"20
*courtyard wall, under the surveillance of the German*
*soldiers.*

SERGEANT: . . . Quick, hurry up!

WOMAN *(off screen)*: My boy!

*Pina and other women listen in anguish to the cries. (HF)*     301:51-2"3

WOMAN *(off screen)*: My boy!

*Two soldiers appear on screen, dragging a young man,*     302:110-4"14
*followed by his weeping mother. One soldier pushes her*
*into the group of women as she continues to scream.*

WOMAN: My boy! My boy! Oh, Giorgio!

*The woman is pushed next to Pina, who pulls her close.*    303:248-10"8

ANOTHER WOMAN: Just look at that!

PINA: Where was he hiding?

WOMAN, *weeping*: I don't know . . . I don't know. . . .
    They took him away . . . what will they do to him?

*At the entranceway of Francesco's building (WF) the*    304:196-8"4
*German corporal, the interpreter, and the Italian lieu-*
*tenant surround the sergeant (camera adjusts slightly left*
*on the lieutenant's entrance).*

CORPORAL: Ist doch unmöglich, dass in diesem Riesenkast
    en keine Männer aufzutreiben sind. Das ist doch
    Quatsch! [It's not possible that there aren't any more
    men in this building. Nonsense!]

INTERPRETER, *to sergeant*: Where are all the men in this
    building?

LIEUTENANT, *to sergeant*: You hear? Where are the men?

SERGEANT: How should I know . . .

*Don Pietro, in white surplice, followed by Marcello in an*    305:130-5"10
*altar-boy's robe, approaches the group from the doorway.*
*The lieutenant moves toward them. (WF)*

SERGEANT: . . . I'm not the doorman here!

CORPORAL, *to Don Pietro*: Halt! *To interpreter*: Was will
    denn der da? [What's that guy want?]

INTERPRETER, *to sergeant*: What's that guy want?

*The lieutenant reaches Don Pietro and Marcello as they*    306:58-2"10
*are about to go up the stairs and stops them. (HF)*

LIEUTENANT: Where're you going?

DON PIETRO: There's a sick man here who needs a priest.

SERGEANT, *to interpreter*: He's the parish priest.     307:34-1"10

LIEUTENANT *(off screen)*: You might as well . . .

    . . . save your breath! There's nobody left up there.     308:572-
We got everybody down for some fresh air.     23"20

DON PIETRO: That's impossible! A very sick man—I must
go up!

*Don Pietro tries to go up the stairs but is again stopped
by the lieutenant. The sergeant, coming on screen from
left, steps in.*

LIEUTENANT: Eh? Stop!

SERGEANT, *to Don Pietro*: You finally made it, Father?
That poor fellow was begging for you. He must be
dead by now!

*The corporal comes on screen (back to camera) followed
by the interpreter.*

SERGEANT, *to Don Pietro*: Go on up!

LIEUTENANT: Just a minute! What is this? They got
everybody out!

SERGEANT: No, not that fellow. He's a paralyzed old guy.
Go on, Father, hurry up!

*Don Pietro and Marcello hurry up the stairs, going off
screen to left. The sergeant continues talking to the
others.*

SERGEANT: What service! They used to be as quick as the
firemen!

*(Stairway, HF)*     309:395-
16"11

*Don Pietro and Marcello (seen from below) are going up
the stairs (camera pans 360° left after them). Music*

*begins. Off-screen sounds of soldiers searching the building are heard.*

*(Wipe to right)*

*Marcello (HF from above) reaches the top of the stairs alone (camera pans right after him). He stops and begins to whistle. Behind him, the railroad tracks can be seen through the window. (LS)*

310:623-
25"23

MARCELLO: Romoletto, Romoletto, open up! It's me! And Don Pietro's here too!

*Don Pietro (WF) comes on screen. Marcello knocks on the terrace door (camera pans right after him).*

ROMOLETTO *(off screen)*: Go away! Get out of here! You're still. . . .

DON PIETRO, *knocking*: Come on, Romoletto, open up!

ROMOLETTO *(off screen)*: No! Go away—or you'll be blown

up with me!

*Don Pietro grasps the top of the door and tries to pull it off its hinges.*

DON PIETRO: I said open up!

*He manages to pull the door open; his cape falls from his shoulders with the effort. He stoops to pick it up before going out onto the terrace.*

*(Terrace, TQ)*                                    311:51-2"3

*Don Pietro enters from the right and looks in horror at Romoletto. (TQ)*

DON PIETRO: What're you doing?

*Romoletto is clutching a rudimentary bomb, which he*      312:177-7"9
*threatens to hurl from the terrace. (WF)*

ROMOLETTO: Nothing. I'm going to kill them all! Go away!

DON PIETRO: You want to murder everybody? You're out of your mind! Give me that thing! *After a brief struggle with the boy, he gets hold of the bomb.*

MARCELLO: Stop, look out!

*Don Pietro seizes a submachine gun lying at Romoletto's feet, then moves forward (to HF) and looks upward toward the sound of a voice.*

WOMAN *(off screen)*: Help! Help!

*(FS; camera subjective from the terrace, looking upward*      313:55-2"7
*through the twisted wire lath of a caved-in floor to the balcony of the next building.)*

*Two Germans are dragging away a screaming woman.*

WOMAN: Help! Help, Antonio! Let me go!

*Don Pietro bows his head and goes off screen. Romoletto*      314:32-1"8 *remains alone at the back of the terrace. Music ends.*

WOMAN *(off screen)*: Let me go!

*At the entranceway (HF) the lieutenant, suspicious, turns to the sergeant.*                                      315:399-
                                                                                                                16"15

LIEUTENANT: What floor is this sick guy on?

SERGEANT, *embarrassed*: I don't know for sure—the third or the fourth.

*The lieutenant signals to two soldiers to follow him and, repulsing the sergeant, starts up the stairs.*

LIEUTENANT: I'll go have a look myself. I'm something of a doctor myself.

SERGEANT: I'll go with you.

LIEUTENANT: No, no, no, I'll go by myself. I don't like your face.

*(Stairway, TQ)*                                                                                                316:89-3"17

*Don Pietro, followed by Marcello, rushes down the stairs (camera pans left after him). Don Pietro is carrying Romoletto's bomb and submachine gun. Music begins.*

*Three floors below, the lieutenant and the two soldiers are coming up the stairs. (FS from above)*             317:101-4"5

*Don Pietro and Marcello continue down the stairs. (WF from below; camera pans left after them)*                318:68-2"20

*The lieutenant and the soldiers enter an apartment. (MS from above)*                                           319:154-6"10

*Don Pietro rushes down the stairs. (TQ; camera pans right after him)*                                          320:101-4"5

LIEUTENANT *(off screen)*: Nobody in here. Let's have a look . . .

*The lieutenant and the soldiers leave the apartment and*                                                       321:48-2" *continue on up the stairs. (FS)*

LIEUTENANT: . . . upstairs.

*Don Pietro and Marcello enter Pina's apartment (HF; camera pans right after them). They shut the apartment door. Music ends.*

322:130-5"10

*In one of the rooms of Pina's apartment (TQ), the grandfather is asleep in bed.*

323:65-2"17

*Don Pietro opens the door to the old man's room and goes over to the table. (TQ; camera pans right after him)*

324:983-
40"23

*Marcello follows him. Don Pietro puts the gun and bomb on the table. The old man sleeps on. Don Pietro removes his cape.*

DON PIETRO, *whispering to Marcello:* The door! The door!

*Marcello whirls around and bumps against the submachine gun, which knocks the bomb off the table. Terrified, Don Pietro catches the bomb on the fly and sighs in relief. He then goes over to the bed (WF), and hides the bomb under it. Marcello has returned to his side; Don Pietro takes the gun, hesitates, and returns to the bed. He raises the bedclothes and hides the gun underneath. The old man sleeps on. The priest straightens his surplice and, sighing, sits down by the head of the bed.*

*The old man awakens. Terrified at the sight of the priest, he pulls himself up. (HF)*

325:105-4"9

GRANDFATHER: Oh, oh! Are you crazy? What are you doing here?

DON PIETRO: Biagio—

*Don Pietro stands up to calm the old man and tries to get him to lie down again. (HF)*

326:477-
19"21

GRANDFATHER: But I'm fine! I'm fine! You hear?

DON PIETRO: Calm down! For the love of God, lie down! Pretend you're sick! (*Their voices overlap.*)

GRANDFATHER, *so upset he cannot understand*: But I'm fine! I'm fine! I'm gonna live till a hundred! Get out of here! Understand?

DON PIETRO: But the SS are coming!

GRANDFATHER: Who's coming?

DON PIETRO: The Germans!

GRANDFATHER: The Germans? I don't give a damn about the Germans or the Fascists either! I'll spit . . .

*Increasingly worried, Don Pietro puts his hand over the old man's mouth.*

DON PIETRO, *to Marcello*: Get me. . . .

GRANDFATHER, *his voice muffled*: . . . in their eye!

(*Stairway, TQ*) 327:103-4"7

*The lieutenant and the two soldiers leave Francesco's apartment and enter Pina's (camera pans right after them). Music begins.*

*In Pina's apartment (WF), the lieutenant and the soldiers* 328:472-
*begin their inspection at the end of the hallway. The* 19"16
*lieutenant comes forward (to TQ), opens a door, and enters.*

LIEUTENANT: You look in there!

*As the soldiers search, the sound of a falling object is heard off screen. The music fades into the sound of Don Pietro's prayers (off screen). The two soldiers, who have evidently broken something, come up to the lieutenant*

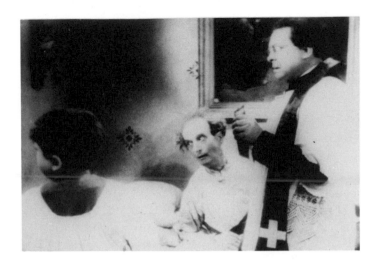

*as he is about to enter the room from which they can hear the priest's voice.*

*The lieutenant and the two soldiers appear in the doorway of the grandfather's room (TQ). Don Pietro, off screen, continues to murmur his prayers.*  329:93-3"21

*The old man is lying still on the bed, his eyes closed. Don Pietro stands by the bedside, reading from his breviary in a low voice. Marcello his face serious, is beside him. The priest stops reading as the three men enter and stares severely at the lieutenant. (WF)*  330:217-9"1

*Perplexed, the lieutenant watches for a moment, then walks out, signaling to the soldiers to follow him.*  331:189-7"21

LIEUTENANT: Come on.

*Don Pietro, off screen, resumes his prayers.*

*Don Pietro waits a moment, then puts down his breviary, bends over the old man, and tries to bring him to. Marcello hands the priest a bottle of water. Don Pietro pours a little on a handkerchief and places it on the old*  332:512-21"8 *man's forehead. (TQ)*

DON PIETRO: Wake up, wake up! Biagio, wake up! *To Marcello*: Give it to me! *To the grandfather*: Come on, wake up!

*Marcello kneels to pick up a frying pan with a twisted handle.*

*Smiling, Marcello observes the frying pan. (TQ)*     333:56-2″8

MARCELLO: Gosh, Don Pie' . . .

   *(TQ)* . . . you really gave it to him!     334:118-4″22

*Shaking his head, Don Pietro takes the frying pan. The old man, reviving, touches his aching head.*

*(Courtyard, TQ)*     335:359-
                                                           14″23

*Pina, lined up with the other women against the wall, holds the woman whose son has been captured. The sound of German voices is heard off screen.*

PINA: Don't worry.

*The German corporal walks back and forth in front of them (camera shifts slightly with him). He stops to look at Pina and caresses her shoulder and arm.*

CORPORAL: Hat Dir schöne Augen gemacht, der Pfarrer? [Has the priest made eyes at you?]

*Furious, Pina slaps his hand.*

*The soldiers have discovered Francesco and some other*     336:75-3″3
*men and are taking them away. (FS)*

*As soon as Pina sees Francesco, she starts toward him*     337:89-3″17
*but is held back by the German corporal. Pina struggles to get free of him.*

PINA: Francesco! Francesco! Francesco!

*Francesco is dragged away by the soldiers. (TQ)*  338:59-2″11

FRANCESCO: Pina! Pina!

*The soldiers take Francesco out through the main en-*  339:62-2″14
*trance. (MLS)*

FRANCESCO: Pina! Pina!

*Struggling, Pina hits the corporal in the face, manages*  340:96-4″
*to get free of him, and runs after Francesco. She goes off*
*screen to right.*

PINA: Francesco!

*Pina runs toward the front entrance as the interpreter,*  341:101-4″5
*coming from the side of the courtyard, tries to stop her.*
*Pina crosses the sill but is stopped on the sidewalk by*
*two soldiers, who cross their rifles to bar her way. (MLS)*

PINA: Francesco! *To the German:* You bastard! *Then:*
    Francesco! Francesco!

*(Street, RA)*  342:46-1″22

*Pina breaks through the gun barrier and races ahead.*
*Don Pietro, who has just returned, and the sergeant try*
*to stop her. (WF)*

PINA: Let me go! Francesco!

SERGEANT: Pina, come back here!

*A soldier pushes Francesco and other prisoners onto the*  343:39-1″15
*truck. (TQ)*

PINA *(off screen):* Let me go!  344:71-2″43

*Pina tries to get away from a soldier. Marcello kicks*
*another, who has caught him.*

*The sergeant and Don Pietro try to stop Pina, but she*  345:72-3″
*sidesteps them, going off screen to left. Don Pietro, in*

*anguish, watches her go. (TQ)*

SERGEANT: Pina, stop!

*Pina runs shouting into the half-empty street (MLS; she*     346:39-1″15
*is facing the camera, which adjusts and tracks briefly*
*back).*

PINA: Francesco!

*Pina runs toward Francesco, one hand outstretched*     347:43-1″19
*toward him, a scarf in the other (TQ; camera tracks*
*rapidly sideways). The street is crowded with people.*

PINA: Francesco! Francesco!

*Don Pietro pulls Marcello close to him and covers the*     348:41-1″17
*boy's face with his hand. (TQ)*

*Francesco, watching anxiously from the truck, which is*     349:39-1″15
*about to pull away, has one foot on the tail gate. (MLS)*

PINA: Francesco!

FRANCESCO: Pina! Hold her back!

*A burst of machine-gun fire is heard off screen.*

*Pina (seen from the front) is running toward the truck when the gunfire fells her (MLS). At the same time Marcello runs on screen. Music begins.* 350:38-1"14

*Marcello runs screaming toward his mother (camera pans left after him).* 351:28-1"4

MARCELLO: Mama! Mama!

*Pina lies face-down in the street, her right leg bared to the garter. Weeping, Marcello throws himself on her. Don Pietro comes on screen, lifts Marcello from his mother's corpse, and hands him over to the sergeant. Screaming, Marcello struggles between the priest and the sergeant. (WF)* 352:94-3"22

MARCELLO: My mama!

*The sergeant holds Marcello back as Don Pietro kneels down beside Pina. In the background the soldiers hold back the crowd. (MS)* 353:203-8"11

MARCELLO, *crying*: Mama!

*Don Pietro, on his knees, holds Pina's dead body in his arms. (TQ)* 354:128-5"8

MARCELLO *(off screen) screaming*: Mama!

*(Dissolve to . . .*

*(Area near World's Fair grounds, ELS)* 355:188-7"20

*A partisan (back to camera) pulls himself up from a ditch and looks cautiously around.*

*(LS from above; camera subjective from the partisan's* 356:137-5"17

*viewpoint.)*

*A column of open trucks, carrying prisoners, appears on the road, preceded by a motorcycle.*

*The man turns and whistles.*                                    357:45-1″21

*Four armed partisans, including Manfredi, are hidden behind a low wall. In the background is the Palace of Civilization in the World's Fair area. (MLS)*          358:613-
                                                                         25″13

MANFREDI: There they are! Get set!

*One of the partisans whistles in reply. Manfredi and the others get into firing position.*

MANFREDI: Ready when they reach the turn. Aim at the drivers!

*(LS from above, at the partisans' position)*                    359:414-17″6

*The motorcycle and the first truck come on screen from left (camera pans right to include a tunnel). The line of trucks enters the tunnel. The music continues, overlapping the noise of the trucks.*

*The partisans are ready to shoot. In the background the motorcycle and the trucks emerge from the tunnel and are about to enter another when the partisans open fire. (LS)*                                                      360:103-4″7

*(LS from above)*                                                361:102-4″6

*Two trucks stop. Soldiers jump out and begin to answer the fire. The prisoners jump out and scatter.*

*The prisoners flee. (LS)*                                       362:69-2″21

*Following the movements of the soldiers, the partisans continue their fire. (MLS)*                              363:87-3″15

*One of the prisoners, among the trucks, takes advantage*        364:100-4″4 *of the confusion to shoot with a rifle taken from a fallen German soldier. (MLS)*

*(A truck, almost empty, MLS)* 365:87-3"15

*A German soldier fires as he tries to reach cover.*

*Same action as preceding shot. (LS)* 366:64-2"16

*The prisoners run toward the hill, from which the partisans cover them. One soldier fires and kills a prisoner but is in turn felled by another prisoner. (LS)* 367:141-5"21

*The battle continues, but the Germans have the worst of it. (LS)* 368:68-2"20

*A soldier is killed. A prisoner takes his gun and escapes with the others (LS). Music ends.* 369:85-3"13

*(Fade-out)*

*(Fade-in)* 370:196-8"4

*(A Roman street in late afternoon, FS)*

*A German military truck approaches and stops in front of a small restaurant (camera pans to right after it).*

*A German soldier gets out of the truck, opens the back door, and with the help of another soldier leads two sheep into the restaurant. (WF)* 371:500-20"20

*Bleating of sheep is heard.*

*(Restaurant, WF)* 372:496-20"16

*The two soldiers enter, leading the sheep on ropes (camera pans left after them).*

FIRST SOLDIER: Flavio!

FLAVIO *(off screen)*: What?

FIRST SOLDIER: We bring meat!

FLAVIO *(coming on screen from left)*: Oh? Where is it?

FIRST SOLDIER: Here!

*Shaking his head, Flavio comes out from behind the checkroom counter.*

FLAVIO: So that's the meat? I'm a cook, not a butcher!

FIRST SOLDIER: We butcher it!

FLAVIO: Oh, yes, you people are specialists.

*Manfredi and Francesco appear in the doorway behind the soldiers. (HF)*    373:35-1″11

FLAVIO *(off screen)*: Oh!

*Manfredi and Francesco come on screen from right and go off to left, passing the soldiers. (WF)*    374:166-6″22

FLAVIO: Good afternoon, sir! Come right on in!

*The waiter in the restaurant greets Manfredi. (TQ)*    375:501-
20″21

WAITER: Oh, hello, sir! Miss Marina's waiting for you!

MANFREDI, *to Francesco*: Let's go!

*They are about to go out again when Marina appears from the right. She takes Manfredi's arm and leads him to a table (camera tracks with them and pans left). They stop at the table.*

MARINA: Oh, Giorgio, at last! I've looked everywhere for you! I hoped you'd come here. What happened to you?

*Francesco comes on screen (camera adjusts slightly to right; all three are in TQ).*

MANFREDI, *taking off his coat*: Nothing. Why? What could have happened? I don't understand you.

MARINA: What? At your place— *Marina stops, noticing Francesco.*

MANFREDI: Oh, this is a friend of mine. Sit down, Francesco.

MARINA, *shaking Francesco's hand*: Pleased to meet you.

*Manfredi sits down. Marina is already seated. (HF)*     376:576-24"

MARINA: The SS were there, weren't they?

MANFREDI: Who told you?

MARINA: Your concierge. But why were they looking for you?

MANFREDI, *taking out a cigarette*: I don't know. Maybe because I'm an officer.

MARINA: And where are you living now?

MANFREDI: I don't really know. We'll be at a friend's tonight.

MARINA: Why don't you come to my place?

MANFREDI: No, not your place.

MARINA: Why not?

MANFREDI, *lighting his cigarette*: No, I don't want to trouble you, and anyway, I'm with him.

MARINA: So? He can sleep on the couch in the living room. *To Francesco*: You'll be very comfortable.

WAITER *(off screen)*: Spaghetti for all three of you?

*The waiter comes on screen from left, sets the wine on the table, and remains at the margin of the frame.*

MANFREDI, *to Marina*: We'll see about it later.

WAITER: Ration cards, please.

FRANCESCO *(MCU)*: I don't have one. 377:44-1"20

MARINA: I'll give you . . .

*The three are seated at the table. (HF)* 378:222-9"6

MARINA: . . . a stamp.

FRANCESCO: Thanks!

WAITER: And for the second course?

*As Marina gives the waiter the ration stamps, Flavio approaches.*

FLAVIO: That's all right, I'll take care of these folks!

*The waiter goes off. Flavio looks around cautiously.*

FLAVIO, *whispering in Manfredi's ear (MCU)*: They've 379:230-9"14
arrested Mezzetta.

MANFREDI, *surprised*: When?

FLAVIO: At six this morning. The painter told me.

MANFREDI: If we don't disappear for a while they'll catch
us all.

VOICE *(off screen)*: Flavio!

FLAVIO: Here I come! *He turns and goes off screen.*

MARINA *(CU)*: I bet that's where you were going to stay. 380:50-2"2

MANFREDI *(MCU)*: Somebody's ratted— 381:180-7"12

*A pistol shot is heard off screen. Manfredi and Marina
turn toward the window. Manfredi stands up (camera
adjusts upward) and approaches the window (camera
pans to right after him). Marina and Francesco follow
Manfredi.*

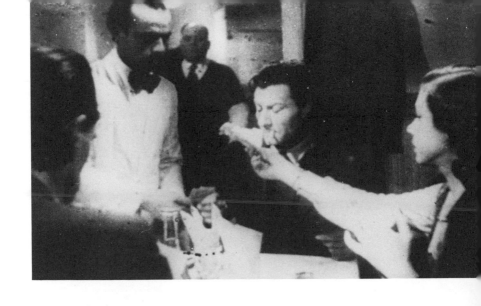

*The three look out the window (they are seen from out-*     382:76-3"4
*side, HF).*

MARINA: Poor animals!

*(Camera subjective from the restaurant window, WF)*     383:61-2"13

*In the courtyard, one soldier is kneeling over the dead sheep. The other soldier is about to shoot the second sheep with his pistol.*

*Marina moves away from the window and hides her face*     384:77-3"5
*on Manfredi's chest (HF). A second shot is heard off screen.*

*(Wipe to right)*

*(Don Pietro's church; camera pans downward until it*     385:182-7"14
*includes Don Pietro, in WF, back to camera.)*

*Don Pietro is before the altar, conducting evening prayers. An altar boy is beside him. Don Pietro's voice, heard first off screen and then on screen, is followed by the responses of the congregation. Organ music mingles with the prayers.*

DON PIETRO: . . . Sancta Dei Genitrix . . . Sancta Virgo
    Virginum . . . Mater Christi. . . .

CONGREGATION: Ora pro nobis . . . Ora pro nobis . . . Ora
    pro nobis. . . .

*(Don Pietro and the altar boy, in profile, TQ)*     386:44-1"20

DON PIETRO: Mater Divinae Gratiae. . . .

CONGREGATION: Ora pro nobis. . . .

*(The congregation praying, FS)*     387:77-3"5

DON PIETRO: Mater Purissima . . . Mater Castissima . . .
    Mater Inviolata . . . Mater Intemerata . . . Mater
    Amabilis . . . Mater Admirabilis. . . .

CONGREGATION: Ora pro nobis . . . Ora pro nobis . . . Ora pro nobis . . . Ora pro nobis . . . Ora pro nobis . . . Ora pro nobis. . . .

*(Don Pietro's rectory, MCU)*

388:1589-
1'6"5

*The Austrian, in civilian clothes, is kneeling in front of the heater, lighting a cigarette with a piece of newspaper. He rises and goes over to the desk (HF; camera tracks with him and pans to right). He stops (camera continues tracking over to Marcello, asleep on the bed). The Austrian comes on screen and covers the boy with a blanket (camera shifts as he bends over and straightens up). The Austrian approaches the bureau (TQ) on which stands a large crucifix. He gazes at it, then turns away. End of organ music.*

*(Living room of Marina's well-appointed apartment, FS)*

389:207-8"15

*Manfredi paces up and down. Marina is kneeling by the radio, tuning it in. Francesco, in despair, sits on a couch.*

MARINA: At this hour there's always an American station playing jazz.

*The jazz comes in on the radio. Marina rises and begins to dance. Manfredi sits on the arm of a chair. Marina (TQ) dances over to the buffet (camera pans right after her).*

*(Francesco and Manfredi, TQ)*

390:1473-
1'1"9

MARINA *(off screen)*: Shall we have a little drink, boys?

*Marina comes on screen from right with a bottle. She sits down beside Francesco (camera adjusts slightly downward). She sets three glasses on the table and opens the bottle.*

MARINA: This gin was a gift. It'll warm us up a little. *She pours a drink and hands it to Francesco.*

FRANCESCO, *absently*: Thanks.

MARINA, *to Francesco*: Don't you feel well?

FRANCESCO: No, no.

MARINA, *feeling his forehead*: But you've got a fever! Giorgio, he's burning! I'll fix your bed right away. *Marina rises and goes off as Manfredi comes over to his friend.*

FRANCESCO: Don't trouble.

MANFREDI: Chin up, Francesco! *He rises as Marina brings over the bedding.*

MARINA: Give me a hand, Giorgio. *To Francesco*: You'll see, you'll be very comfortable. When you're in bed I'll give you some aspirin.

*Francesco gets up. With Giorgio's help, Marina prepares a bed on the couch.*

MARINA, *to Francesco*: Would you please hand me that blanket? You have to be careful—there's flu going around. The way things are these days, it's the only thing that is going around! *The doorbell rings off screen.* Who can that be at this hour?

*She goes off screen to right. Manfredi goes to turn off the radio (camera pans left after him), then goes to close the door (camera pans right after him).*

MARINA *(off screen)*: Who is it?

*Marina stops a moment in the front hall (facing away*    391:513-21″9
*from camera toward the door), then moves forward to open the door. (WF)*

LAURA *(off screen)*: It's me, Marina!

MARINA, *annoyed*: Oh, it's you.

*Marina opens the door. Laura, giggling and evidently tipsy, enters and sets her suitcase down on a chest in the hall. Then she picks it up again (both women come toward the camera, HF).*

LAURA: Oh, hello, darling! You see, I did come! Fritz didn't want me to go, but I—

MARINA: Are you drunk?

LAURA: Oh, just a little high.

MARINA, *pushing her toward the bedroom*: Then go straight to bed!

LAURA, *curious*: Who's in there—company? *She goes to open the living room door (camera pans left after her).*

*(RA)*                 392:193-8″1
*Followed by Marina, Laura (MS) opens the door and enters the living room (camera tracks out until all four are included in TQ).*

LAURA: Oh, it's Mr. Manfredi! *She giggles.*

MARINA: Lauretta, go to bed!

LAURA: I'm not going to eat him up! *She turns and sees Francesco.*

LAURA, *surprised (MCU)*: Francesco!       393:24-1″

*(Francesco, MCU)*            394:33-1″9

LAURA *(off screen)*: What're you doing here?

*Manfredi comes on screen next to Laura. (MCU)*     395:113-4″17

LAURA, *giggling*: Ah, Pina's kicked you out right on your wedding night!

MANFREDI: Lauretta, I think Marina's right.

*(TQ of all four)*                                      396:61-2"13

MANFREDI, *to Marina*: Put her to bed!

*Marina (WF) leads the giggling Laura off (camera pans right with them).*

*Marina and Laura cross the hall (FS; camera tracks after*      397:181-7"13
*them).*

MARINA: Come on!

LAURA: Hey, what long faces! What a welcome! I should have stayed with Fritz! I'm going to tell Pina as soon as I see her.

*Manfredi, in the background, closes the living room door.*

*Francesco is sitting up on the couch as Manfredi walks*      398:203-8"11
*through the living room. (FS)*

MANFREDI: Go to bed, Francesco. You've got a fever. I'll get you some aspirin.

*In the bedroom, Laura and Marina are both getting*      399:806-
*ready for bed. (WF)*                                             33"14

LAURA: I've had a fight with my sister. I'm never going back there again.

MANFREDI *(off screen)*: Marina!

MARINA: Come on in!

*Laura slips quickly into the bathroom, going off screen to right.*

LAURA: Oh, don't look at me!

MANFREDI *(off screen)*: I just wanted the aspirin.

MARINA: Oh, that's right. Look in the drawer—there must be a bottle there.

*Manfredi comes on screen from left (camera tracks right up to HF). He looks through the drawer. In the background Marina is putting on a dressing gown as she talks.*

MARINA: That dope was just what we needed! Now what'll we do? Where'll you sleep?

MANFREDI: Oh, don't worry. I'll be all right in the armchair in there.

MARINA: You'll be uncomfortable. You'll be cold. What a shame!

*The telephone on the night table rings. Marina flings herself across the bed to answer it. Manfredi sits down on the bed too.*

MARINA: Hello. . . .

*(Marina, on the bed, answering the telephone, MCU)*     400:101-4"5

MARINA: Oh, it's you. Hello.

*(Bergmann's office in Gestapo Headquarters, HF)*     401:439-18"7

*Ingrid is telephoning. Bergmann is behind her, with a cigarette and a drink in his hand.*

INGRID: How are you, darling? I was waiting for you to phone. Why didn't you? You're not alone?

BERGMANN: Und er? [Is he there?]

*Ingrid covers the receiver and frowns at him, signaling him to keep quiet.*

INGRID: Have you seen him? He's there? Oh, it's our little Lauretta!

MARINA: She's come to stay with me for a few days.     402:34-1"10

*Manfredi, on the bed, lights a cigarette. As he puts the lighter into Marina's handbag he sees the little bottle of*     403:179-7"11 *cocaine. He takes it out and looks at Marina. (TQ)*

MARINA *(off screen)*: No . . . No . . . Yes, of course. . . .

MARINA: All right.                                                404:53-2″5

*Manfredi slips the bottle into his pocket. (TQ)*               405:92-3″20

MARINA *(off screen)*: We'll talk tomorrow.

*Marina puts down the receiver and turns to Manfredi.*         406:103-4″7

MARINA: Good night!

MANFREDI *(CU)*: What's this stuff doing in your bag?          407:58-2″10

MARINA *(CU)*: What is it?                                      408:23-0″23

*Manfredi shows her the little bottle. (CU)*                    409:24-1″

*(Marina and Manfredi on the bed, CU; resume on Man-*          410:789-
*fredi showing the bottle.)*                                         32″21

*Marina gets up to take the bottle, but Manfredi tosses it
toward her on the bed.*

MARINA: Oh, of course, the dentist gave it to me, when my
    tooth was hurting me so. Remember?

MANFREDI, *coldly*: No, I don't remember.

*He stands up (camera adjusts slightly upward) as Marina
comes closer to show him the tooth (as they talk they
come closer into HF).*

MARINA: Yes you do—this tooth here. I had to use it to
    kill the pain.

MANFREDI: You still have the pain?

MARINA: No, it was a while ago.

MANFREDI: Oh, but just to be careful, you still carry the
    painkiller around with you? *He picks up the bottle.*

MARINA: I was going to bring it back to the dentist.

MANFREDI: Oh, so that's it. That explains everything. *He puts the bottle in his pocket.*

MARINA: What're you doing?

MANFREDI: I'll keep it. We'll stop by the dentist's together.

*Marina, her face suddenly contorted, struggles to get the bottle back. (ECU)*     411:45-1″21

MARINA: Don't kid around! Give me back that stuff!

*Manfredi (CU) hands her the bottle.*     412:91-3″19

MANFREDI, *scornfully*: Here!

MARINA: You might lose it, and with the price what it is, there'd be a fine mess! *She goes off screen for a moment, leaving Manfredi alone.*     413:128-5″8

*Marina puts the bottle in a drawer of her dressing table, then goes toward Manfredi, who appears on screen (TQ; camera pans to right with Marina).*     414:494-20″14

MARINA: Why're you looking at me like that? Oh, Giorgio, you don't think? . . .

MANFREDI: No, no, I don't think anything. Besides, you're your own boss. I haven't any right to tell you what to do. Who am I, anyway? Just a guy who's passed through one moment of your life.

MARINA: You were going to say, "one of the many guys."

MANFREDI: I didn't say it.

*Marina goes off screen to right.*

*Marina sits on the bed and begins to take off her stockings. (TQ)*     415:491-20″11

MARINA: But you thought it. Yes, I've had lovers, of

course. What was I supposed to do? How do you think I bought this furniture, my clothes, everything? With my pay? My pay covers my stockings and my cigarettes, that's all! I've just looked out for myself, like everybody else. That's life.

MANFREDI *(HF)*: Life is what we want it to be.                416:51-2″3

MARINA *(CU)*: Words, words! Life's dirty and ugly. I     417:297-12″9
know what poverty is, and I'm scared of it. If I hadn't done what I did, today maybe I'd be married to a bus driver, and I'd be dying of hunger . . .

*Marina gets up. Manfredi is standing, listening to her.*     418:276-
*(TQ)*                                                                      11″12

MARINA: . . . me, my kids, and him. *(Camera shifts slightly to follow Marina over to the wardrobe.)*

MANFREDI: Poor Marina! And you think happiness means having a fancy apartment, fancy clothes, a maid . . .

*Marina hangs her dress up in the wardrobe. (HF)*           419:416-17″8

MANFREDI *(off screen)*: . . . rich lovers.

MARINA: If you'd really loved me, you'd have changed me. But you're just like all the others—no, worse, because at least the others don't preach at me!

*Manfredi comes on screen from left (camera pans slightly left after him). He goes out of the room to the right. Sound of door opening off screen is heard.*

MANFREDI, *coldly*: You're right. Forgive me!

MARINA: Giorgio!

*Laura, in her nightgown, enters the bedroom from the*        420:107-4″11
*bathroom and goes to the bed (WF; camera pans left after her). Marina comes on screen from right.*

LAURA: You've had a fight for a change!

*Marina goes toward the bed (CU; camera pans left after her).*    421:107-4″11

MARINA: You were listening, of course!

LAURA *(off screen)*: No, I wasn't, but I heard. You hear everything in this place.

*Laura is in bed. Marina stands beside her, thinking. (WF)*    422:140-5″20

*(Dissolve to . . .*

*(Living room, TQ)*    423:106-4″10

*Francesco is lying on the couch. Manfredi, sitting in the armchair, is talking softly as he rolls a cigarette. Marina opens the door behind them and listens.*

MANFREDI: Tomorrow we'll go to Don Pietro's. He offered to hide me for a while in a monastery.

*Unobserved, Marina eavesdrops, then she closes the door. (HF)*    424:158-6″14

MANFREDI *(off screen)*: We'll go together.

FRANCESCO *(off screen)*: No, I can't now. Now I have to work . . .

. . . even more than before. She's dead!    425:1100-
45″20

MANFREDI: Yes, I understand. But look, Francesco, you're a wreck right now. Your work would do more harm than good. Don't be afraid of missing the boat. It'll be a long fight. We've hardly started.

*The door opens, and Marina enters with a glass and some blankets.*

MARINA: Here's the aspirin.

FRANCESCO: Oh, thanks!

*Francesco sits halfway up. Manfredi's cigarette is ready;*

*he looks for a match, doesn't find one, is exasperated, and throws the cigarette on the table. Marina remains next to Manfredi for a moment; then, realizing that he will not even look at her, she starts to leave the room.*

MARINA: Good night.

MANFREDI: Good night.

FRANCESCO: Good night.

*(Wipe to right)*

*(Bedroom, WF)*                                               426:797-33″5

*Laura is asleep in Marina's bed. Marina sits on the bed beside the telephone, thinking. Finally she comes to a decision, picks up the receiver, and, after checking to see that Laura is asleep, dials a number. Laura awakes, and Marina puts down the receiver.*

LAURA: Marina!

MARINA: What?

LAURA: You know, maybe Manfredi's right. We're dopes!

MARINA: Quiet down! Go to sleep!

*Laura falls back to sleep; Marina picks up the telephone again and begins to dial.*

*(Fade-out)*

*(Street in front of Don Pietro's church the next day, MLS)*   427:370-
                                                               15″10

*An overcrowded double streetcar comes to a stop (camera pans left after it). Manfredi gets off the second car, crosses the street, and enters the church (camera tracks left after him).*

*(Wipe to left, following Manfredi)*

                                                               428:254-
*(Don Pietro's rectory, CU)*                                   10″14

*Don Pietro is seated at his desk, looking over an identi-*
*fication card. The sexton appears and whispers in the*
*priest's ear.*

AGOSTINO: There's a man to see you. He says you're expecting him.

DON PIETRO: Oh, yes. Show him in.

*The sexton goes to the door and opens it (WF). Manfredi*      429·1330-
*enters (camera pans slightly right after him to include*        55"10
*the seated Austrian deserter; all four now in TQ).*
*Manfredi and Don Pietro shake hands.*

AGOSTINO: Come in.

MANFREDI: Hello, Don Pietro.

DON PIETRO: Oh, fine! I was waiting for you! I've got your
ID card.

*Manfredi takes the card and, after reading it, puts it in*
*his pocket.*

MANFREDI, *reading*: Giovanni Episcopo. . . . You've taken
two years off my life! Thanks! Who's that?

DON PIETRO: That's the Austrian. Didn't Francesco tell
you?

MANFREDI: Oh yes, that's right.

*Manfredi and Don Pietro come over to the Austrian*
*(camera pans to right with them). The Austrian stands*
*up.*

DON PIETRO: He's a fine person. *To the Austrian*: May I
introduce you? This is the gentleman who'll be
coming with us.

*Manfredi and the Austrian shake hands.*

MANFREDI: Glad to meet you.

AUSTRIAN: My pleasure.

*Don Pietro goes to a bureau at the rear of the room and puts some things in a drawer.*

DON PIETRO: I've spoken to the prior of the monastery, and he's expecting us.

MANFREDI: What about Francesco?

DON PIETRO: He's out in the courtyard with Marcello. We'd better hurry. *To Agostino:* Give me my. . . .

*Agostino goes off screen and returns with Don Pietro's hat and coat. Don Pietro starts to put them on.*

DON PIETRO, *to the other two men*: After you. . . .

MANFREDI, *to the Austrian*: After you. . . .

DON PIETRO: Agostino, I'll be back a little late.

AGOSTINO: When are you going to stop . . .

*Agostino talks as he helps Don Pietro on with his coat.* 430:515-
*(TQ)*                                                       21"11

AGOSTINO: . . . getting yourself into this kind of fix!

DON PIETRO: Ssh! You and the boy have dinner and then go to bed.

AGOSTINO: Sure! Who could sleep? Oh, Don Pietro!

DON PIETRO: What now?

AGOSTINO, *gesturing with his fingers to indicate money*: If I have to feed the kid, I need—

DON PIETRO: I get it. *He takes some coins from his pocket and hands them to the sexton.* Hm . . . here. That'll be enough.

AGOSTINO, *counting the money*: But you've got nothing left!

DON PIETRO, *as he leaves*: No, no. I've got some, I've got some!

AGOSTINO, *skeptically*: Sure, of course you do.

*(Courtyard of the church, TQ)*                    431:194-8″2

*Francesco, seated on a bench with Marcello, has his arm around the boy, who is wearing a black mourning band on his arm. Music begins.*

FRANCESCO: We won't see each other for a while. But then I'll come back and we'll stay together always.

MANFREDI *(off screen)*: Let's go, Francesco!

FRANCESCO: I'm coming!

*Don Pietro, Manfredi, and the Austrian are walking*     432:26-1″2
*toward the entrance to the courtyard. (MLS)*

*Francesco and Marcello stand up. Francesco caresses the*     433:233-9″17
*boy's cheek, then goes off screen to left. Marcello calls to him.*

MARCELLO: Papa!

*Francesco (in TQ) turns as the other three men, in the*     434:371-
*background, are about to leave the courtyard. Marcello*          15″11
*appears on screen from right and gives Francesco Pina's scarf. (LS)*

MARCELLO: Maybe you'll be cold. Mama gave it to me.

*Francesco goes off. Marcello remains (back to camera).*

*(Street in front of Don Pietro's courtyard, WF)*     435:52-2″4

*Don Pietro, Manfredi, and the Austrian walk along the sidewalk (backs to camera).*

*Francesco leaves the courtyard, hurrying to catch up*     436:37-1″13
*with the others. (WF)*

*As Don Pietro, Manfredi, and the Austrian turn the corner onto the Via Casilina, two cars approach them from behind. Brakes screeching, the cars stop just in front of and just behind them. German soldiers jump out of the cars and stop the three men. Manfredi tries to turn back but is stopped by a German.*    437:201-8"9

GERMANS: Halt! Hände hoch! Los! [Halt! Hands up! Quick!]

*Francesco stops at the corner and watches the action. (MCU)*    438:40-1"16

*The Germans arrest Manfredi, Don Pietro, and the Austrian, and force them into the second car.*    439:142-5"22

GERMANS: Keinen Wiederstand Einsteigen, los, los! Jawohl, marsch! *Los, los!* Vorwärts los, los! Abfahrt! [Don't try anything! Get in, quick, quick! In you go, quick, quick! Let's go!]

*Francesco hides behind the wall.*    440:35-1"11

*A streetcar passes by. The German car pulls away with the prisoners. Two soldiers watch, their submachine guns at the ready, before starting to reenter the other car.*    441:204-8"12

*(Dissolve to . . .*

*(The Gestapo office that night, TQ)*    442:850-35"10

*Bergmann is seated at his desk. Ingrid, beside him, toys with a piece of paper. The telephone rings. Bergmann answers.*

BERGMANN: Hello? Bergmann. Gut . . . ach . . . Gut. *To Ingrid*: Die Auskünfte waren richtig. Ausgezeichnet! [Hello? Bergmann. Good . . . ah . . . good. The tip was right. Splendid!]

*Smiling, Ingrid holds her hand out to Bergmann, who takes a little bottle from a drawer and hands it to her.*

*Satisfied, Ingrid goes off screen to left (camera adjusts left to Bergmann).*

*(Gestapo drawing room, HF)*  443:496-
20"16

*Ingrid opens the door and enters. She stops to look at the bottle, then puts it in her jacket pocket. She continues on (camera pulls back with her) and comes up behind Marina, who is sitting in an armchair. She caresses Marina's head.*

INGRID: The information was correct. Good girl! *She goes off screen.*

*Ingrid picks out a fur coat from a trunk, glancing back*  444:415-17"7
*at Marina as if to gauge her size. (TQ)*

*Ingrid brings the fur over to Marina, who rises, removes*  445:781-
*her own coat, and tries on the fur. (TQ)*  32"13

INGRID: You like it? Try it on! Come on, darling! It's magnificent! Look at yourself, Marina!

*Ingrid leads her to a mirror (camera tracks laterally with them to the left). The two women (backs to camera, in HF) are reflected in the mirror. Ingrid straightens the hair on Marina's shoulders.*

MARINA: They've arrested him?

INGRID: Yes.

MARINA: What'll they do to him?

INGRID: Nothing, nothing at all.

*(RA)*  446:169-7"1
*Ingrid lays her head on Marina's shoulders. (HF)*

INGRID: We need some information. As soon as he gives it, we'll let him go.

MARINA: What if he refuses?

*(RA)*                                                    447:525-
*They both turn their backs to the mirror. (MCU)*         21"21

INGRID: Nonsense! Don't worry, he'll talk!

MARINA: What if he doesn't?

INGRID: Why shouldn't he?

MARINA: Yes, why not?

INGRID, *taking Marina by the chin*: Are you in love with
    him?

MARINA: Me? I'm not in love with anybody!

*Marina shakes herself brusquely loose and goes off screen.*
*Ingrid remains alone.*

*Marina sits down in the armchair again. Ingrid follows*    448:581-24"5
*and sits down beside her (camera tracking forward with*
*her). Ingrid leans close as if to kiss Marina, who pays*
*no attention. (TQ)*

INGRID: Why are you being so mean to me tonight?

MARINA: Let me go away from here!

INGRID: No, you must stay here, with me!

MARINA: No, I don't want to! I don't want to anymore!
    Let me go!

INGRID, *gently*: Why, Marina?

MARINA, *weeping*: What have I done? What have I done?

*To calm her down, Ingrid reaches for the bottle in her*
*pocket. At this gesture, the meaning of her betrayal is*
*brought home even further to Marina. Instead of calming*
*down, she bursts into tears.*

*(Another angle of the preceding scene, TQ)*            449:156-6"12

*Marina, weeping, lays her head on Ingrid's shoulder.*

*(Corridor in Gestapo Headquarters)*

450:472-<br>19″16

*Don Pietro, Manfredi, and the Austrian, escorted by four soldiers, come forward from the far end of the corridor. One of the soldiers speaks to the corporal on duty at the desk.*

FIRST SOLDIER: Heil Hitler!

CORPORAL: Heil Hitler!

FIRST SOLDIER: Welche Nummer? [What number?]

CORPORAL: Vierzig. [Forty.]

*The group continues along the corridor. Don Pietro and the Austrian are pushed forward (camera tracks out in front of them). Don Pietro, noticing something, hesitates.*

*(RA)*

451:57-2″9

*Two soldiers cross the corridor with a man who has*

*fainted (WF). Sound of kicking at a door is heard.*

*A soldier pushes Don Pietro and the other prisoners into*       452:259-
*a bare room (camera continues tracking out).*                        10"19

FIRST SOLDIER: Los! [In you go!]

*(The Gestapo prisoners' room, HF)*                               453:399-
                                                                     16"15
*Shoved violently into the dark room by the soldier, Don
Pietro falls to the floor, losing his glasses. Manfredi and
the Austrian enter after him. The door closes behind
them. They bend down to help Don Pietro to his feet.*

MANFREDI: Are you hurt, Don Pietro?

DON PIETRO, *looking for his glasses*: No . . . my glasses. . . .
*The Austrian picks up the glasses; then, with Manfredi,
helps Don Pietro up.*

AUSTRIAN: They're broken!

DON PIETRO: Never mind!

*The two men steady Don Pietro on his feet. (HF)*                 454:443-
                                                                     18"13
DON PIETRO: Thanks.

MANFREDI: It was my fault! They must have shadowed
    me! *He goes off screen to right.*

DON PIETRO: No, I think just the opposite. They must
    have been spying on me for a long time now. I
    shouldn't have had you come to the church.

AUSTRIAN, *looking about fearfully*: Keep quiet! The walls
    have ears!

MANFREDI *(CU)*: Let them listen. We've nothing to tell      455:93-3"21
    each other.

    *(off screen)*: Right, Don Pietro?                           456:424-
                                                                     17"16
DON PIETRO: Of course, we've nothing to tell each other.

*A blood-curdling scream is heard off screen. The Austrian moves toward the wall. Manfredi, coming on screen from right, approaches Don Pietro, who is still in the middle of the room.*

AUSTRIAN: Did you hear that? We too—we too will scream like that!

*The Austrian goes toward the bricked-up window. Don Pietro follows him (camera tracks forward and cuts out Manfredi).*

DON PIETRO: Take it easy!

*In the Gestapo office (TQ), Bergmann (back to camera) is seated at his desk, listening to a noncommissioned officer (NCO) who is emptying the contents of a briefcase onto the desk. Krammer is beside him.*

457:493-
20"13

NCO: Das ist in der Wohnung des Pfarres gefunden worden, Herr Sturmbannführer, und dieses sind die Ausweise der Verhafteten, selbstverständlich alle falsch. [This was found in the priest's place, sir, and these are the prisoners' documents, all forged, of course.]

BERGMANN: Haben Sie die Wohnung des Pfarres durchsucht? [You searched the priest's apartment?]

NCO: Jawohl, auch die Sakristei. [Yes, sir, and the sacristy too.]

BERGMANN: Das war unklug! [That wasn't very clever!]

NCO: Es war nur ein Kirchdiener und ein Junge am Beten, Herr Sturmbannführer. Sie haben so Angst, das sie bestimmt nicht sprechen werden. [There was only a sexton and a boy praying there, sir, and they were so scared they won't talk for sure.]

*(RA; Bergmann, with the officer on the margın of frame,*   458:70 2"22
*TQ)*

BERGMANN: Beruhigen Sie sich, sie werden sprechen. Danke. [Rest assured, they'll talk. Thanks.]

*The NCO salutes and goes out. (TQ)*   459:149-6"5

BERGMANN, *to Krammer:* Räumen Sie auf! [Straighten up in here!]

KRAMMER: Jawohl! [Yes, sir!] *He begins to straighten up the desk.*

*In the prisoners' room (FS), Manfredi is sitting on the*   460:551-
*floor. Don Pietro leans against the wall nearby. The*   22"23
*Austrian paces up and down, then approaches Manfredi.*

AUSTRIAN: You're not afraid?

MANFREDI: Yes, I'm very much afraid. But I feel very calm too. Strange, isn't it? But I don't know why, I just—

DON PIETRO: I understand you.

AUSTRIAN, *forcefully*: You people! You're crazy! Listen! I know you must have something . . . *He kneels down beside Manfredi.*

> . . . to hide. People's lives depend on your silence. You think you can stand the torture? *(HF)*     461:250-10″10

> But you don't know how it is! They make cowards even out of heroes! *(MCU)*     462:119-4″23

MANFREDI *(MCU)*: We're not heroes, but they'll never get anything out of us, I assure you! *The Austrian's hand can be seen.*     463:149-6″5

*(Gestapo office, TQ)*     464:416-17″8
*Bergmann, leaning against the desk, lights Ingrid's cigarette. From the other side of the desk Krammer approaches and lights Bergmann's cigarette. Bergmann begins to pace nervously up and down the room.*

BERGMANN: Wie spät ist es? [What time is it?]

KRAMMER: Halb neun, Herr Sturmbannführer. [Eight-thirty, sir.]

BERGMANN: Diese Männer müssen, bevor die Sperrstunde vorüber ist, sprechen, damit ihre Gefangennahme sich nicht unter den Verschwörern verbreitet. Wir haben zehn Stunden vor uns. [These men must talk before the curfew is over; their arrest must be kept secret, so the rebels don't get wind of it. We have ten hours to work in.]

*(Dark prisoners' room, TQ)*     465:960-40″
*Don Pietro, Manfredi, and the Austrian are all on their feet. Manfredi comes up to the priest.*

MANFREDI: Look, Don Pietro, I don't know if we'll be together much longer, and if we'll see each other again or not. But—but I want to thank you for everything you've done for me and for us. *Don*

*Pietro gestures to cut him off.* No, let me go on! I have to tell you the truth. I'm not the man you think I am. I'm—

AUSTRIAN, *interrupting as he approaches*: Listen, they're coming! I beg you, don't betray me! *The door opens. Two German soldiers gesture to Manfredi to follow them.*

SOLDIER: Sie! [You!]

*(Gestapo office, HF)*     466:306-
*Bergmann, sitting at his desk, examines Manfredi's file*     12"18
*card. Someone knocks at the door. Bergmann puts out the cigarette he is smoking, places the document in a drawer, and adjusts the desk lamp to shine on the chair opposite him.*

BERGMANN: Krammer, machen Sie das Licht aus! Herein! [Krammer, turn out the light! Come in!]

*The door opens. A noncommissioned officer enters,*     467:526-
*salutes, and shows in Manfredi, who comes forward*     21"22
*(camera pans left after him). Manfredi ignores the soldier's gesture toward the chair and stands in front of the desk, looking fixedly at Bergmann, who gestures for him to sit down. (HF)*

BERGMANN: Please. . . .

*Manfredi sits down (camera pans left after him).*

BERGMANN: What is your name?

*The light glares on Manfredi's face. He appears calm and*     468:76-3"4
*indifferent as he watches Bergmann. (MCU)*

MANFREDI: Giovanni Episcopo.

BERGMANN, *reading from the forged identification papers*:     469:151-6"7
    Of course. Episcopo, born in Bari, businessman. . . .

*Manfredi and Bergmann eye each other across the desk.*     470:1208-
*(HF)*     50"8

BERGMANN: You deal in? . . .

MANFREDI: Oil and wine.

BERGMANN, *sarcastically*: Oil and wine! *Ausgezeichnet!* [Splendid!] Listen, Mr. Episcopo . . .

*Bergmann (TQ) rises and leans over the desk toward Manfredi (camera pans left after him). Manfredi, taking no notice of him, folds down his coat collar.*

BERGMANN: . . . if I had time to waste, I'd have some fun talking about your wine business, but unfortunately I am pressed for time, and I also respect you. Therefore I make you an offer. I know everything about you: your real name, your political activity in the past.

*He takes the file card from the drawer and puts it on the desk. Manfredi takes it, observes it for a moment, then hands it back, indifferently, as if it did not concern him.*

BERGMANN: As for the present, I know from my informers that you are one of the leaders of the military command of the Committee of National Liberation, and in contact with the Badoglio military command. *He slaps the file card on his open palm for emphasis.* It it absolutely imperative and urgent for me to know the details of this organization . . .

*Krammer waits at the typewriter. (MCU)*     471:39-1"15

BERGMANN *(off screen)*: . . . and you are precisely the man to tell me!

*Bergmann goes off screen (camera tilts slightly down).*     472:272-11"8
*Manfredi replies calmly, following Bergmann with his eyes. (MCU)*

MANFREDI: You say you know who I am, what I've done, and what I'm doing now. Then why do you make me this offer? Why do you think I would suddenly turn traitor?

*Bergmann listens angrily, twisting his hands together.*   473:94-3″22
*(MCU)*

MANFREDI *(off screen)*: I know that here in this building, perhaps right in this office, the same offer . . .

  . . . was made to Italian generals, to the Badogliani,   474:250-
as you people say. I know that they paid for their     10″10
loyalty and their silence with their lives. I hope . . .

*Bergmann is standing behind the desk. (HF)*   475:846-35″6

MANFREDI *(off screen)*: . . . I am up to the same mark.

BERGMANN: I'm sorry to see you refuse such a—reasonable proposal. But I must say I expected it. *He sits on the desk and takes out his cigarette case.* You Italians, whatever party you belong to, are all addicted to rhetoric. But I'm quite sure that you will see things my way before dawn. Cigarette? *He holds the cigarette case out to Manfredi, who pretends not to notice it.* Come now, a cigarette won't make you talk.

*Manfredi takes the cigarette, Bergmann lights it for him.*

BERGMANN: There are so many peculiar rumors about the Gestapo.

*(TQ; resume on Bergmann lighting Manfredi's cigarette.*   476:173-7″5
*Manfredi's back is to the camera. Krammer can be seen in the background.)*

BERGMANN: Krammer!

KRAMMER: Jawohl, Herr Sturmbannführer!

BERGMANN: Bringen Sie den Mann heraus! [Take him out!]

*Krammer stands up, crosses the room, and, seizing Man-*
*fredi's arm, leads him to a side door (camera pans right*
*after him).*

*Manfredi, with Krammer at his right, comes forward*          477:132-5"12
*(HF; camera tracks slightly out). The German goes off*
*screen to right while Manfredi comes forward (to MCU).*
*He looks straight ahead, his cigarette still lit.*

*(RA)*                                                        478:202-8"10
*Manfredi steps forward through the open doorway*
*(HF; camera adjusts slightly to right). From the other*
*room, two men immediately seize him and force him*
*into a chair. Krammer reappears on screen and closes the*
*door behind Manfredi, then goes off screen to left.*

*Bergmann, at his desk, puts some documents away in a*       479:107-4"11
*drawer.*

BERGMANN: Der Pfarrer, Krammer! [The priest, Krammer!]

KRAMMER: Jawohl!

*(Prisoners' room, WF)*                                       480-535-22"7
*Don Pietro is leaning against the closed window. The*
*Austrian is sitting on the floor, leaning against the wall.*
*The door opens, and the shadow of a soldier appears in*
*the strip of light.*

SOLDIER *(off screen)*: Sie! [You!]

*Don Pietro steps forward and rests a hand on his com-*
*panion's head. Then he comes forward (to HF; camera*
*pans right with him) and goes off screen to right.*

DON PIETRO: Keep steady, my son. Try to pray!

*The Austrian, in despair, sits in the dark. Then he looks*    481:695-
*up, as if searching for something. He rises and goes down*        28"23
*the length of the room (HF; camera pans right after him).*
*He stops in front of two radiator pipes, which run along*

*over the door. He stretches his hand out toward them (camera adjusts slightly upward).*

*(Gestapo office, HF)*            482:34-1″10
*Don Pietro is seated in front of Bergmann, who takes a package of fliers from his desk drawer.*

BERGMANN: We found this material . . .

*Don Pietro looks at the fliers Bergmann has laid on the*   483:105-4″9
*desk. (MCU from above)*

BERGMANN *(off screen)*: . . . in your home.

DON PIETRO: Ah!

BERGMANN, *harshly (MCU)*: Your purpose is clearly to   484:117-4″21
    harm the Reich and its armed forces.

DON PIETRO, *calmly*: That was not exactly my purpose—   485:58-2″10

*Bergmann jumps to his feet (camera adjusts upward) and*   486:314-13″2
*pounds his fist on the table.*

BERGMANN: What would you call a man who not only
    furnishes refuge and forged papers to Italians who
    are preparing attacks on our troops, but who even
    assists German deserters?

DON PIETRO, *looking calmly at Bergmann*: A man who is   487:84-3″12
    unworthily trying to exercise charity.

BERGMANN: He is a traitor who must be punished accord-   488:106-4″10
    ing to the rules . . .

*Resigned, Don Pietro lowers his eyes.*   489:83-3″11

BERGMANN *(off screen)*: . . . of war of the Reich!

DON PIETRO: God will judge!

*Somewhat calmer, Bergmann sits down (camera pans*   490:69-2″21
*downward).*

BERGMANN: Then listen to me!

*He nervously extinguishes his cigarette. Don Pietro listens calmly.*

491:446-
18"14

BERGMANN: Your friend Episcopo is the leader of a military organization of which you too have full knowledge. *He joins his hands; his voice sharpens.* If you talk, and you persuade your friend to do the same, you will only have fulfilled your duty as a priest and as a citizen. I shall tell you why. . . .

These men who attack and sabotage the German forces are violating the rights of an occupying power, which are guaranteed by international treaties.

492:286-
11"22

*Don Pietro listens intently, as if perplexed.*

493:201-8"9

BERGMANN *(off screen)*: Therefore they are bandits and must be consigned to the forces of justice. Is that clear?

DON PIETRO: Your words have deeply . . .

*Satisfied, Bergmann turns to his aide.*

494:73-3"1

DON PIETRO *(off screen)*: . . . shocked me.

BERGMANN: At last! Krammer!

*Krammer is ready at the typewriter. (HF)*

495:26-1"2

KRAMMER: Jawohl, Herr Sturmbannführer!

BERGMANN: Nehmen Sie die Aussagen auf. [Take down his statement.]

496:21-0"21

*Krammer puts a fresh sheet of paper in the typewriter.*

497:57-2"9

DON PIETRO: But there's a problem.

498:40-1"16

BERGMANN, *vexed*: What is it?

499:28-1"4

DON PIETRO, *calmly (off screen)*: Personally, I . . .

. . . have nothing to tell, because I don't know any- 500:231-9″15
thing. What little I knew has been told to me in
confession, and those secrets must die with me. That
is our rule.

BERGMANN, *furious*: I'm not interested in your rule! 501:55-2″7

DON PIETRO, *calmly*: But it interests Someone Who is 502:114-4″18
higher than you—and me!

BERGMANN: Then persuade your friend to talk! 503:526-
21″22

DON PIETRO *(off screen)*: I don't think he knows anything
about what you suspect—

*Bergmann rises and comes close to Don Pietro (camera*
*pans left after him and tracks back until Don Pietro is*
*included in HF).*

BERGMANN: You're trying to tell me you don't know what
his real activity is? His true identity? Uh!

DON PIETRO: I only know that he is a man who needed
my modest help.

*Bergmann turns wrathfully and sits on the edge of his*
*desk (camera pans right after him).*

BERGMANN: Ah, is that so? Then I shall tell you who this
man is! He is a subversive . . .

*(Camera tracks forward until only Don Pietro is seen.)* 504:115-4″19
*He listens, motionless, then lowers his eyes. (CU)*

BERGMANN *(off screen)*: . . . an atheist, an enemy of yours!

*Bergmann listens scornfully. (CU from below)* 505:62-2″14

DON PIETRO *(off screen)*: I am a Catholic priest . . .

. . . and I believe that a man who fights for justice 506:215-8″23
and liberty walks in the pathways of the Lord—and
the pathways of the Lord are infinite.

BERGMANN: You're not going to preach to me, I hope!  507:92-3″20

DON PIETRO: That is not my intention.  508:67-2″19

*Bergmann turns and takes a few steps (camera tracks right  509:203-8″11
after him), then suddenly swings around again.*

BERGMANN: Listen, I have no time to waste. You've made
up your mind not to talk?

*Don Pietro lowers his eyes, then raises them again.*  510:67-2″19

BERGMANN, *vexed*: You don't even want to try to persuade  511:235-9″19
your friend?

*Bergmann comes forward (camera tracks left after him,
until he is again in CU from above).*

BERGMANN: You can save him from suffering that you
cannot even . . .

*(off screen)* . . . imagine!  512:293-12″5

DON PIETRO, *submissively at first, then with irony*: I
imagine it better than you think. But I think there'd
be no point to it. Besides, if he's the man you say he
is, it will be difficult to persuade him to talk, don't
you think?

BERGMANN, *scornfully*: Don't worry, he'll talk!  513:87-3″15

DON PIETRO, *firmly convinced*: I don't believe it. He  514:67-2″19
won't talk.

*Hands in pockets, Bergmann has an arrogant sneer on  515:17-0″17
his face (TQ). Behind him. Krammer waits at the typewriter.*

BERGMANN: Really?

DON PIETRO, *shaking his head, smiling*: He won't talk.  516:122-5″2
I will pray for him!

BERGMANN, *smiling scornfully*: That won't help you much    517:272-11"8
with your Heavenly Father!

*Bergmann turns and goes toward the torture room*
*(camera pans after him until he is in WF). He enters,*
*closing the door behind him.*

*Don Pietro, who has been very calm up to now, no longer*    518:214-8"12
*hides his anguish; he bows his head on his hand. The*
*door opens again. Don Pietro pulls himself together.*
*(Wide CU)*

*Bergmann appears in the doorway of the torture room.*    519:302-
*He pushes the door further open and steps aside to reveal*    12"14
*Manfredi, bare-chested, strapped to a chair, with two*
*Gestapo men hovering over him. One of them holds an*
*acetylene torch; the other passes in front of the door with*
*a cat-o'-nine-tails. Manfredi waits impassively. Bergmann,*
*satisfied, watches Don Pietro's reaction.*

*Don Pietro, squinting without his glasses, makes an effort*    520-72-3"
*to watch.*

*(WF; camera subjective from Don Pietro's viewpoint.)*    521:62-2"14

*Manfredi is between the two Gestapo men. One of them*
*lights a cigarette with a sheet of paper lit at the acetylene*
*torch.*

*Don Pietro looks on in anguish. (CU)*    522:56-2"8

*The Gestapo men continue their preparations (WF;*    523:214-8"22
*camera pans left to include Bergmann, in CU). Bergmann*
*turns to his aide.*

BERGMANN: Es wird noch einige Zeit dauern. Ich geh in
mein Zimmer. Sobald es etwas Neues gibt, rufen Sie
mich bitte. [This will take a while. I'm going in the
other room. As soon as you get somewhere, call me.]

KRAMMER: Jawohl, Herr Sturmbannführer!

BERGMANN, *as someone knocks at the door*: Herein!

*The door opens, and a noncommissioned officer enters,*   524:100-4″4
*saluting. (HF)*

SOLDIER: Herr Sturmbannführer, Deserteur hat sich . . .

    *(off screen)* . . . aufgehängt. [Sir, the deserter has   525:78-3″6
hanged himself.]

BERGMANN, *disgusted*: Idiot! *He goes off screen to left,*
*followed by Krammer.*

DON PIETRO, *in anguish, bowing his head*: Requiem aeter-   526:153-6″9
nam dona eis, Domine . . .

*Bergmann comes on screen from right, crossing over to*   527:48-2″

*the desk. Watching Don Pietro, he takes out his cigarette case. (HF)*

DON PIETRO *(off screen):* . . . et lux perpetua luceat . . .

*A scream of pain is heard. Don Pietro's head jerks up.*　　528:63-2″15

DON PIETRO: . . . eis.

*Bergmann puts his cigarettes back in his pocket. He*　　529:45-1″21
*watches the priest with satisfaction.*

*Don Pietro suffers as he listens to the screams, which*　　530:123-5″3
*become more strangled but no less intense.*

*Bergmann goes toward the drawing-room door (camera*　　531:226-9″10
*pans left after him to include the priest in CU). Don*
*Pietro listens in anguish to Manfredi's screams. Berg-*
*mann, in the background, opens the door, turns a moment*
*to observe the priest, then opens the second of the double*
*doors to the drawing room, from which piano music can*
*be heard. Don Pietro turns to look, then turns back to*
*face the torture room. Manfredi screams.*

*Bergmann opens the door to the drawing room, then goes*　　532:294-12″6
*over to the liquor table (HF; camera pans left after him).*
*He pours himself a drink.*

*Marina, looking lost, is leaning against Ingrid's shoulder,*　　533:46-1″22
*drinking (Wide CU). Ingrid turns toward Bergmann.*

*Carrying his drink, Bergmann comes over to a group of*　　534:236-9″20
*four officers seated around a table, playing cards (camera*
*pans to right with him and tracks forward to include the*
*card players).*

BERGMANN: Wer gewinnt? [Who's winning?]

FIRST OFFICER: Ah, immer der selbe! [Oh, always the same
　　one!]

*Bergmann leaves the card players and comes over to Marina and Ingrid, who are sitting on the couch (camera pans left with him, keeping him in HF). He watches them silently, then takes a cigarette from the table and goes over to the piano (camera tracks with him and pans left). He lights the cigarette at a candlestick standing on the piano. An older officer, Hartmann, settled comfortably in a baroque armchair with a drink in his hand, addresses Bergmann. (Pan ends on Hartmann.)*

HARTMANN *(off screen)*: Viel Arbeit *(on screen)* heute Abend? [Much work this evening?]

BERGMANN: Nicht so viel, aber interessant. [Not much, but interesting.]

*Bergmann looks at Hartmann. (MCU)*

535:731-
30″11

HARTMANN *(off screen)*: So, was denn? [So, what's up?]

BERGMANN: Ich habe einen Mann erwischt, der vor morgen früh sprechen muss, und einen italienischen —*he picks up his glass from the table, walks a few paces away (camera follows him with pan to left, to HF)*—Pfarrer, der das Gegenteil behauptet, weil er für ihn beten wird. [I've picked up a fellow who's got to talk before tomorrow morning, and an Italian priest who says he won't because he's going to pray for him.]

HARTMANN *(off screen)*: Und wenn er doch nicht sprechen sollte? [And if he doesn't talk?]

BERGMANN, *turning toward Hartmann*: Oh, gut! [You're joking!]

HARTMANN: Und wenn er doch schweigen sollte? [And if he doesn't talk, no matter what?]

BERGMANN: Wenn er schweigen sollte, so würde das bedeuten, dass ein Italiener einem Deutschen gleichgekommen wäre. *Bergmann sits down on the arm of a chair.* Es würde bedeuten, dass es keinen Unterschied zwischen dem Blut einer Sklaven und Herrenrasse gäbe. *He drinks.* Welchen Sinn hatte der Kampf, den wir führen? [If he doesn't talk, it would mean an Italian is as good as a German. It would mean that there was no difference between the blood of a slave race and a master race. What would be the meaning of our struggle then?]

HARTMANN *(MCU)*: Vor fünfundzwanzig Jahren befeh-
ligte ich eine Kompanie in Frankreich. Damals war ich ein junger Offizier, damals glaubte ich, auch die Deutschen gehören zu einer Herrenrasse. [Twenty-five years ago I was commanding a company in France. I was a young officer then, and I also believed the Germans were a master race.]          536

*Bergmann, annoyed, turns away and drinks. (HF)*          537:122-5″2

HARTMANN *(off screen)*: Aber die französischen Patrioten liessen sich lieber hinrichten als etwas auszusagen. [But the French patriots chose to die rather than talk.]

*The young officer at the piano listens as he plays. (MCU)*          538:99-4″3

HARTMANN *(off screen)*: Etwas wollen wir Deutschen nie begreifen, dass die Völker frei leben wollen. [We Germans will never understand one thing, that people want to live free.]

BERGMANN, *whirling around*: Sie sind betrunken, Hartmann! [You're drunk, Hartmann!]          539:32-1″8

*Piano music ends.*

HARTMANN: Ja, ich bin betrunken! *(off screen)* Ich
betrinke mich ja jeden Abend . . .          540:54-2″6

*The four card players turn to listen. (HF)*          541:62-2″14

HARTMANN (off screen): . . . um zu vergessen.

HARTMANN: Und das Endergebnis? Ich sehe immer klarer!  542:78-3″6

Marina looks lost and insensible. Ingrid follows the  543:58-2″10
conversation with interest.

HARTMANN (off screen): Wir bringen es nicht weiter als . . .

He puts his glass on the table. (MCU)  544:469-
                                        19″13

HARTMANN: . . . morden, morden, morden! Ganz Europa
   haben wir mit Leichen übersäht; und aus diesen
   Kriegen wächst unaufhaltsam der Hass, Hass, überall
   Hass! Wir werden vom Hass vertilgt ohne Hoffnung!
   [Yes, I'm drunk! I get drunk every evening . . . to
   forget. And the result? I see it more and more clearly.
   We bring nothing but . . . death, death, death! We
   have filled all Europe with corpses. And from these
   wars spring hate, hate, everywhere hate. We will be
   wiped out by this hatred, there is no hope for us!]

Exasperated, Bergmann suddenly stands up (camera shifts  545:22-0″22
slightly upward).

BERGMANN: Genug! [That's enough!]

HARTMANN, smiling bitterly: Alle werden wir sterben,  546:97-4″1
   sterben ohne Hoffnung. [We will all die, die without
   hope.]

Bergmann comes forward, greatly agitated (camera  547:205-8″13
tracks after him and pans right to include the seated
Captain Hartmann). Bergmann smacks his hand on the
piano.

BERGMANN: Ich verbiete Ihnen fortzusetzen! [I forbid you
   to continue!]

HARTMANN: Ohne Hoffnung . . .

BERGMANN: Ich verbiete . . .

HARTMANN: . . . ohne Hoffnung. . . .

BERGMANN: . . . zu sprechen! Sie vergessen ein deutscher Offizier zu sein? [I forbid you to speak! Have you forgotten that you are a German officer?]

*(RA)* 548:168-7″
*As Bergmann glares indignantly at Hartmann, the four card players listen in the background (WF). Krammer, who has just entered, salutes. Bergmann turns and immediately goes toward him (camera adjusts slightly to right).*

*Bergmann stops in front of Krammer. (HF)* 549:113-4″17

BERGMANN: Hat er gesprochen? [Has he talked?]

KRAMMER: Nein, Herr Sturmbannführer. Wendel sagt niemals eine derartige Hartnäckigkeit vorgefunden zu haben. [No, sir. Wendel says he's never seen such stubbornness.]

*Marina is leaning against Ingrid's shoulder.* 550:51-2″3

KRAMMER *(off screen)*: Der Mann hat eine völlige Insensibilität erreicht. [The man has now passed out.]

Was sollen wir tun, Herr Sturmbannführer? [What should we do now, sir?] 551:188-7″20

*Furious, Bergmann throws away his cigarette and moves rapidly to the door (WF), which the soldier opens for him (camera adjusts slightly downward). The door closes behind him.*

*(Bergmann's office and torture room, TQ)* 552:405-
16″21

*The aide opens the door and Bergmann enters (camera tracks out in front of him as he comes toward Don Pietro). Bergmann stops a moment (in HF) to look at the priest, who is in the same attitude as before. Then he continues toward the door of the torture room (camera pans and tracks to right with him in TQ). Wendel (WF) awaits him at the door.*

BERGMANN: Na, Wendel? [Well, Wendel?]

WENDEL: Es ist unmöglich, Herr Sturmbannführer. Man muss warten, wieder bu Kräften kommen lassen. [It's impossible, sir. We have to wait until he comes around.]

BERGMANN: Das ist unmöglich . . . [It's impossible . . .]

*(Closer HF of Bergmann; Wendel is in right foreground,*   553:190-7"22
*back to camera.)*

BERGMANN: . . . das ist bereits zu spät. [. . . it's already too
late.]

WENDEL: Vielleicht mit psychologischen Mitteln, Herr
Sturmbannführer? [Shall we try psychological
methods, sir?]

BERGMANN: Sie sind ja wahnsinnig? Der Mann muss
doch noch sprechen! [Are you crazy? This man must
talk right now!]

*He comes forward (camera pans right).*

*In the torture room (wide CU), Bergmann comes on*   554:278-
*screen from left (camera tracks and pans right) and moves*   11"14
*toward Manfredi. He bends over to examine Manfredi*
*(camera tilts downward). His back hides Manfredi from*
*view. Bergmann straightens up and goes off screen, re-*
*vealing the unconscious Manfredi's bloodied head and*
*chest (in HF). One of the two Gestapo men pulls Man-*
*fredi's head up by the hair from behind, then lets it drop*
*back on the chest.*

WENDEL, *to Gestapo man (wide CU):* Spritze! [Syringe!]   555:43-1"19
*The man goes off screen.*

*(Insert: a small table with instruments of torture—many*   556:106-4"10
*types of pincers, needles, a lighted acetylene torch, and*
*other instruments—lying about in disorder, with blood*
*spots everywhere. The bloodied hands of the Gestapo*
*man open a small case and take out a syringe.)*

*Bergmann waits (CU). Behind his shoulders is the shadow*   557:46-1"22
*of a large torture instrument, like a wine press.*

*Manfredi's head lies on his chest (CU). The two Gestapo*   558:283-
*men are behind him. One injects the contents of the*   11"19
*syringe into Manfredi's upper arm, then hands the syringe*
*to the other man, who goes off screen.*

*Bergmann watches.*                                                      559:58-2″10

*As the injection takes effect, Manfredi slowly raises his*             560:170-7″2
*head and opens his eyes with effort.*

BERGMANN, *persuasively*: Listen, Mr. Ferraris, I have told             561:214-8″22
    you before, I admire you very much, and, believe me,
    I appreciate this proof of your courage, of your
    spirit of sacrifice . . .

*Manfredi glowers at Bergmann. (ECU)*                                   562:111-4″15

BERGMANN *(off screen)*: . . . but you must understand that
    this cannot go on any longer.

*(A wall map is seen on the background.)*                               563:180-7″12
BERGMANN *(CU)*: You're a Communist. Your party has
    allied itself with the reactionaries.

*Manfredi glowers at Bergmann.*                                         564:170-7″2

BERGMANN *(off screen)*: You are all working together
    against us now. But tomorrow, when Rome is
    occupied . . .

  *(on screen)* . . . or—liberated, as you people say—        565:187-7″19
    will these monarchist army officers still be your allies?

*Don Pietro watches through the open door. (WF)*                        566:73-3″1

BERGMANN *(off screen)*: I offer you the solution to this
    problem.

*[Shots 567–571: alternate close-ups of Bergmann and of*
*Manfredi.]*

BERGMANN *(off screen)*: Give me the names of the                      567:92-3″20
    Badogliani generals.

    Make it possible for me to arrest them, and I         568:86-3″14
    guarantee your release . . .

*(off screen)* . . . and immunity for the men in your    569:102-4″6
party.

Well . . .    570:33-1″9

*(off screen)* . . . Mr. Ferraris?    571:34-1″10

*Manfredi's only answer is to spit in Bergmann's eye.*

*Manfredi (CU; back to camera) is leaning forward toward*    572:37-1″13
*Bergmann, facing him (HF). Astonished, Bergmann steps*
*back, wipes his face with his left hand, and furiously*
*snatches up a whip.*

GESTAPO MAN *(off screen)*: Verfluchter Hund! [Damned
    dog!]

*(Manfredi, wide CU)*    573:16-0″16

*Bergmann lashes Manfredi's face repeatedly with the*
*whip.*

*Bergmann continues to lash Manfredi.*    574:19-0″19

*Bergmann stops, angrily throws the whip aside, and stalks*    575:51-2″3
*off screen to right. (HF)*

BERGMANN, *as he goes*: Setzen Sie fort, bis auf Ende!
    [Keep after him to the end!]

*The Gestapo men get ready to start in again on Manfredi,*
*whose head has now dropped on his bloody chest.*

*Bergmann (CU), apparently calmer now, is back in his*    576:557-23″5
*office. He comes up to Don Pietro (seated in HF; camera*
*tracks and pans left after him). Blows and muffled cries*
*can be heard from the torture room. Bergmann turns*
*again and passes by Krammer, who is sharpening a pencil*
*(camera tracks and pans right with Bergmann). He goes*
*off screen for a moment and returns, going toward the*
*left to sit down angrily on his desk.*

*Manfredi is now strapped to two iron rings on the wall, arms outstretched (CU). His face is sweaty and contorted with pain. He screams.*  577:22-0"22

*A Gestapo man burns Manfredi's chest with the acetylene torch. (HF)*  578:44-1"20

*Bergmann turns his head to the left.*  579:93-3"21

*Ingrid, carrying a wineglass, appears in the doorway leading to the drawing room (TQ). She closes the door and comes forward to Don Pietro (camera tracks out and pans right). She looks at the priest for a moment, then comes up to Bergmann and looks questioningly at him. He stiffens and turning his eyes away, stands up. He remains at right margin of frame. Ingrid (HF) leans against the desk, smiling ambiguously.*  580:849-35"9

INGRID: Geschiht? Ich sagte es dir, dass es nicht so leicht sein würde! [Well? I told you it wouldn't be so easy!]

*Manfredi is heard groaning. Ingrid looks to the right and goes past Bergmann and Krammer to the doorway of the torture room (camera tracks and pans after her). She stops and looks in. One of the Gestapo men bows to her. Manfredi is breathing with difficulty.*

*The two Gestapo men lift Manfredi up from the floor and sit him on a chair (WF; camera pans right and tracks briefly forward).*  581:264-11"

*Ingrid smiles. (CU)*  582:85-3"13

*Ingrid (back to camera) turns and comes back toward the priest, passing in front of the seated Krammer (TQ; camera pans and tracks left after her). Bergmann is pacing nervously. Ingrid stops behind the desk.*  583:228-9"12

*One Gestapo man applies the pincers to Manfredi's fingernails; the other circles around the chair. (HF)*  584:46-1"22

*Ingrid sits down behind the desk (TQ). Bergmann paces nervously to left and to right (ECU), coming on and off screen. Manfredi screams.*

585:563-23″11

INGRID: Eine Zigarette?

*Bergmann goes over to her and holds out his cigarette case. Ingrid takes a cigarette. Bergmann takes one too and lights both. Don Pietro glares at them. Bergmann goes off screen to right.*

*Bergmann comes on screen from left and stops at the door of the torture room. He looks to the right, then turns his head, reflecting. Then he throws his cigarette away angrily. (HF)*

586:271-11″7

BERGMANN: Der Pfarrar, sofort! [The priest, quick!]

*Bergmann goes off screen to right as two Gestapo men (in CU) come on screen from right and go off to left.*

*The two Gestapo men, coming on screen from right, seize*

587:134-5″14

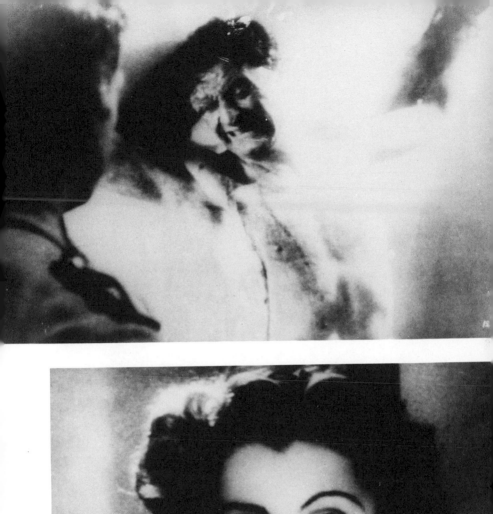

*Don Pietro's arms and pull him out of his chair (TQ).*
*They go off screen to right.*

*Bergmann, now in the torture room, turns to Don Pietro*   588:53-2"5
*as he is pushed in. Don Pietro stops, gazing at Manfredi.*

BERGMANN: Look, priest! Look!

*A Gestapo man pulls up Manfredi's battered head. (CU)*   589:63-2"15

BERGMANN *(off screen)*: Are you satisfied now? This . . .

*Bergmann motions toward Manfredi, whom Don Pietro is*   590:66-2"18
*contemplating with pity and horror. (HF)*

BERGMANN: . . . is your Christian charity! This is your love
   for your brother in Christ!

*The two Gestapo men are in the foreground. Behind*   591:99-4"3
*them, Ingrid and Krammer enter the room. (HF)*

BERGMANN *(off screen)*: You preferred to see him like this
   rather . . .

*Don Pietro, bending over Manfredi, in profile on the*   592:90-3"18
*right, gazes at him with love and pity. (CU)*

BERGMANN *(off screen)*: . . . than talk. But don't hope to
   save yourself, you hypocrite . . .

*A Gestapo man pulls up Manfredi's face; the eyes are*   593:49-2"1
*closed.*

BERGMANN *(off screen)*: . . . or your accomplices either!

*Don Pietro is still bending over Manfredi.*   594:72-3"

BERGMANN *(off screen)*: You'll be shot as a traitor!

*Manfredi slowly opens his eyes; his swollen lips part.*   595:53-2"5

BERGMANN *(off screen)*: We will destroy all of you, all of
   you! To . . .

*Don Pietro is moved to tears. He gently and wonderingly smiles at Manfredi.*  596:91-3"19

BERGMANN *(off screen)*: . . . the last man!

DON PIETRO, *to Manfredi*: You didn't talk!

*Manfredi's head falls to his chest. Music begins.*  597:53-2"5

*Don Pietro is stunned. He raises the dead man's face and gazes at it, then lets it fall again. He raises his tear-filled eyes, turns for a moment, and again gazes pityingly on Manfredi. He stretches his hand out to lift Manfredi's face again.*  598:450-18"18

*The hand of Don Pietro, who is at the left (back to camera), closes the dead man's eyes, then lets the head fall back to the chest again.*  599:136-5"16

*Overwhelmed, Don Pietro gives absolution to Manfredi.*  600:317-13"5

DON PIETRO, *almost inaudible*: Suscipiat. . . .

*(Resume on Don Pietro, in profile, MCU)* Don Pietro makes the sign of the cross, then turns toward  601:89-3"17

*the unseen Bergmann, to the right. The background is
blank.*

*Bergmann looks at him. (MCU)* 602:38-1″14

DON PIETRO *(off screen):* It is finished! *He is overcome by
wrath.*

It is finished! You wanted to kill his soul, but you 603:158-6″14
have only killed his body! *(MCU)*

*Bergmann takes a step backward. (MCU)* 604:43-1″19

DON PIETRO *(off screen):* You're all damned!

*Tears in his eyes, Don Pietro shakes his fist.* 605:34-1″10

DON PIETRO: You're damned!

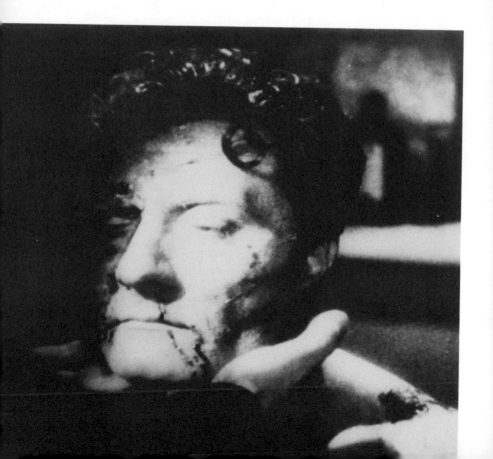

*Ingrid, Krammer, and another Gestapo man, who are listening in the doorway, also step back. (HF)*   606:34-1"10

DON PIETRO *(off screen)*: You will be crushed . . .

*(on screen)* . . . in the dust, like worms!   607:48-2"

*All stand stock-still, listening.*   608:34-1"10

DON PIETRO *(off screen)*: You are damned!

*Don Pietro stops short and, closing his eyes, weeps. Then he shakes his head, repenting of his curses. One hand on his breast, he lifts his eyes to heaven and falls to his knees.*   609:332-13"20

DON PIETRO: No, my God, what have I said!

*(Resume on Don Pietro, falling on his knees, FS)*     610:209-8″17
*He joins his hands in front of the dead man tied to the
chair. All the others look on, motionless, in a semicircle
to the rear. The flaming torch is in the foreground.*

DON PIETRO: Forgive me, my God, forgive me. De pro-
fundis clamavi . . .

*Smiling, Marina and Hartmann come arm-in-arm through*     611:379-
*Bergmann's office. (WF)*     15″19

DON PIETRO *(off screen)*: . . . a te, Domine, Domine exaudi
vocem meam. . . .

*Marina laughs (when she and Hartmann reach HF,
camera tracks over to Krammer and Ingrid, at the sides
of the doorway). The background music fades out into
the piano music coming from the drawing room. Marina
looks toward the torture room. She laughs nervously
again; then her smile suddenly dies out, she covers her
face with her hands, screams, and falls to the floor in a
faint.*

*(Resume on Marina's fall, near Ingrid's and Krammer's*     612:46-1″22
*feet, MCU)*

BERGMANN *(off screen)*: Raus! Raus! [Out! Out!]

BERGMANN, *furious (MCU)*: Bringt den Pfarrer weg . . .     613:44-1″20
[Get the priest . . .]

*Boots—Bergmann's—step over Marina's body.*     614:55-2″7

BERGMANN *(off screen)*: . . . schnell, alle raus! [. . . out of
here, quick! Everybody out!]

*Hartmann comes on screen from right (CU) and sits*     615:165-6″21
*down in front of Bergmann's desk. Ingrid is behind the
desk, drinking. Bergmann comes on screen from right and
joins Ingrid behind the desk. (WF)*

BERGMANN *(off screen)*: Diese dummen Italienen! *(on screen)* Verdammt! Nun haben sie es verfehlt! Dieser verdammte Pharrer hat mich aus dem . . . [These stupid Italians! Dammit! You've failed! This damned priest has . . .]

*Ingrid (back to camera) turns toward Bergmann. (HF)*     616:163-6"19

BERGMANN *(off screen)*: . . . Konzept gebracht. [. . . flustered me.]

INGRID: Ich sagte es dir, dass es nicht so leicht sein würde. [I told you it wouldn't be so easy.]

BERGMANN, *smiling, takes Ingrid's hand*: Du hast immer recht. [You're always right.]

KRAMMER *(off screen)*: Herr Sturmbannführer . . .

*at attention (HF)*: . . . die Meldung! [Sir, the statement!]     617:24-1"

*(Bergmann and Ingrid, HF)*     618:183-7"15

BERGMANN: Ach, ja, wegen des Hinscheidens—Herzeschlag! [Oh, yes, the cause of death—heart attack!]

*Ingrid laughs. She and Bergmann are about to leave, but Krammer has another question.*

KRAMMER *(off screen)*: Jawohl, Herr Sturmbannführer . . .

. . . und das Fräulein? [What about the girl, sir?]     619:31-1"7

BERGMANN, *turning to Ingrid*: Das betrifft die Dame. [That's your affair.]     620:147-6"3

INGRID, *to Krammer*: Sperren Sie sie eine Zeitlang ein und dann. . . . [Shut her up for a little while and then. . . .] *She goes off screen.*

BERGMANN, *following her*: Komm mit, denn jetzt muss ich etwas Kräftiges zu mir nehmen! [Come with me,

I need something strong!]

KRAMMER: Verzeihung, Herr Sturmbannführer, welchen Namen muss ich eintragen? [Excuse me, sir, what name should I put?]

        621:91-3"19

*Ingrid and Bergmann have stopped. He thinks for a moment before answering. (MCU)*

        622:257

        10"17

KRAMMER *(off screen)*: "Manfredi" oder "Ferraris"? ["Manfredi" or "Ferraris"?]

BERGMANN: Einfach "Episcopo—Giovanni Episcopo." Sonst schaffen wir einen Märtyrer. Es gibt schon genug davon. [Just "Episcopo—Giovanni Episcopo." Otherwise we'll make a martyr. There are already enough of them.]

*Music begins. Bergmann, laughing ironically, starts going off screen to right.*

INGRID, *stopping him*: Ein moment, bitte! [Just a minute, please!] *She goes off screen to right.*

*(The torture room, HF from above)*

        623:235-9"19

*Marina is still lying in the doorway. Ingrid comes on screen from left, her head and shoulders unseen. She bends down over the girl and removes the fur coat. She straightens up again (camera tilts slightly upward with her), shakes out the fur, and goes off screen with it to left.*

*Returning to Bergmann's office (TQ), Ingrid comes on screen from right. She passes the seated Hartmann, takes Bergmann's arm, and goes off screen to left with him.*

        624:254-

        10"14

INGRID: Für das nächste Mal! [For the next time!]

*Piano music ends. (Camera tracks in on Hartmann.)*

HARTMANN: Wir sind eine Herrenrasse! [We are a master race!]

*(Dissolve to . . .*

*(The rifle range at Fort Bravetta, LS)*                          625:184-7"16

*Two plainclothesmen are setting up a chair for an execu-
tion on the grassy, tree-bordered range. Some of the
soldiers of the Italian firing squad can be seen. Its com-
mander moves toward the right to meet Hartmann, who
comes on screen looking at his watch.*

HARTMANN: What time do you have?

*The Italian officer (back to camera) faces the evidently*          626:230-9"14
*nervous Hartmann. (MCU)*

ITALIAN OFFICER: Eight-fourteen.

HARTMANN: Correct. I'm late!

ITALIAN OFFICER: Yes.

HARTMANN, *taking out his cigarette case*: Cigarette?

ITALIAN OFFICER: Thanks.

*(RA)*                                                              627:48-2"
*A number of soldiers and some buildings are seen in
the background. The Italian officer takes a cigarette.
(MCU)*

HARTMANN, *sharply*: A match!                                      628:46-1"22

*The Italian officer takes out a box of matches and is*           629:180-7"12
*about to strike one when Hartmann seizes the box from
his hand. The Italian is disconcerted and intimidated.*

*(Side view of the two men, HF)*                                   630:302-
                                                                       12"14
*Hartmann lights his own cigarette and hands back the
matches. In the background the two plainclothesmen
finish preparing the chair. While the Italian officer lights
his own cigarette, Hartmann draws on his glove. Both
turn toward the left as they hear a vehicle approaching.*

*A military-police wagon drives onto the range (LS). The*         631:312-13"
*firing squad gathers on the right, while one of the plain-*

*clothesmen fixes the chair firmly to the ground by pound-
ing on a wedge with a brick. The two men then move off
toward the wagon.*

ITALIAN OFFICER: In position . . . in position!

ITALIAN SOLDIER, *to plainclothesmen*: Are you ready?

*The soldiers (wide WF) line up in two ranks. The
officer, taking up his position in front of them, un-
sheathes his sword. The military-police wagon appears
on screen from the right, in the background, and drives
toward the building just behind them. (LS)*

632:214-8"22

ITALIAN OFFICER: Attention!

*The wagon stops. An Italian officer steps down from the
front, carrying a rifle. He comes around to the back door
(camera pans left with him) and opens it. Two soldiers
and a young priest step down (TQ). Don Pietro follows.
(WF)*

633:682-
28"10

PRIEST, *apologetically*: Your hat, Don Pietro.

DON PIETRO: Oh, yes. *He removes his hat slowly and hands
it to the officer on the left. Then he comes forward
(camera pans slightly right with him).* Thanks.

*The execution chair is all set on the range. (LS)*

634:46-1"22

*Don Pietro and the young priest (HF) come forward
(to MCU; camera tracks right with them).*

635:482-20"2

PRIEST: Come! Be strong!

DON PIETRO: Oh, it's not hard to die well. It's hard to
live well!

PRIEST: Pater noster, qui est in caelo, santificetur nomen
tuum . . .

*Hartmann is smoking his cigarette. (HF)*

636:100-4"4

PRIEST (off screen): . . . adveniat regnum tuum. Fiat
voluntas tua . . .

Murmuring prayers, Don Pietro and his companion ap-  637:168-7"
proach the chair from the left. Don Pietro sits down,
facing the back of the chair. The two plainclothesmen
begin to strap him to it. (MS)

PRIEST (off screen): . . . sicut in caelo et in terra. Panem
nostrum quotidianum da nobis hodie . . .

The firing squad marches forward. (wide WF)  638:47-1"23

PRIEST (off screen): . . . et remitte nobis debita nostra . . .

Don Pietro is strapped to the chair as the firing squad  639:171-7"3
halts behind him. Hartmann, smoking, moves forward.
(MS)

PRIEST: . . . et ne nos inducat in tentationem. Semper
libera nos a male . . .

Don Pietro joins his hands. The young priest is beside  640:148-6"4
him. The plainclothesmen continue to fasten his bonds.
(MS)

PRIEST: Ave Maria, benedicta tu in mulieribus, et . . .

Hartmann motions for the plainclothesmen to leave. (TQ)  641:39-1"15

PRIEST (off screen): . . . benedictus fructus ventris tui
Jesus . . .

The two plainclothesmen nod. (HF)  642:32-1"8

The plainclothesmen, in the background, motion to the  643:65-2"17
priest to come away.

PRIEST: . . . Sancta Maria, mater Dei, ora pro nobis . . .

The young priest, beside Don Pietro, nods. (HF)  644:127-5"7

PRIEST: Sancta Maria, mater Dei, ora pro nobis.

Beyond the wire fence surrounding the rifle range, the young children of the parish, led by Romoletto with his crutch, climb up the slope. (LS)

645:31-1"7

(RA)
The children climb up to the fence (backs to camera).

646:32-1"8

The children (coming into WF) begin to whistle a tune to catch Don Pietro's attention.

647:33-1"9

Three soldiers in the firing squad turn slightly (HF). The children (off screen) continue whistling. The priest's prayers can be heard dimly.

648:35-1"11

The young priest squeezes Don Pietro's arm to give him courage, then goes off. Don Pietro bows his head. (HF)

649:118-4"22

Three soldiers face the camera (HF). Don Pietro, in the background (back to camera) waits. The young priest murmurs the "Gloria Patria." The children continue to

650:61-2"13

*whistle.*

*The children are still whistling at the fence.* 651:41-1″17

*Don Pietro hears the whistling and squints toward the* 652:188-7″20
*sound (CU). In the background the firing squad about-*
*faces and aims its rifles.*

PRIEST: Sicut era in principio et nunc et semper *(off*
*screen)* et in saecula saeculorum . . .

*Children whistle off screen.*

*Three soldiers (backs to camera) aim their rifles (HF).* 653:27-1″3
*The children's whistling continues off screen.*

*Four other soldiers aim their rifles low.* 654:16-0″16

*Don Pietro (back to camera) is in the background; the* 655:21-0″21
*soldiers' helmets are seen in the foreground (MS). They*

*shoot, but the bullets hit the ground at Don Pietro's feet: the soldiers have refused to kill him. The children's whistling ceases.*

*Don Pietro (seen head-on) bows his head at the sound of the gunfire (HF). The air behind him is full of smoke.*     656:28-1″4

*The children lower their eyes.*     657:37-1″13

*Don Pietro, in anguish, raises his face. (CU)*     658:56-2″8

*Hartmann, among the soldiers, urges them on furiously. (HF)*     659:43-1″19

HARTMANN: Feuer! [Fire!]

*Don Pietro lifts his face and prays. (CU)*     660:112-4″16

HARTMANN *(off screen)*: Feuer! Machschluss! [Fire! Stop this!]

DON PIETRO: God, forgive them, for they know not what they do. . . .

*Hartmann's voice, swearing at the soldiers, drowns out Don Pietro's.*

*Hartmann unbuckles the holster of his pistol and goes off screen to right. (HF)*     661:30-1″6

*The pistol is aimed at Don Pietro's head from the right, and the shot is fired. (CU)*     662:33-1″9

*The children lower their heads (HF). Music begins.*     663:65-2″17

*Don Pietro's head hangs over the back of the chair (TQ). The young priest and the plainclothesmen come toward the dead man, while the firing squad goes off screen to right.*     664:114-4″18

*Marcello sadly lowers his eyes. (CU)*     665:53-2″5

*Other children drop their heads. (CU)*     666:75-3″3

*The two plainclothesmen check to see that Don Pietro is dead, then untie him.*

667:160-6"16
668:62-2"14

*The children (backs to camera) start down the slope again. (Wide HF)*

669:219-9"3

*Only Marcello and one slightly older boy are left at the fence (HF). The other boy puts his arm around Marcello, and they start off together (backs to camera, which pans left after them).*

*(Dissolve to . . .*

670:575-
23"23

*(Via Trionfale, wide WF)*

*The children (backs to camera) return toward the city (camera pans right after them up to LS). Rome, with the dome of St. Peter's, is in the valley below them. Coming slightly after the rest of the group are Marcello and the older boy, whose arm rests protectively around Marcello.*

## THE END

*(Fade-out)*

# Paisan (1946)

# Credits

Presented by La Cineteca Nazionale
 Metro-Goldwyn-Mayer

Produced by Roberto Rossellini for O. F. I.
 with the collaboration of Rod Geiger

Written by Sergio Amidei
 in collaboration with Klaus Mann, Frederico Fellini,
 V. Hales, Marcello Paglieri, Roberto Rossellini

Scenario and Script by Sergio Amidei, Federico Fellini, and
 Roberto Rossellini

Directed by Roberto Rossellini

Photography by Otello Martelli

Music by Renzo Rossellini

*Cast:*

EPISODE I
*Carmela*                    Carmela Sazio

*American Soldiers*          Robert van Loon
                             Benjamin Emanuel
                             Raymond Campbell
                             Harold Wagner
                             Albert Heinze
                             Merlin Berth
                             Mats Carlson
                             Leonard Penish

EPISODE II
*Joe*                        M. Johnson

| | |
|---|---|
| *Pasquale* | Alfonsino |

Note: In the original Italian version, the characters normally speak their own tongues, and are therefore frequently incomprehensible to one another. Exceptions are herein indicated by notes in the text or by an asterisk placed after the speaker's name, signifying his use of his interlocuter's language.

# EPISODE I

*(Sicily, daytime, LS; a bomb bursts in the sea.)*[1]          1:155-6″11

SPEAKER: On the night of July 10, 1943, the Allied fleet . . .

*(Allied landing craft among columns of thick smoke, LS)*          2:65-2″17

SPEAKER: . . . opened fire against the southern coast . . .

*(Columns of water and black smoke over the sea, LS)*          3:63-2″15

SPEAKER: . . . of Sicily.

*(A ship turning, LS)*          4:105-4″9

*(A number of ships turning, LS)*          5:44-1″20

SPEAKER: Twelve hours later, the first . . .

*(Landing craft, LS)*          6:61-2″13

SPEAKER: . . . great Allied landing on the European continent . . .

*(Landing craft, LS; narrower than shot 4)*          7:53-2″5

SPEAKER: . . . had begun.

*(A long line of ships with antiaircraft balloons, LS)*          8:64-2″16

*(Other ships and landing craft are seen from aboard an Allied ship, LS)*          9:44-1″20

*(An Allied landing craft full of soldiers, LS)*          10:41-1″17

---

[1] Shots 1–13 are stock shots.

*(A few yards from the shore, groups of soldiers jumping out of landing craft into the waves, MS)* 11:62-2″14

*(Two lines of soldiers running toward the shore, MS)* 12:37-1″13

*(On the beach, a truck pulling a cannon along behind, while a second truck follows, FS)* 13:162-6″18

SPEAKER: Under cover of the first shadows of evening, Allied patrols penetrate into Italian territory.

*Music begins.*

*(Dissolve to . . .*

*(Coast of Sicily at night, FS; a soldier climbing down from some rocks and coming forward to meet other soldiers.)* 14:438-18″6

*(Dissolve to . . .*

*(The soldiers climbing down from rocks near a burning house, FS; camera pans left.)* 15:280-11″16

*(Dissolve to . . .*

*(The soldiers stopping, HF)* 16:770-32″2

FIRST SOLDIER: Is the only way out of this hole up them steps?

SERGEANT: Yes, I'm afraid so. We'll have to take a chance. Tony and Junior! Go first! Cover!

*The sergeant orders two soldiers to scout ahead. The patrol moves (followed by pan to left, to FS) to a stairway going up between two walls. The soldiers warily go up one at a time.*

*(Village street, MS)* 17:487-20″7

*The soldiers advance in Indian file along a narrow street bordered by high walls. (The first two soldiers come into HF; camera adjusts slightly left.)*

FIRST SOLDIER: We got out of that hole just to find ourselves in this village! I don't think we're a damn bit better off than we were.

SERGEANT: Yeah, it makes me almost as happy as it does you!

*He signals to the others to advance. (Camera tracks out and adjusts slightly left to follow them.)*

*The patrol has reached the junction of the street and the village square (HF; camera pans slightly left following the soldiers and revealing the square). One American is left on guard behind the corner (camera adjusts slightly right).*    18:347-14″11

SERGEANT, *to soldiers behind him*: If we're seen in this village, we may have the whole German army on our necks! Keep your eyes open and come out one at at time. First man!

*Music ends.*

*The sergeant gestures three times for three men to move out.*

*The first soldier comes forward and stops beside one of the boats drawn up in the center of the village square. (FS)*    19:80-3″8

WOMAN *(off screen)*: Ricuzzo! Ricuzzo!

*(Camera pans slightly left to show the figure of a child in the doorway of the church.)*

*The American soldier looks around. (CU)*    20:23-0″23

WOMAN *(off screen)*: Ricuzzo!

*The boy is standing outside the church entrance. The woman comes out of the church.*    21:82-3″10

WOMAN: Ricuzzo! *She spots the soldiers and comes*

*toward them, unafraid.* Heavens! What do you want? Who are you?

SOLDIER, *with a gesture of annoyance (HF)*: What can I do?  22:40-1″16

SERGEANT *(off screen)*: Follow that earthquake!

*The soldier moves toward the church. (MS; camera pans left)*  23:72-3″

WOMAN: What do they want? What do they want?

*Several peasants come out of the church and approach the Americans. (WF)*  24:30-1″6

MAN: Maybe they're looking for their buddies.

*Rifles at the ready, the soldiers have now come closer to the boats in the center of the square.*  25:32-1″8

*Luca and a young man come out of the church and un-hesitatingly approach the soldiers.*  26:102-4″6

BOY: Your buddies left this morning. They're gone, they're gone. They're not here.

AMERICAN *(off screen)*: What did he say?

WOMAN *(off screen)*: Dear God!

*Guns still ready, the Americans are on one side of a long-boat; the peasants, who have still not understood who these people are, are on the other. (WF)*  27:528-22″

AMERICAN: They take us for Germans.

AMERICAN: That's what happens when you got a face like Swede's!

LUCA: Welcome comrades! Welcome! They didn't land, did they?

AMERICAN: There's a helluva mess!

BOY: But these are Americans!

LUCA: What do you mean, Americans! If they put a foot on land here, they'll stay put, horizontally. *He gestures horizontally to underline his meaning.*

AMERICAN: They're beginning to catch on that we're Americans.

AMERICAN: Let's have a look at the inside of the church.

LUCA: Are you Americans?

AMERICAN: Yes. American army.

*The soldiers move toward the church.*

*The soldiers go up the steps leading to the church. Rifle at the ready, the sergeant enters, pushing the peasants in the doorway back inside.*    28:105-4″9

VOICES: Americans! Americans!

*In the church (HF) the sergeant looks around and moves forward (camera pulls back and pans right).*    29:285-11″21

SERGEANT: Merlin and Joe! Guard the door. Harry and Junior, check the rear!

*Harry and Junior (backs to camera) move forward. (MS)*    30:173-7″5

AMERICAN: Boy, this ain't no place for me!

*A woman comes up to the sergeant from the back of the church and takes him by the arm.*

WOMAN: My son . . .

*Harry and Junior go warily toward the altar, which is covered by a black cloth. At the foot of the altar stands a coffin surrounded by burning candles. (TQ)*    31:269-11″5

WOMAN *(off screen)*: . . . was at Licata till ten days ago.

He was a soldier. Did you hurt him? My blessed boy, with these terrible things happening!

SERGEANT *(off screen)*: What's she moaning about?

*The black-shawled woman (back to camera) is talking to two soldiers, one of whom is named Tony. (HF)*    32:526-21″22

TONY: She's worried about her son. She wants to know where the fighting was.

SERGEANT: Well, I feel for her and all that stuff *(off screen)* but try and get some information, will you?

*The sergeant goes off screen. Another soldier takes his place.*

TONY\*: Don't be afraid, ma'am. No one'll hurt you. But what's happened here?

WOMAN: Dear God, he's talking Italian! Are you an Italian like us?

TONY\*: Yes, my father's Sicilian. He was born in Gela.

WOMAN: Really?

OLD MAN, *joining the woman and the two Americans*: Gela? I'm from Gela too! Luca!

*Luca turns (CU). Behind him (TQ), other villagers gather around the sergeant.*    33:714-29″18

OLD MAN *(off screen)*: The American is from Gela!

MAN *(off screen)*: Is that what he says?

SERGEANT, *surrounded by villagers (TQ)*: Come here, Tony!

TONY: Never mind, never mind.

WOMAN: The last few days it's been terrible.

MAN: The planes have been bombing all day long.

MAN: The Germans left this morning, every last one of them.

WOMAN: We haven't left the village. We're holding a wake.

MAN: Everybody's left, even the grave-digger.

WOMAN: We can't leave the village, we can't go anywhere else. We can't even lay my daughter-in-law to rest in peace.

SERGEANT, *to Tony*: What's the deal?

TONY: The Germans were here before.

SERGEANT: Is that all? Look, kid, we can't stay here all night! Shake a leg, will ya?

TONY*: How many Germans left?

OLD MAN: So the American's from Gela!

*(Luca and the woman worried about her son, HF; also shots 36, 38, 41, 45, 48.)*    34:24-1″

LUCA: What's your name?

*(Tony and the old man, HF; also shots 37, 40, 42, 44, 47, 50, 52.)*    35:111-4″15

TONY: Tony Mascali.

LUCA *(off screen)*: He's not from Gela.

TONY\*: Yes, my father's really from Gela. Then he came to America.

LUCA *(HF)*: There aren't any Mascalis in Gela.    36:48-2″

*Annoyed by Luca's tone of voice, Tony reacts angrily but is immediately restrained by the sergeant. (HF)*    37:92-3″20

LUCA *(off screen)*: He's not from Gela. They come here and tell a pack of lies, and they want you to believe them.

*(on screen)*: . . . Some fix!    38:34-1″10

*(The sergeant surrounded by the villagers, HF; also shots 43, 46, 49, 51.)*    39:22-0″22

SERGEANT, *to Tony*: What's he say?

*Tony questions a villager standing by him.*    40:77-3″5

TONY, *to the sergeant*: He just says . . . *To the villager, in Italian*: When did the Germans leave?

VILLAGER *(off screen)*: They set mines all over the place this morning.    41:43-1″19

TONY, *to the sergeant*: . . . the Germans left this morning . . .    42:36-1″12

*The sergeant claps his hands on his helmet in a gesture of mock despair. (HF)*    43:51-2″3

TONY *(off screen)*: . . . the place is lousy with mines.

SERGEANT: Amazing!

SERGEANT *(off screen)*: It took you this long to find that out?　44:88-3″16

TONY: Sergeant, I'm sorry, but I just . . .

TONY *(off screen)*: . . . don't speak Italian in a hurry . . .　45:60-2″12

OLD MAN: So the American's from Gela!

TONY: . . . it takes a little time to talk to these people.　46:59-2″11

SECOND SOLDIER, *to Tony*: Take it easy, kid! You know what you're . . .

*Tony questions another old man.*　47:137-5″17

SECOND SOLDIER *(off screen)*: . . . doing, just take your time.

TONY\*: How many Germans were there?

OLD MAN: Lots, my boy, lots—three thousand, or more, even more.

*The first old man makes his way forward from behind Luca.*　48:63-2″15

OLD MAN: Thirty thousand!

LUCA, *making a broad gesture*: Thirty million!

SERGEANT: Say, kid, if you don't understand this stuff, just say so. We'll forget the whole thing.　49:71-2″23

SERGEANT: Ask him where the Krauts went, will ya?　50:203-8″11

TONY\*: Which direction did they go, can you tell me?

OLD MAN: They went north, maybe toward Scopina. For sure they were headed north.

TONY, *to sergeant*: This guy says the Krauts went north.

SERGEANT: Well, I guess that's as much as we'll get ·out　51:72-3″

of him. Ask him if they know where the mines are.

TONY*, *to the villager*: Where'd they lay the mines?   52:196-8″4

VILLAGER: Along the coast, on the way north. The only
way to get through is over the lava. It's dangerous
by night.

BOY *(off screen)*: You need somebody . . .

*The crowd of villagers surrounding the sergeant and*   53:332-13″20
*Tony, TQ.*

(on screen) . . . that knows the path, like Carmela.
She's gone that way twice already to look for her
folks.

TONY, *to sergeant*: The only clear way is through the bed
of an old lava canal—he says it'll be rough going.

BOY: Come with me! *He motions to the Americans to
follow him as he goes toward the rear of the church.*

TONY: Let's find out!

*Followed by the soldiers, the boy comes on screen from*   54:619-25″19
*left and passes through the crowd (HF; camera pans
right).*

BOY: Come!

MAN *(off screen)*: Who'll give me a cigarette? Yes, yes, a
cigarette.

*Tony starts to give him a cigarette, but the sergeant
calls him.*

BOY: Carmela, these are Americans. They want to talk
to you.

SERGEANT *(HF)*: Come here, Tony!

*Tony approaches the group (TQ; camera tracks forward
after him).*

TONY* *(HF)*: Are you the one that knows the way over
the lava?

CARMELA: I go that way every day to take my father his lunch.

TONY*: Is it a path or a road?

CARMELA: It's lava.

TONY*: Isn't there somebody who can lead us? Someone in your family?

CARMELA: No. My brother and my father have been away four days. Twice I tried to leave the church to look for them . . .

*(Joe, an American soldier, chewing gum, MCU)*      55:100-4″4

CARMELA *(off screen)*: . . . but the other people were afraid to let me go alone. I'll lead you . . .

   . . . I know the way. I'll come with you.      56:104-4″8

*A woman clutches Carmela's arm, trying to hold her back, but the girl pulls away.*

WOMAN: But you can't go alone with these strangers. Where are you going? Where are you going?

*Joe turns to start out of the church. (MCU)*                    57:72-3″

*Amid the loud protests of the villagers, the Americans*         58:218-9″2
*begin to follow Carmela toward the church door (HF;*
*camera tracks left with them).*

SERGEANT: What's she saying?

TONY: It's just like I told you—the whole coast's nothing but rocks and mines. The only way north is through this old lava canal.

SERGEANT: Okay, let's try it. Al, you and Swede stay here. Don't leave the place and keep an eye on the Eyeties!

*Two soldiers in the doorway of the church (TQ) watch*           59:30-1″6
*Carmela (back to the camera).*

SERGEANT *(off screen)*: Where does she think she's going?

TONY*, to Carmela: You're really coming with us?                 60:274-11″10

CARMELA: Yes.

TONY, *to sergeant*: This dame wants to lead us through the canal.

SERGEANT: Are you in your right mind? How do you know this girl? How do you know where she'll lead us? Grow up, will ya? This dame stays here with the rest of the Eyeties.

JOE: Well, it's one or the other—either we trust the girl    61:207-8″15
or try our luck with the mines. You might know, I'm less afraid of the girl than I am of the mines. Here we are, six men with guns . . .

   *(off screen)* . . . and afraid of a little girl!                62:362-15″2

SERGEANT: Okay, if that's the way you feel about it, don't come crying to me later!

*The soldiers again start toward the church door (camera tracks and pans left). Luca and the villagers protest loudly.*

LUCA: Where are you taking that girl?

*The soldiers become more wary. Fending Luca off with one hand, Tony hurries Carmela out.*

TONY*: Let's go, baby.

LUCA: Carmela, don't go!

*(Village square, MS)*        63:300-12″12

*Music begins. The soldiers and Carmela come out of the church and start off (camera pans left).*

SOLDIER: Hold it! Take care of the girl, Bill!

*(Dissolve to . . .*

*(Sicilian countryside, nighttime, MS)*        64:159-6″15

*The soldiers come forward from the background and stop in the foreground (TQ). The sergeant sits down on the ground. The others gather around him.*

*(A tower, seen dimly, LS)*        65:81-3″9

SERGEANT *(off screen)*: Well, this is it, I guess. This must be the place the . . .

*The soldiers are spread out behind the seated sergeant. Bill keeps an eye on Carmela, standing to the rear on the left.*        66:675-28″3

SERGEANT: . . . old man wanted for his O.P. Some joint! Hey, Junior, remember Frankenstein? This reminds me of the old mill there!

JUNIOR: Ha ha! It does, now that you mention it. What a place for a murder!

SERGEANT: Harry, what would you say if I suggested you go along and scout the joint?

HARRY: Offhand, Sarge, I'd reply with a firm, polite "no thanks!"

SERGEANT: Nevertheless, I think we'd better split up. Merlin! You and Harry go around that way! Junior, you take the other side! Make it snappy, but be careful!

*The soldiers begin to move out, going off screen to left.*

*The soldiers make their way up the hillside toward the tower. (MS)*                                           67:30-1"6

*Taking advantage of a moment in which she is un-observed, Carmela tries to escape. Hearing the noise, the sergeant turns quickly. Two soldiers chase after her.*                                           68:37-1"13

*They catch the girl and bring her back. (WF)*          69:236-9"20

TONY: That old chicken tried to fly the coop!

*The sergeant comes on screen from left and stops, observing Carmela. Then he turns to watch his men's progress.*

*The soldiers approach the tower. (MS)*                 70:145-6"1

*(Overall view from the base of the tower, LS)*         71:108-4"12

*Two soldiers cautiously enter.*

*The sergeant (CU) and Joe, half-hidden in the rear, watch their companions' progress. (MCU)*               72:200-8"8

SERGEANT: If Junior ever gets out of this, South Norwood'll never hold him. He'll be writing about it for six months!

JOE: I wouldn't mind being in South Norwood myself right now!

*One soldier can be dimly seen on the tower, signaling*    73:139-5″19
*with his arms. Two whistles are heard.*

*The sergeant and Joe sigh in relief.*    74:62-2″14

JOE: Ah! They made it!

*(Dissolve to . . .*

*(The stairway between two floors of the tower, seen from*    75:372-15″12
*above, WF)*

*The two soldiers who have scouted ahead welcome the*
*others. One waits at the top of the stairs for the sergeant,*
*who goes up. Carmela, Joe, and Tony follow part way.*

SOLDIER: Come on in and make yourself at home!

SERGEANT: Excellent! In that case you can draw my bath!

*Music ends.*

*The sergeant glances at the upper floor, then returns*
*down the stairs and motions to Tony to come up. Tony*
*is followed by Carmela and Joe.*

SOLDIER *(off screen)*: There's a million bats in there and
    that's all!

ANOTHER SOLDIER: I hope we find a treasure up here!

TONY: Why, what would you do with a million bucks?

JOE: Aw, he'd go to a . . .

*On the upper floor, the sergeant inspects the tower. He*    76:48-2″
*looks through an opening and observes his companions.*
*(HF)*

JOE *(off screen)*: . . . medic and get his face lifted!

*One soldier puts his gun down by a wall. Feeling safe,*    77:83-3″11
*the Americans joke among themselves. (WF)*

JOE *(off screen)*: Notice the lovely interior decorating,

complete with running water and room service!

*The sergeant finishes his inspection (HF) and goes off*    78:73-3"1
*screen to right while Joe continues to point out the*
*attractions of the tower.*

JOE *(off screen)*: But you haven't seen anything yet! Come
   on downstairs—there's another room underneath
   here. Watch your step on these stairs.

*Bracing his hands against the wall, the sergeant makes his*    79:232-9"6
*way carefully down the ruined stairway (WF; camera tilts*
*slightly down).*

JOE *(off screen)*: I think there's ten or fifteen—I don't
   know.

SERGEANT: Hell! Do you call these stairs? It's as dark as a
   graveyard at midnight!

*A soldier, waiting for the sergeant in the room below,*    80:313-13"1
*flicks on his cigarette lighter to help him see his way. (TQ)*

SERGEANT: Damn it! It's dark!

SOLDIER: Is this any better?

SERGEANT: Put that light out, you damn fool! Do you want
   to get us all killed?

*(Camera pans right toward the center of the room.) The*
*sergeant stops at an aperture from which the sea can be*
*seen, but the soldier motions for the sergeant to follow*
*him. They both go off screen to right.*

SOLDIER *(off screen)*: Come on!

*The soldier leads the way for the sergeant (HF; camera*    81:165-6"21
*tracks forward and pans right to WF).*

SOLDIER: Let me show you around! This place is the real
   McCoy! This place has a trapdoor too, a deep, dark
   trapdoor. Hey, you're not scared, are you?

*Two soldiers look down from the upper floor at the*    82:34-1″10
*sergeant approaching the trapdoor (WF). Sound of the*
*sea is heard.*

SOLDIER *(off screen)*: Stop worrying, will ya? The place is
    deserted . . .

*The sergeant and his companion reach the open trapdoor.*    83:189-7″21
*The sergeant kneels down and looks in.*

SOLDIER: . . . I tell you. Take a look for yourself!

JOE: Hey! Any witches or stiffs down there?

*As voices call out from upstairs, the sergeant stands up.*

*The soldier goes toward his companions, who are playing*
*with his canteen.*

SOLDIER: Even smiling, you look scared to death up there!
    You don't look overjoyed to me.

*The two soldiers upstairs are grinning at their*    84:66-2″18
*companion.*

SOLDIER: Well, are you satisfied now?

*Tony is squatting down with his rifle in his hands*    85:45-1″21
*(HF from above). Carmela, standing beside him, is at*
*right margin of frame.*

TONY*: Why'd you try to escape?

CARMELA, *angrily (CU from below)*: I didn't come here to    86:58-2″10
    look at your pretty faces!

*(Tony, HF)*    87:375-15″15

CARMELA *(off screen)*: I haven't seen my father and my
    brother for four days. I'm going to look for them.

*The sergeant and two other soldiers come up the stairs.*

*Tony stands up (camera tilts upward) and goes toward*

*them (camera pans right). Then he returns toward Carmela (camera pans right). The girl comes on screen from right.*

SERGEANT: All right, let's break it up! Let's take off!

TONY: She still intends looking for her old man and her brother.

SERGEANT: Well, there's nothing we can do but trust her now. She stays here. Joe, you stay with her!

JOE: What?

SERGEANT: That's right—you stay!

*(Joe, the sergeant, and Tony, MCU)*                88:509-21″5

JOE: All right, so somebody's got to stay. Why me? Let Tony stay—he can talk to the girl.

SERGEANT, *clapping a hand on Joe's shoulder*: Well, it's like this—first, we have to take Tony along to do the interpreting. Then, Ike[1] and I had a long talk. He said, "Sergeant, you have a man in your outfit that is an expert in towers." So, Joe, that's you!

JOE: It's nice to know the old man's got confidence. Are you sure I'm the Joe he's talking about?

ONE SOLDIER: Yeah, Sarge. Are you ready to see him, Joe?    89:1110-46″6

SERGEANT, *to soldier*: Oh, blow it! *To Tony*: Say, kid, thank the girl and tell her we'll be back shortly to take her home. *He goes off screen to left with the soldier.*

TONY: Right. *He slings his rifle over his shoulder. To Carmela*\*: Good girl, Carmela. Don't worry about your folks. If we find them we'll bring them back with us. You stay here—Joe'll keep you company.

---

[1] General Eisenhower.

Look what a cute guy he is! *Grinning, he slaps his
companion, then starts off.*

CARMELA: I want to go back to the church. Can I go
back to the church?

TONY*, *turning back*: We'll all go back to the church
together, later. *(off screen)* See you!

*He goes off screen to left. Joe follows him down the stairs
a little way (camera pans left and tilts slightly downward).*

*Joe and Tony say good-bye (HF; seen from the top of the
stairs).*                                                          90:101-4″5

TONY: Well, take it easy, old boy!

JOE: Don't get low, now!

*(Tower, LS)*                                                      91:125-5″5

*The soldiers go down the hillside from the tower.*

*(Overall view from the base of the tower, LS)*                   92:91-3″19

*(Inside the tower, WF)*                                           93:2257-
                                                                  1′34″1

*Music begins. Joe goes back up the stairs, taking out his
cigarettes (camera adjusts slightly to right and upward
to include Carmela in WF).*

JOE, *offering her a cigarette*: Smoke? *She refuses, shaking
her head.* No? Okay!

*He goes to look out of a window (camera tracks and pans
left). He returns toward the girl (camera tracks out in
front of him and pans right to include her).*

JOE: Are you scared? You a Fascist? I bet you're a Fascist.
I'm a Fascist. *He stops in front of her and starts to
light his cigarette.*

CARMELA, *slapping his hand*: No light!

JOE: You're a good girl! You're not Fascist, really!

*Music ends.*

*Joe gives her a friendly slap on the shoulder. Vexed, Carmela digs her elbow into him and steps away, going off screen to left. Joe moves behind a corner to light his cigarette, then decides against it and follows the girl outside the tower (camera tracks and pans left until Carmela is included, HF). Joe gestures to try to make himself understood as he talks to her.*

JOE: Maria? You Maria? What's your name? Maria?

CARMELA: What in the world's he saying?

JOE: Look! I'm Joe, from Jersey. You?

CARMELA: Ah! I'm Carmela.

JOE: Me Joe—you Carmela. What beautiful scenery!

CARMELA: Ah, sea! [*mare*]

JOE: *Mare?*

CARMELA: My father and my brother went out to sea. You understand?

JOE: Yeah, *mare!* In Jersey we have the same blue sea!

CARMELA: The boat is good and the sea is calm. Maybe they didn't come back because of the war. I'm going to find them and you stay here. I go. *She starts to leave.*

JOE, *stopping her*: Where are you going? You can't leave now. There's fighting out there! Understand? Boom-boom! War!

*Carmela pulls free and goes off to left, into the tower, followed by Joe. (WF)*

CARMELA: You're all alike, you, the Germans, the Fascists!

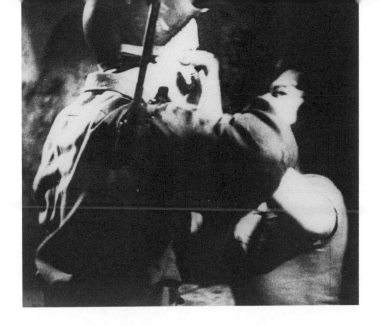

All you people with guns! You're all the same!

*Joe comes up to Carmela as she stands by a window; he attempts to distract her with friendly conversation. (HF)*

94:6065-
4'12"17

JOE: Don't look at me like that—it's not my idea. Come on! We got a couple of hours in here together—I'm in no mood for an argument! Come on, Carmela, smile! Grr! Look, I'm Joe from Jersey—I've said that before! *He casts his cigarette aside angrily.* I wish they'd send me home! Fifty-four! Shooting star! See? Whee! No! I don't mean bombs! Shooting star! Understand? Shooting star! Where I live, if you wish on a shooting star, you get whatever you wish for. So far I've counted fifty-three, and always the same wish! Then, if you see another one in two minutes, it's a sure sign you get your wish—you can't miss! See? What did I tell you? Now I'm only waiting time on the first one I made!

*He points out another shooting star to Carmela.*

CARMELA: Ah, shooting star! [*stella cadente*]

*Joe is vexed at not making himself understood. He moves toward the camera and goes to lean against the wall (camera tracks back and pans right). Then he returns to Carmela (camera pans left). He removes his helmet and sits down (camera tracks and adjusts left to include the standing Carmela). The sea can be seen in the background. Music begins.*

JOE: No, *stella cadente!* Shooting star! You know, you don't see so many where I come from. If this story about wishing were true, you people'd be the happiest in the world—all your wishes'd come true. I want a bottle of whisky! . . . A bottle . . . ah! Now I want . . . no, I don't want C ration! C ration goes to the bottom of the drink. Don't stand there with a mouthful of teeth! . . .

*Joe continues to gesture broadly as he talks. Carmela, standing beside him, listens without interest. Vexed, Joe finally gets up (camera pans left after him).*

JOE: Say something! You may be more scared than I am, but I doubt it! I don't mind telling you, sweetheart, I wish I were home!

*Carmela picks up his last word, which she misinterprets as the Italian* comme, *"what."*

CARMELA: *Comme?*

JOE: What?

CARMELA: You said *comme.*

*Disappointed, Joe sits down again; Carmela does the same. He counts off his stock of foreign words on his fingers.*

JOE: You got me! Tony can follow you, but I can't. Look —*paisan, spaghetti, bambina, mangiare, tout de suite, c'est la guerre*—that's it. Oh, yes, and Carmela! Now how about you? Is your English any better than my Italian? Let's try you now. Go—me Joe. Understand? Joe.

CARMELA: Joe.

*Delighted by the success of his pupil, Joe squeezes her hand to congratulate her.*

JOE: Good! Good! Move to the head of the class! Okay, now try this: me Joe, boy—you Carmela, girl.

CARMELA\*: Ah, girl!

JOE: Fine, fine! You're doing this fine! We're friends, understand? Friends!

CARMELA\*: Friends.

JOE: Good girl! Good girl! Look, Carmela—you're dark —you dark, me blond, huh?

CARMELA: Ah, blond! [*biondo*]

JOE: *Biondo?* You know, I can almost imagine I'm home —it's quiet at night like this where I come from. I'm sorry, just thinking about home.

CARMELA, *again mistaking his last word*: *Comme?* You say that the same way in America?

JOE: Home! Yeah! In America I was a truck driver for a milk company. You like milk? I bring the milk . . . see? Drive . . . milk. . . . *He gestures as if driving, then as if milking a cow.*

CARMELA: Ah, ding-dong?

JOE: No ding-dong! Look! Look . . . moo! Aaaah!

*He imitates a cow, making horns with his hands, mooing and repeating the gestures of milking; then he pretends to pour milk into a glass and to drink it avidly. Carmela finally understands.*

CARMELA: Milk. Uncle Luca used to have cows. Up on that cow he once put seven children. [*bambini*]

JOE: *Bambini?* You *bambini?*

CARMELA: No.

JOE: Me . . . yes . . . oh, no! no! My sister has a little boy, Dick. He's seven and lives with us. You know, we've got a garden . . . my mother grows tomatoes. My sister and I tied a rope on two pear trees to swing on. One day I loosened the rope and my sister got an awful surprise! *He takes his wallet out of his back pocket and shows some photographs to Carmela.* This is Pop and Mom. This is Dick and my sister Ellen. You don't understand.

*Carmela takes the photographs from him and examines them almost jealously.*

JOE: It's my sister! See? Little boy and his mother?

*Seeing that the girl does not understand, Joe takes out his cigarette lighter and flicks it on, bringing the photographs close to her face.*

JOE: She's my sister. Here, look! See? You know, she's much better looking than this. People say she looks a little like me.

CARMELA: Sister.

*Sound of rifle shot. Joe drops the lighter and falls to the floor.*

*Music.*

*(Sicilian countryside)*                                   95:61-2"13

*A German soldier puts down his rifle. (CU)*

*Four German soldiers are crouched down, hiding among*    96:304-12"16

*the rocks and the prickly pears. (MS)*

FIRST GERMAN: Was ist los? Warum hast du geschossen?
[What's going on? Why did you shoot?]

SECOND GERMAN: Ich habe Licht gesehen. [I saw a light.]

FIRST GERMAN: Du musst die Nerven besser kontrollieren.
Die Leute leiden seit einiger Zeit an Schreckgespen-
stern. Komm, wir gehen! [Keep a tighter grip on
your nerves. People are so scared these days they're
seeing things. Come on, let's go!]

SECOND GERMAN: Und doch habe ich es gesehen! [But I
did see it!]

*The soldiers get up to go.*

*The Germans (seen from behind) come on screen and*   97:223-9"7
*make their way down the cliff. The sea can be seen below*

*them.  They  stop.  One  points  to  something  in  the
distance.  (WF)*

FIRST GERMAN: Neumann, siehst du . . . [Neumann, see
there . . .]

*(Tower, ELS, seen from another angle, rising on a rocky     98:77-3"5
strip overlooking the sea.)*

FIRST GERMAN *(off screen)*: . . . von dort hätte das Licht
kommen können. [. . . the light might have come
from there.]

SECOND GERMAN *(off screen)*: Schon möglich, wollen wir
nachschaun? [It could be. Shall we have a look?]

*The German soldiers continue down the cliff. (WF)*      99:77-3"5

*(Dissolve to . . .*

*(Inside tower, HF)*                                        100:70-2"22

*The Germans come forward.*

FIRST GERMAN: Schlosspiraten. [Pirates' castle.]

SECOND GERMAN: Was für ein? [What is it?]

*Carrying Joe's rifle, Carmela climbs up the ladder       101:61-2"13
through the trapdoor. (WF from below)*

*Carmela climbs out through the trapdoor and bends       102:44-1"20
down to close it after her. (TQ from above)*

*Joe lies still on the straw, diagonally across the frame.   103:42-1"18
(TQ)*

*Carmela straightens up (TQ) and starts to go get some    104:131-5"11
straw (camera pans left and tracks back, WF). She turns
as she hears the voices of the Germans.*

FIRST GERMAN *(off screen)*: Pass auf, dass keiner rein-
kommt. [Keep a lookout so no one comes in.]

*Carmela turns again and hurriedly picks up handfuls*     105:115-4″19
*of straw. (HF)*

SECOND GERMAN *(off screen)*: Bleib hier! [Stay here!]

FIRST GERMAN *(off screen)*: Nein, kommt nichts! [No, don't
    come!]

*Chatting, the Germans come forward (HF).*     106:109-4″13

SECOND GERMAN: Hier könnte ich romantisch werden.
    [Here I could be romantic.]

*Carmela covers the trapdoor with straw.*     107:54-2″6

FIRST GERMAN *(off screen)*: Und die Amerikaner? [Any
    Americans?]

*Music ends.*

*In one of the upper rooms of the tower the two Germans*     108:58-2″10
*shine a flashlight on the rooms below. (HF)*

SECOND GERMAN: Hast doch Recht gehabt . . . [You were
    right, it's a . . .]

*(A wall illuminated by the flashlight, MS)*     109:25-1″1

SECOND GERMAN *(off screen)*: . . . ein richtiges Piratenloch.
    [. . . real pirates' den.]

*Carmela crouches down near the wall as the flashlight*     110:52-2″4
*plays against the wall just over her head. (HF)*

*(FS; camera pans downward and to right, following the*     111:46-1″22
*light through the room whose floor is scattered with*
*straw.)*

*Another soldier joins the two exploring the tower with*     112:264-11″
*the flashlight. (HF)*

FIRST GERMAN: Jetzt kannst es nicht abwarten—Mensch,

hier ist sogar das notwendige Stroh. [Now you can't wait for it—hey, here there's even the straw we need.]

SECOND GERMAN: Na, dann los, wollen wir die Zimmer einrichten und das Hauptquartier aufbauen? [Well, come on, let's fix up this room and set up head-quarters.]

*They go off screen to right.*

*Carmela is in the dark. (CU)*                                    113:57-2″9

*The Germans go down the stairs, lighting their way with*        114:86-3″14
*the flashlight. (WF from below)*

THIRD GERMAN: . . . finster wie ein Loch. [. . . as dark as a hole.]

FIRST GERMAN: Die richtige Gegend um sich das Genick zu brechen. [Just the place to break your neck.]

*Carmela moves closer to the wall. (CU)*                          115:62-2″14

FIRST GERMAN *(off screen)*: Mensch, halt an! [Hey, stop!]

SECOND GERMAN *(off screen)*: Na, Gott sei Dank . . . [Well, thank God . . .]

*Joe, lying on the straw, tries to move. (TQ)*                    116:66-2″18

SECOND GERMAN *(off screen)*: . . . dieses Mal ist's wieder glatt gegangen. [. . . this time it's all right.]

*The Germans have reached the bottom of the stairs. (TQ)*        117:57-2″9

FIRST GERMAN: Und die Amerikaner?

*Joe manages to roll over on his side. (TQ)*                      118:61-2″13

SECOND GERMAN *(off screen)*: Ich glaube, da sind wir nicht . . . [I think we're not too . . .]

*The Germans pass in front of the window (HF) where*          119:132-5"12
*Joe and Carmela had been sitting (camera tracks right*
*and then pans right with them until Carmela is revealed*
*in the light of their torch).*

SECOND GERMAN: . . . weit vom jenseit. [. . . far from there.]

FIRST GERMAN: Nee, kuck mal an, da ist doch jemand.
   [Hey, look, there's somebody there.]

*The two Germans (seen head-on) flash their light on*          120:34-1"10
*Carmela. (HF)*

SECOND GERMAN: Mensch, was machst du denn hier?
   [Hey, what're you doing here?]

*(Carmela, TQ)*                                                121:502-
                                                                    20"22
*The two Germans come on screen from left and begin to*
*question her.*

FIRST GERMAN*: Why did you leave the village?

CARMELA: I was afraid.

*From above, a third German calls to his companions.*

THIRD GERMAN *(off screen)*: Was ist los? [What's up?]

FIRST GERMAN: An die Arbeit! [To work!]

THIRD GERMAN: Schick sie mal hoch. [Send her upstairs.]

FIRST GERMAN*, *to Carmela*: You afraid?

CARMELA: Of the Americans.

FIRST GERMAN*: Nothing to be afraid of!

*One soldier picks up some straw behind Carmela as she*
*moves away (camera tracks back and adjusts left).*

FIRST GERMAN *(off screen)*: Sogar Menschen sind hier zu
   finden. [Even here you find people.]

THIRD GERMAN *(off screen)*: Was hast du gefunden?
[What've you found?]

*The other German picks up some straw too and pushes
Carmela on ahead of him.*

FIRST GERMAN*: We won't hurt you. We're friends. Did
you make light?

CARMELA: No. *(Camera tracks and pans left after them.)*

FIRST GERMAN: Sie scheint die Sprache nur zu haben . . .

*Joe is dragging himself along toward the trapdoor ladder.* 122:190-7″22
*(TQ)*

FIRST GERMAN *(off screen)*: . . . Zeichen für ein Frauen-
zimmer. [She seems to have only a tongue . . . bad
sign for a harem.]

SECOND GERMAN *(off screen)*: Warum ist sie hierherge-
kommen? Das könnte gefährlich sein. Wenn sie . . .
[Why did she come here? It could be dangerous.
If she . . .]

*The Germans, still carrying their straw, have stopped at* 123:34-1″10
*the bottom of the stairs. Carmela is between them. (HF)*

SECOND GERMAN: . . . Licht gemacht hat, müssen auch
andere Menschen hier sein. [. . . struck a light, there
must be other people here.]

*(RA)* 124:35-1″11
*The first German starts up the stairs. (HF)*

FIRST GERMAN: Ach, Quatsch! [Nonsense!]

*Carmela waits at the foot of the stairs with the second* 125:90-3″18
*German, who is talking with his companion as the latter
goes up. (HF)*

SECOND GERMAN: Junge, wat die de reife Birne. Jetzt gibt
die uns . . .

*The first German comes up the stairs (toward the camera,*   126:313-13″1
*HF). Carmela turns away to allow the soldier behind her*
*to pass by, then follows him up (camera pans right,*
*adjusts upward, and pans right again).*

SECOND GERMAN *(off screen):* . . . drei noch was zu tun und
    da bleibt doch noch was übrig. [Boys, this girl's
    really stacked. She'll keep us three busy for now . . .
    and there'll be some left over.]

THIRD GERMAN: Das ist eine ewige Plünderei. Zeig mal her,
    was du gefischt hast? [Here's the Eternal Loot. Let's
    see, what've you caught?]

SECOND GERMAN*, *to Carmela:* What are you doing here?
    You're not here because you're afraid. No, no. You
    were supposed to meet your boy friend, eh? *He puts
    down the straw and lays a hand on Carmela's
    shoulder.*

*(The German and the girl face the camera almost head-*   127:321-13″9
*on, TQ)*

*He tries to paw her, but she pulls away from him.*

CARMELA: Keep your hands off!

SECOND GERMAN*: Your boy friend's very stupid not to
    come. I'm right aren't I? I've guessed right?

FIRST GERMAN, *to Second:* Ich glaube, du hast schlechte
    Absichten [I think you have evil intentions.]

SECOND GERMAN: Ich bin völlig untauglich dafür, völlig
    untauglich. *He sits down on the floor.* [I'm com-
    pletely impotent, completely impotent.]

*(WF from above; resume on German sitting down.)*   128:136-5″16

SECOND GERMAN: Bei der Post und der ewigen Rennerei.
    [Because of the news and all this running around.]

FIRST GERMAN: Ich glaube, es wäre dir lieber gewesen, ein Fass Wein zu finden. [I think you'd rather have found a barrel of wine.]

*Carmela listens to the Germans talking. (MCU)*　　129:44-1″20

SECOND GERMAN *(off screen)*: Beides, ein Fass Wein . . .

*He gestures broadly. (MCU)*　　130:21-0″21

SECOND GERMAN: . . . und das Mädchen obendrauf. [Both a barrel of wine . . . and a girl on top of it.]

*The third soldier loosens the scarf around his neck.*　　131:120-5″
*(MCU)*

THIRD GERMAN: Mir würde auch Wasser genügen. Ich habe nur Durst. [Just water'd be enough for me. I'm just thirsty.]

SECOND GERMAN *(off screen)*: Hast du vielleicht Komplexe . . .

*(MCU)* . . . willst du vielleicht noch Milch haben.　　132:29-1″5
[Maybe you have complexes . . . maybe you still want milk.]

THIRD GERMAN*, *turning to the girl (MCU)*: We're thirsty.　　133:156-6″12
Can you find water?

*Carmela nods. (HF)*　　134:30-1″6

THIRD GERMAN* *(CU)*: Good! Is it very far?　　135:40-1″16

CARMELA, *starting to leave (MCU)*: I'll go.　　136:33-1″9

*As Carmela starts to leave, the second German, who is*　　137:191-7″23
*seated, touches her. She slaps him. (WF from above)*

SECOND GERMAN: Junge, heute nacht wird's Überraschungen geben. [Boys, we're in for some surprises tonight.]

*Music begins.*

FIRST GERMAN: Natürlich, der Herr immer vornehm.
[Naturally, the gentleman is always refined.]

THIRD GERMAN: Ich möchte nicht . . .

*One German takes her hand to help her pass by. Carmela
(WF) starts up the stairs.*

*Carmela comes on screen from right (HF; camera tracks
and then pans left with her). She begins to run. (WF)*

138:149-6″5

THIRD GERMAN *(off screen):* . . . bei unseren Aussehen?
[I hope it's not . . . our appearance?]

*The soldiers laugh.*

*(Dissolve to . . .*

*(Carmela, coming on screen from left)*

139:189-7″21

*As she is about to go down the stairs, aircraft and gunfire
are heard. She stops. (HF)*

*(Seen from the coast, rockets shoot up into the sky, LS)*

140:101-4″5

*The Germans crowd around the window to watch. (HF)*

141:120-5″

*Carmela (HF) has reached the floor with the trapdoor.
She stops, looks around, then goes to uncover the trapdoor. (MS)*

142:188-7″20

*(Dissolve to . . .*

*(Carmela approaching Joe's body at the foot of the ladder)
She bends down over him. (HF)*

143:118-4″22

*Carmela straightens up, her head by the ladder. (MCU)*

144:31-1″7

*Carmela looks at Joe and then upward, as if trying to
make a decision. Tormented, she leans against the wall.
(CU)*

145:265-11″1

CARMELA: Joe!

*Music ends. The fourth German, named Fritz, listens to the third German. (MCU)*    146:129-5"9

THIRD GERMAN *(off screen):* Fritz, Fritz, glaubst du dass sie noch weiterkommen? [Fritz, Fritz, do you think they'll come any farther?]

*(Third German, MCU)*    147:101-4"5

FOURTH GERMAN *(off screen):* Ja.

THIRD GERMAN: Das wir noch mehr zurückziehen müssen, vielleicht bis Palermo, denkst Du? [You think we'll have to pull back even farther, maybe even to Palermo?]

FOURTH GERMAN *(MCU):* Bei uns gibt's kein Zurückrug.    148:237-9"21
Morgen gibt er einen Gegenangriff und da werden sie laufen wie die Hasen, bis wach Aegypten, ach, bis zum Teufel. [We never retreat. Tomorrow there'll

be a counterattack, and they'll run like rabbits all
the way to Egypt, or straight to the devil.]

*Carmela weeps silently. (CU)*                      149:198-8″6

*Carmela takes Joe's rifle and starts up the ladder (HF;*   150:201-8″9
*camera adjusts upward).*

*Carmela climbs up the ladder. (TQ)*               151:57-2″9

*Carmela raises the trapdoor and creeps out slowly, with-*   152:285-
*out a sound. (MS)*                                        11″21

FIRST GERMAN *(off screen)*: Junggesellen haben vorrecht.
  [Youth before age.]

SECOND GERMAN *(off screen)*: Würfeln wir doch aus . . .
  drei. [We'll throw dice for it . . . three.]

THIRD GERMAN *(off screen)*: Acht. [Eight.]

*Carmela runs toward the Germans (camera pans and*
*tracks first in front of her and then after her).*

FOURTH GERMAN *(off screen)*: Zwölf. [Twelve.]

*Carmela takes aim and fires a shot.*

FIRST GERMAN *(off screen)*: Achtung! [Look out!]

*Sound of shot.*

*The wounded soldier claps his hands to his forehead*    153:31-1″7
*and falls backward (WF). Music ends.*

*(Sicilian countryside, MS)*                          154:293-12″5

*The American soldiers are crouching down . on the*
*ground. The sergeant calls a man, who runs up.*

AMERICAN: Sergeant, sounds like a carbine!

SERGEANT: Maybe Joe's in trouble!

AMERICAN: I hope not, damn it!

SERGEANT: Hurry up! *They stand up and begin to move forward cautiously.*

*(Dissolve to . . .*

*(Inside the tower, WF)*

155:636-
26"12

*The Americans are in the room with the trapdoor. They pick something up from the floor. The sergeant is perplexed. He moves forward (camera tracks out in front of him and pans right). As he sees the open trapdoor, he stops, then runs toward it (camera pans right). Music begins.*

*(MS; camera subjective from sergeant's viewpoint, looking down through the trapdoor; only the sergeant's feet are seen.)*

156:57-2"9

*Joe's body lies at the foot of the ladder.*

*The sergeant stands up. The others come silently up to him.*  157:217-9″1

*(The trapdoor seen from above)*  158:74-3″2

*The soldiers look down through the trapdoor. (MCU)*  159:203-8″11

SERGEANT: Why, that dirty little Eyetie!

*He goes off screen to right. The others follow him (camera pans right). Sound of shot.*

*(The three German soldiers, seen head-on, looking downward, HF)*  160:97-4″1

*(LS from below; the Germans seen atop a rock overlooking the sea)*  161:296-12″8

GERMAN: Da weg . . . Los. [Let's go.]

*They move off (camera pans downward). Carmela's shattered body lies on the rocks below. Music ends.*

*(Fade-out)*


## EPISODE II

*(Paestum, daytime, LS; camera pans left over the temple of Paestum.)[1]*  1:667-27″19
*Music begins.*

SPEAKER: The war passed quickly through southern Italy. On September eighth, the day of the Italian surrender, the cannons of the Allied fleet were trained on Naples. When the German resistance was broken at Salerno . . .

*(Wipe to right)*

*(Vesuvius at night, ELS; camera pans left over Mount Vesuvius.)*  2:198-8″6

1 Shots 1–3 are stock shots.

SPEAKER: . . . the Allies landed on the Amalfi coast. A few weeks later, Naples was liberated.

*(Wipe to left)*

*(Port of Naples, daytime, ELS)*        3:76-3"4

SPEAKER: The port of Naples became the most important . . .

*(Dissolve to . . .*

*(Moving cranes and men busy unloading enormous quantities of matériel, FS; camera pans left.)*    4:109-4"13

SPEAKER: . . . logistics center for the war in Italy.

*Music ends.*

*(Camera pans right as a crane swings a piece of tank track over to a truck, where several men are waiting, FS)*   5:67-2"19

*A gun-carriage is being unloaded from the stern of a boat. Men are watching the operation from the shore. (FS)*   6:65-2"17

*(Dissolve to . . .*

*(Naples, LS)*        7:100-4"4

*A crowd throngs around the Capuan Gate.*

*(A crowded Neapolitan marketplace, LS)*   8:79-3"7

*(Street in Naples, MS)*     9:166-6"22

*A man holding a torch drinks from a small bottle, then blows on the torch, creating a jet of flame. A small crowd looks on. (MS)*

FIRE-EATER: Egyptian fakir defies death . . . lungs of steel. . . .

*(A shoeshine boy, several street venders, and, in the back-*   10:77-3"5

*ground, a small boy doing acrobatic tricks, MS)*

PASQUALE: Look here, look here, watch him jump!

*Pasquale and two other boys loudly advertise their*      11:119-4″23
*friend's prowess. (HF)*

PASQUALE: Ladies and gentlemen, he could break his neck,
but he doesn't miss!

SECOND BOY: Look here, look here, watch him jump!

PASQUALE: Hey, Joe, come on!

*Pasquale calls on Joe, an elderly Neapolitan, to go*      12:248-10″8
*through his tricks. The old man turns a somersault and*
*then goes off. The boys watch him. (WF)*

SECOND BOY: Look at that! He's a wonder!

*Pasquale decides to leave. His friends try to dissuade him.*      13:274-11″10
*(HF)*

THIRD BOY: Pasquà, you going?

PASQUALE: We can't get anything here!

SECOND BOY: Get this stuff out of my way!

PASQUALE: I'm going down to the port to pick up some
dough!

SECOND BOY: You're leaving us all by ourselves.

PASQUALE: You better learn to eat fire!

*Another boy, in profile, points to the fire-eater. (MCU)*      14:42-1″18

BOY: Look at that dirty Arab!

*Pasquale goes off screen to left. (HF)*      15:41-1″17

PASQUALE: Those fire-eaters make a lot of dough!

*The fire-eater continues his act.*      16:29-1″5

STREET VENDER *(off screen)*: Tarallare, tarallare!

*Pasquale walks along the street. Some boys are playing*     17:344-14″8
*against a wall (camera pulls back in front of Pasquale).*
*He walks along the filthy street, stops to pick up a*
*cigarette butt. A boy comes up to him. The street is*
*crowded with people and objects. A street vender moves*
*through the crowd, peddling pastries. (WF)*

STREET VENDER: Tarallare!

BOY, *to Pasquale*: Gimme a light, will you?

*Another boy appears from around a corner. He looks*     18:77-3″5
*around. Seeing Pasquale (off screen), he motions to him.*
*(WF)*

BOY: Hey, come here!

*(Pasquale, MCU)*                                                   19:26-1″2

BOY *(off screen)*: You want to make fifty lire?

*The two boys bargain rapidly. (TQ)*                 20:454-18″22

PASQUALE: No, make it two hundred!

BOY: A hundred. All right?

PASQUALE: No, I want two hundred!

BOY: A hundred and fifty.

PASQUALE: All right. What do I have to do?

BOY: You stay here and look out for the M.P.s. We're
     picking up some dough.

*He gives the money to Pasquale and goes off screen to*
*right, around the corner from which he had appeared.*

*Pasquale follows him (camera pans slightly left onto*
*him). He counts the money and puts it in his pocket.*

BOY (*off screen*): Look at those big feet!

*Pasquale peers around the corner.*

*A drunken black American soldier—Joe—is propped up*     21:650-27"2
*against the wall, while a swarm of boys look him over,*
*touch his clothing, and verbally divide it up among them-*
*selves. (TQ)*

FIRST BOY: I got a hundred lire off him!

SECOND BOY, *opening the soldier's jacket*: Look at what a
    jacket the guy has!

FIRST BOY, *indicating the soldier's shoes*: Why don't you
    take his shoes?

*The second boy opens the soldier's jacket again.*

FIRST BOY: Why don't you take his jacket?

*The soldier pays no attention to them. He mutters*
*drunkenly to himself.*

SOLDIER: Angelina . . . I want to go to Angelina! Angelina
    . . . beautiful, beautiful . . . Toro! You promised to
    take me to Angelina . . . take me to Angelina! (*sings*)
    Angelinaaa! Take me to Angelina!

SECOND BOY: Wait, three thousand lire!

*Pasquale comes on screen and joins the bargaining of the*
*other two boys.*

PASQUALE: I'll give you three thousand and two packs
    of cigarettes.

FIRST BOY: Get away, go back there!

*Suddenly a man appears and breaks into the bargaining.*

MAN: Here, three thousand!

PASQUALE: I already offered three thousand and two packs
    of cigarettes.

*The man roughly hands the money over to Pasquale and without further ado goes off with the soldier. The boys protest in vain.*    22:124-5″4

MAN: Go on, go on! Three thousand's enough.

PASQUALE: You're taking advantage because I'm just a kid.

*The man pulls the soldier along through a crowded square. (MS)*

*The two men move along with the crowd (MS; camera pans slightly left with them).*    23:60-2″12

*Pasquale makes his way through groups of people who*    24:93-3″21 *are bargaining. (HF)*

PASQUALE, *shouting*: The M.P.s, the M.P.s! Run for it! Run for it!

*The people begin to run. The drunken soldier is shoved*     25:288-12″
*this way and that (MS; camera tracks and pans left with*
*him).*

VOICES: The M.P.s, the M.P.s! Run for it!

*Pasquale recaptures the soldier and pulls him along*     26:140-5″2
*through the streets (FS; camera pans right). They run*
*as a streetcar bears down on them.*

*(Wipe to right)*     27:256-10″16

*They run across the street and onto the sidewalk (FS;*
*camera tracks and pans left with them, then up a few*
*steps into a doorway).*

*(Puppet theater, HF)*     28:69-2″21

*Pasquale and the soldier enter.*

FIRST PUPPETEER *(off screen)*: Hurrah for Orlando . . .

*Pasquale pushes the soldier forward into the room, look-*     29:78-3″6
*ing about cautiously (MCU). They go off screen to left.*

PASQUALE: Joe, Joe, move, move!

FIRST PUPPETEER *(off screen)*: . . . the Roman Senator . . .

*Pasquale and Joe look for places along the side of the*     30:150-6″6
*room (camera tracks left after them). They stop to see*
*better. (HF)*

FIRST PUPPETEER *(off screen)*: . . . the famous paladin and
    adventurer.

SECOND PUPPETEER *(off screen)*: To arms, to arms,
    Christians, to . . .

*Five puppets are lined up on the stage. (WF)*     31:89-3″17

SECOND PUPPETEER *(off screen)*: . . . war against the black
   Saracen.

FIRST PUPPETEER *(off screen)*: God summons us. We seek
   not . . .

*Pasquale and Joe move through the room looking for*          32:212-8″20
*seats (camera tracks and pans left after them). Members*
*of the audience protest as they push by. (MS)*

FIRST PUPPETEER *(off screen)*: . . . riches and gold.

THIRD PUPPETEER *(off screen)*: Justice and civilization.
   Death to the Moors!

*The puppets begin to march off stage.*

*The puppets march off stage. (WF)*                          33:20-0″20

*Amid the protests of the spectators, Pasquale and Joe*      34:211-8″19
*find seats in the middle of a row (MS). On stage, the*
*painted background-curtain representing an army camp*
*is removed, and another, showing a bridge, is substituted.*

*Two puppet warriors enter from the opposite wings of*       35:74-3″2
*the stage and begin to duel. (WF)*

FIRST PUPPETEER *(off screen)*: Here am I, the white
   Orlando . . .

*(Closer view of the stage, WF)*                             36:101-4″5

*The puppet Orlando swings his sword.*

FIRST PUPPETEER *(off screen)*: . . . and you, the black Moor.
   Here am I, the great Orlando.

*The three musicians (piano, violin, and percussion) begin*  37:35-1″11
*to play. (HF)*

*The two puppets continue their battle. (WF)*                38:60-2″12

*The audience watches the duel, enthralled. (MS)*            39:47-1″23

*The two puppets battle energetically, leaping about to*        40:88-3″16
*the rhythm of the little orchestra. (WF)*

*(Closer view of the audience, MS)*        41:47-1″23

*Among the audience, Pasquale and Joe are enjoying*
*themselves too.*

*Pasquale turns toward Joe. (CU)*        42:26-1″2

*Joe begins to smile. (CU)*        43:58-2″10

*The puppets continue their battle. (WF)*        44:81-3″9

*Pasquale and Joe urge the warriors on. (MCU)*        45:50-2″2

*The puppets battle on. (WF)*        46:47-2″23

*Joe starts to stand up. (MS)*        47:15-0″15

*(RA)*        48:91-3″19
*Joe gets up, climbs onto the stage, and begins to box*
*with the puppets. (MS)*

PUPPETEERS, *protesting against the intruder (MCU)*: Get        49:38-1″14
out of here, get out of here! Damn . . .

*(Puppets and Pasquale, WF)*        50:45-1″21

*Pasquale has followed Joe onto the stage, tries to drag*
*him away.*

PUPPETEER *(off screen)*: . . . it! You touch that puppet and
I'll . . .

*Joe's head and shoulders disappear behind the upper*
*section of the curtain. Pasquale pulls his jacket, but Joe*
*continues to box the puppets.*

*(The puppeteers, furious, MCU)*        51:33-1″9

PUPPETEER: . . . slam it in your face.

*Joe continues to box, then lifts his hands to eye level*        52:63-2″15
*to protect his face from the puppets' blows (HF).*

*Pasquale, behind him, keeps pulling on his jacket. The puppet's shield is on right margin of frame.*

PUPPETEER *(off screen)*: We're working here . . .

*The enraged puppeteers try to free the puppets from Joe's grasp. (MCU)*      53:25-1″1

PUPPETEER: . . . understand?

*Pasquale tries to prevent Joe from grabbing a puppet, which the puppeteers have freed from his grasp. The other puppet is lying on the floor. The audience, enraged, protests loudly. Two puppeteers come on stage from left and from right and try to hold Joe back. Another spectator climbs on stage and joins the fight. (MS)*      54:140-5″20

*Joe and the other spectator box on stage. (TQ)*      55:58-2″10

*The puppeteers and the spectator join forces against Joe. Other spectators come toward the stage. The orchestra plays on. The stage fills with people. (MS)*      56:82-3″10

*Many hands reach out to stop Joe (HF; camera pans down toward Pasquale).*      57:54-2″6

*Joe struggles. (HF)*      58:36-1″12

*Pasquale makes his way among the brawlers, trying to get Joe away.*      59:50-2″2

*The stage is filled with people.*      60:73-3″1

*Joe is climbing up behind the puppet stage. (HF)*      61:33-1″9

*Joe is stopped by one of the puppeteers before he can climb up onto their platform. (TQ)*      62:77-3″5

*As Pasquale follows Joe up behind the puppet stage, various hands try to stop him and to push him on. (HF)*      63:53-2″5

*Pasquale reaches the platform and manages to pull Joe*      64:163-6″19

*free from the puppeteer's grasp (TQ). They go off from
behind the puppet stage (camera tracks and pans right).*

*(Dissolve to . . .*

*(Street, WF)* 65:625-26″1

*Pasquale pulls the reluctant Joe along a street obstructed
with barbed wire.*

PASQUALE: Come on, move your feet!

JOE: Let me go, boy . . . let me go, boy . . . let me go . . .
let me go, boy . . . I'm tired . . . I'm tired now, I'm
tired! I've got nothing . . . I've got nothing . . . I've
got nothing. Aw, go away!

*He staggers along, falls down on the sidewalk, then sits
up (TQ). A passerby stops to watch them. Pasquale
bends over Joe, trying unsuccessfully to get him moving
again.*

PASQUALE: Come on!

*As he bends over, a harmonica falls out of his pocket. He
picks it up and begins to play on it as he walks off.*

JOE: Come here . . . come on, little boy, let me try it . . .
let me try it! Come on, paisan, let me try it!

*Joe gets up and staggers after Pasquale. They go off
screen to right.*

*They come on screen from left (WF). A ship can be seen* 66:268-11″4
*in the background. Pasquale continues to play his
harmonica. Joe follows after him, calling to the boy to
stop (camera pans right after them).*

JOE: Come here, boy . . . come on, let me try it! Come
here, paisan, let me try it!

*Pasquale's only answer is to throw Joe's army cap on
the ground.*

PASQUALE: Here, catch!

*Joe bends down to pick it up.*

*(Dissolve to . . .*

*(Joe following the sound of the harmonica down the rubble-bordered street, TQ; camera tracks out in front of him and pans right until he stops in HF.)*     67:151-6″7

*(Rubble, MS from above)*     68:169-7″1

*Pasquale continues to play the harmonica, holding it with his mouth alone. He pulls on his jacket and starts to pick up his shoeshine box.*

*The soldier has identified the direction from which the music is coming (HF). He moves off (camera pans right) and staggers (back to camera) toward the sound (WF). The music is coming from the ruins of a building. (MS)*     69:286-11″22

*Still playing the harmonica, Pasquale picks up his shoe-shine box.*     70:83-3″11

*Joe stops at the bottom of a pile of rubble (MS). A bell*     71:108-4″12
*tower can be seen in the background, among the ruins.*
*Joe tries to climb up the pile of rubble but slips and falls*
*amid a heap of rattling tin cans.*

JOE: Come on! Come here . . . let me try it, please!

*Pasquale puts down his box again and, still playing his*     72:204-8″12
*harmonica, comes up toward the camera and goes off*
*screen to left. (HF)*

*Joe is still lying among the tin cans. Pasquale appears on*     73:621-25″21
*top of the pile of rubble, and Joe climbs up to meet him.*
*They sit down. (MS)*

JOE: Help me up, paisan! Let me try it. . . .

*The soldier takes the harmonica and tries to play it from*
*the wrong side.*

PASQUALE: You got it the wrong way around. Give it to
    me!

JOE: I'll show you how to play this! I'll show you how to
    play this thing like a maestro! This is for you,
    Angelina—are you listening?

*Pasquale takes the harmonica back from Joe and begins*
*to play.*

*(Closer view of the two atop the rubble, WF)*     74:328-13″16

*Pasquale plays until Joe begins to sing. Then the boy*
*stops playing to listen. He wipes the instrument on his*
*sleeve and puts it in his pocket.*

JOE, *singing*: "Nobody knows the trouble I've seen . . ."

JOE *(CU)*: "Nobody knows my sorrow!"     75:93-3″21

*Pasquale listens inattentively. (CU)*     76:48-2″

JOE *(off screen)*: "Nobody knows . . .

JOE *(CU)*: ". . . the trouble I've seen, Glory Hallelujah!"     77:257-10″17

PASQUALE, *toying with a key (CU)*: This's a house key, but     78:116-4″20
    the doors are all open, the key's no use.

*Pasquale and Joe are still sitting on the rubble (WF).*    79:85-3″13
*The bell tower is in the background.*

PASQUALE: You sang good, but I didn't like it at all!

JOE, *looking curiously at Pasquale's key (CU)*: I wonder    80:303-12″15
how much can I get for that, young man?

*His attention is caught by the sound of a siren coming
from the port.*

JOE, *imitating the sound*: Zzz . . . Zzz. . . .

*Pasquale is astonished by Joe's sudden imitation. (CU)*    81:29-1″5

PASQUALE: What're you doing?

JOE *(CU)*: Do you like this ship, Mr. Errol?    82:125-5″5

PASQUALE *(CU)*: What'd you say?    83:30-1″6

JOE *(off screen)*: Oh, its . . .

    *(CU)*: . . . wonderful! Would you like to have a little    84:241-10″1
    storm for your personal amusement, Mr. Errol?
    Yeah! Bring it on, bring it on, admiral! Bring on
    the storm!

PASQUALE *(off screen)*: What's with you?

JOE: Brmmm! Brmmmmmmm!

PASQUALE *(CU)*: He's off his rocker!    85:27-1″3

*Joe is facing Pasquale, who listens wonderingly to Joe's*    86:181-7″13
*excited monologue. (CU)*

JOE: Brmmmmmmmm. I love that, Mr. Admiral! Bring it
    on, bring it on! You see that storm, paisan? I love
    that! Bring it on, Mr. Admiral!

*Joe continues his fantastic patter, imitating the Morse*    87:2243-
*code and the sound of loudspeakers. Then he takes*    1′33″11
*Pasquale's hand and uses it to imitate an airplane in
flight.*

JOE: Du-du-du-du! Du-du-du-du! Du-du-du! What do we do now, admiral, in this storm? Brmmm! The admiral says there's a plane ready . . . come on, paisan, and we'll get into the plane! Come on, paisan! Brmmm, brmmm!

PASQUALE: A plane, a plane!

JOE: I love this plane! Ummm! Look at the sky, look at the sky! There's not a cloud in sight! And a million stars! If I had two ropes I could swing here forever! I love this, paisan. . . .

PASQUALE: What're you saying?

JOE: I love this, paisan! Ummmm! There's New York! New York . . . New York! And there's Coney Island over there! Yeah, and there's a million skyscrapers with a thousand lights, to welcome me home! I'm a hero, I'm a hero, paisan! And I'll take you up Wall Street! Up Wall Street!

*Continuing to imitate the airplane, Joe pretends to fly over New York, which he points out to Pasquale. The boy plays along, pretending to see the city and pointing to it.*

PASQUALE: New York!

*Joe catches up some bits of paper and throws them into the air. Pasquale, too, enthusiastically snatches up a paper, tears it to bits, and throws the bits into the air.*

JOE: It's full of ticker tape for me! Yes, for me! A celebration for me! Yeah! For me, for me! And you! And there's City Hall over there. I'll introduce you to the mayor! Hi, Mr. Mayor! He says everything's prepared for me. Now we'll go up Broadway. Broadway's the biggest street in the world, and it's my street! I own Broadway to the Waldorf Astoria . . . when we go into the Waldorf Astoria, you have to be careful, only the elite! Now we're at the Waldorf, and look at the big, thick cushions and the gold furniture! A thousand servants all for me! To serve me because I'm a hero! I'm a hero! Now we're gonna eat! Look at the food, look at the food! Caviar! There's chicken, there's turkey! Wine! Whiskey! Beer! Champagne! Everything for me! Eat as much as you want, paisan! Eat it! I've done enough eatin'. I think we'll go to sleep. Come on, we'll go to sleep.

*Joe straightens his clothes and Pasquale's. Then, exhausted, he falls back and is about to go to sleep when the sound of a siren bestirs him. Pasquale watches in amazement.*

JOE: Ready now, paisan! Come on! The train! We'll have to get ready to go home. It's gonna take me home for another celebration, and that celebration's gonna be every day! Every. . . .

JOE, *imitating the rhythm of a train (CU):* Goin' home! Goin' home! Goin' home! Goin' home! Goin' home! Goin' home! Goin' home!  88:88-3″16

*Pasquale watches Joe with delight. (CU)*  89:47-1″23

JOE *(off screen):* Goin' home! Goin' home! Goin' home! Goin' home!

*Exhausted, Joe slows down and begins to think (CU). He turns sad and lets himself fall back (camera adjusts slightly).*  90:380-15″20

JOE: Goin' home! Goin' home? I don't want to go home! My house is an old shack with tin cans at the doors! I don't need that key! I don't want to play no more, paisan. I don't want to go home.

*Lying back on the rubble, Joe stretches out his legs. The tin cans rattle. Pasquale watches him.*  91:150-6″6

JOE: I don't want to go home! I don't want to go home!

PASQUALE *(CU)*: Joe! Joe!                                      92:17-0"17

*Pasquale bends over the sleeping soldier and shakes him.*      93:127-5"7

PASQUALE: If you go to sleep I'll steal your shoes.

*(Fade-out)*

*(Street, LS)*                                                  94:57-2"9

*A Military Police jeep comes on screen from left. The
ruins of Naples are in the background.*

*Joe is at the wheel of the jeep (MCU; toward the camera).*     95:70-2"22

*(Dissolve to . . .*

*(The jeep following a loaded Allied army truck through a central street of Naples, LS)*  96:63-2"15

*(Jeep seen head-on, MCU; camera centers on the driver.)* Joe shields his eyes against the sun.  97:44-1"20

*(Pasquale moving among the boxes on the back of the truck, WF)*  98:31-1"7

JOE, *pointing at the boy (MCU):* Hey, you!  99:53-2"5

*Pasquale, hearing Joe, puts back the box he has taken, but another falls to the floor of the truck.*  100:100-4"4

JOE, *still pointing:* Drop it!  101:45-1"21

*Pasquale puts back the second box. (WF)*  102:51-2"3

*Joe's jeep passes the truck and stops in a large square. (FS)*  103:143-5"23

*(Dissolve to . . .*

*(Street, MCU)*  104:1230-
51"6

*Pasquale and Joe are in the jeep (facing the camera). Joe scolds the boy; he does not recognize him from the other day. (MCU)*

JOE: Dirty little wretch! Yeah, I'm talkin' about you and thousands of little kids just like you! Why do you steal?

PASQUALE: I don't understand. [*Non capisco.*]

JOE: No *capish!* I'll make you *capish!* To steal, to take things that don't belong to you! Yeah, America's rich and kind, but not me! And it's your fault! Yeah, I'm thinking about my first days in Italy—how my friends used to tell me stories about you little . . . If they could see me now! Just three days ago a little

hoodlum like you stole my shoes right off my feet!
If I could get my hands on him! And I will! And
when I do I'll boot him in his pants so hard he'll
see stars! No!

*Pasquale listens to the scolding, then smiles, without
having understood a word. Joe takes out his pack of
cigarettes. It is empty, and Pasquale is quick to offer him
one of his own, but Joe turns it down.*

JOE: Trying to bribe me! Well, I'll be! Come on, now
get out!

*As Joe speaks, Pasquale tries again with another brand.
Joe stares at him in amazement, then stops the jeep.*

*The jeep stops. Joe gets out, circles around it, and pulls     105:460-19″4
Pasquale out from the other side. (MS)*

JOE: Come on, get out and let's have a look! Why do you
steal, huh? Why do you steal, huh? Let's have a
look! I wouldn't be surprised to find a battleship in
your pocket! Take it off! And where did you get
this sweater?

*Joe (TQ) begins to search Pasquale, pulling out the
contents of the boy's pants pockets. Then he removes the
boy's jacket.*

JOE: Where did you get that sweater? Where did you get
that sweater?

*Pasquale begins to pull it off, protesting.*

*Pasquale finishes taking off his sweater and throws it     106:60-2″12
to Joe, on left margin of frame.*

JOE: I suppose you wanna fight me now, huh? Why
you. . . .

PASQUALE: Here, ugly puss.

*Pasquale runs off screen to right. (TQ)*  107:56-2″8

JOE: Come back here! Come here!

*Pasquale comes on screen from left (MS) with Joe in hot*  108:235-9″19
*pursuit (camera pans slightly right). Joe catches the boy*
*and brings him back toward the jeep (camera pans left).*
*They go off screen to left.*

JOE: Come here! Didn't think I'd run after you, huh?
Stealing! You don't get. . . . Come on, put this hat on!

*Pasquale protests.*

*Joe drags Pasquale back to the jeep (TQ). They come*  109:822-34″6
*on screen from right.*

JOE: You don't get away with it like that. Put it on! Put
it on! Put this coat on before you catch cold. You
don't think it's all over, do you? You don't have me
runnin' after you. . . . Come on, put it on . . . put it
on! Put it on!

PASQUALE, *whimpering*: Oh, damn it!

*Joe puts the boy's cap back on and helps him into his*
*jacket. Then he searches Pasquale's jacket pockets and*
*finds the harmonica. Surprised, he puts it to his mouth*
*and plays. Suddenly Joe realizes that Pasquale is the same*
*little thief who stole his shoes.*

JOE: It was you! It was you stole my shoes! Where do you
live? Take me to your home. *In Italian*: Where's
your home?

PASQUALE: I already told you I ain't got one!

*Joe throws the harmonica into the jeep and, in a burst of*
*wrath, seizes the boy by his lapels and lifts him into the*
*jeep.*

JOE: Come on, you take me home. Get inside there.

PASQUALE: I ain't got a home.

*(Wipe to left)*

*(Outskirts of Naples, LS from above)*                                110:160-6"16

*The jeep drives through a shantytown (camera pans left).*
*Raising a cloud of dust, the jeep goes off screen to left.*

*The jeep drives along a road skirting some large caves*              111:120-5"
*(LS) and stops at the foot of the slope leading up to them*
*(the jeep comes forward toward the camera, which pans*
*right and adjusts downward as it stops).*

*Joe gets out of the jeep and looks around (WF; camera*               112:412-17"4
*pans and tracks right up to TQ). Yelling boys encircle*
*him.*

JOE: Come on, get out and get my shoes! Come on, get
    my shoes. *Half-deafened by the shrieks of the boys,*
    *Joe covers his ears.*

*(Closer view of end of previous shot, TQ)*                           113:418-
                                                                           17"10

*Joe picks up one of the screaming boys like a puppy.*
*Pasquale, carrying a pair of shoes, makes his way through*
*the crowd and holds them out to Joe.*

PASQUALE: Joe, Joe, hey, here's your shoes! Hey, here's
    your shoes!

JOE: You brought 'em back! That's the way!

*He sets the child down and takes the shoes. Another boy*
*points to the soles.*

BOY: These are good soles.

*Joe tries on the shoes; they are too small for him.*                 114:97-4"1
*Puzzled, he looks at the soles, realizes that the shoes are*
*not his. He bends down to check the size against the shoes*
*he is wearing. (HF)*

JOE: Wait a minute! Wait, wait a minute! Wait! Wait!

*He grasps Pasquale's arm and pulls him away from the group.* 115:40-1″16

JOE: These are not my shoes ! Come on, take me to your mother and father! How many shoes do you have?

*Holding the shoes in one hand and the boy with the other (TQ), Joe starts toward the cave. (LS)* 116:89-3″17

*(Cave, MS)* 117:97-4″1

*The enormous cave encloses a filthy, poverty-stricken collection of huts and shanties. Many women and children, dressed in rags, run toward the front of the cave to watch the soldier approaching.*

*(Joe dragging Pasquale up the slope toward the cave, LS)*     118:125-5"5

*(Cave, TQ; camera pans right and tracks out in front of*     119:62-2"14
*Joe and Pasquale as they come forward into the cave,*
*with the daylight outside at their backs.)*

*Joe looks around and begins to understand the strange*
*setting.*

*(WF; camera subjective from Joe's viewpoint.)*     120:66-2"18

*A crowd of women and children turn toward the intruder*
*from among the huts and the smoke of the open fires.*

*Joe, increasingly disconcerted as he continues to look*     121:495-
*about him, drags Pasquale along more slowly (TQ;*          20"15
*camera tracks sideways with them and pans right into*
*WF). He stops, obviously shaken by the spectacle, then*
*goes slowly on.*

*Joe and Pasquale move slowly into the shadows at the*     122:182-7"14
*back of the cave (TQ). Joe lets the boy go and moves a*
*little farther on to have a better look (camera pans right,*
*TQ).*

*(FS; camera subjective from Joe's viewpoint; an overview*     123:105-4"9
*of the shantytown inside the cave.)*

*Joe (back to camera) looks around. (TQ)*     124:33-1"9

*(Joe seen from the legs down, his left hand in the fore-*     125:66-2"16
*ground as he turns, TQ)*

*Pasquale (in TQ behind him) faces Joe with eyes closed.*
*The shoes appear (in CU) as Joe turns.*

*(CU; resume on Joe's turn.)*     126:119-4"23

*Joe's head is lowered; he wants to see no more.*

JOE: Where's your mother and father?

*(The shoes are in the foreground. Joe is standing at right*     127:93-3"21

*margin of frame.)*

*Pasquale comes forward and looks up at Joe.*

PASQUALE: I don't understand.

*Joe (CU) looks up and around once more. Without meet-* 128:95-3"23
*ing Pasquale's eyes, he questions the boy again.*

*Pasquale (CU) looks at the shoes (resume on Joe turn-* 129:53-2"5
*ing, at margin of frame).*

*Joe (CU) continues to look around without meeting* 130:76-3"4
*Pasquale's eyes.*

JOE, *in Italian*: Where's Mama and Papa?

*Pasquale moves around to face Joe (camera pans right).*    131:121-5″1
*He looks up toward the soldier's face. (HF)*

PASQUALE: I don't have any more mama and papa.
     They're dead—the bombs.

*Joe (CU) continues to look around, avoiding the boy's*    132:183-7″15
*eyes and turning his back to him.*

PASQUALE *(off screen)*: Boom, boom! Understand? The
     bombs! Boom, boom!

*Pasquale (CU) looks up at Joe.*    133:51-2″3

*Joe slowly drops the shoes and departs (TQ), going off*    134:173-7″5
*screen to left. Pasquale bends down to pick them up and*
*looks after the soldier (camera pans left and adjusts*
*slightly downward).*

*Pasquale (CU) looks after the departing soldier.*    135:105-4″9

*(Outskirts of Naples, FS)*    136:129-5″9

*Joe speeds off in the jeep along the dusty road.*

*(Fade-out)*


# EPISODE III

*(Devastated buildings, with bare mountains in the back-*    1:134-5″14
*ground, seen in daylight, LS)*[1]

SPEAKER: A long, tragic halt at Cassino.

*Music begins.*

*(Dissolve to . . .*

*(The ruins of the Abbey of Monte Cassino, LS)*    2:87-3″15

*(Dissolve to . . .*

---

1 Shots 1–43 are stock shots.

*(A ruined village, LS)*                                                            3:84-3″12

SPEAKER: On February 22, 1944, the Allies landed . . .

*(Dissolve to . . .*

*(Buildings in ruins, FS)*                                                          4:64-2″16

SPEAKER: . . . at Anzio.

*(Dissolve to . . .*

*(Rome seen from the Pincian Hill, LS; camera pans right.)*        5:150-6″6

SPEAKER: Rome waited. After a series of bloody, arduous
 battles . . .

*(Dissolve to . . .*

*(Two boys exploring the remains of a tank; Castel*               6:66-2″18
*Sant'Angelo in the background, LS)*

SPEAKER: . . . the German defense was broken.

*(A horse-drawn wagon, led by a soldier, passing in front*       7:79-3″7
*of the basilica of San Giovanni, LS)*

SPEAKER: Kesserling's troops retreated northward . . .

*A long line of German troops heads into the city on foot*        8:66-2″18
*at the San Giovanni Gate. (LS)*

SPEAKER: . . . through the streets of Rome.

*The cart, drawn by two horses is loaded with German*            9:86-3″14
*soldiers. One soldier walks beside the cart, hanging onto*
*it. (LS)*

*(FS; looking down from a building)*                                          10:70-2″22

*A German patrol passes through the street. An old man*          11:76-3″4
*freezes as he watches them pass by.*

*A line of German soldiers walks past the basilica of San*
*Giovanni. (LS)*

*A group of German soldiers walks along a sidewalk*     12:53-2″5
*behind a gas pump. Several passersby watch them*
*indifferently. (FS)*

*A group of Germans walks along the sidewalk on the Via*     13:77-3″5
*dei Fori Imperiali (LS). The Colosseum is in the back-*
*ground.*

*A German tank towing a cannon passes through the San*     14:52-2″4
*Giovanni Gate (FS from above). Both vehicles are loaded*
*with soldiers (camera pans right).*

*A tank enters the square outside the San Giovanni Gate.*     15:50-2″2

*German tanks (FS from above) head rapidly northward*     16:94-3″22
*down the New Appian Way, towing cannons (camera*
*pans upward).*

*A German tank passes in front of the monument to Saint*     17:45-1″21
*Francis in the square of San Giovanni. (FS)*

*A German tank loaded with troops passes down the Via*     18:99-4″3
*dei Fori Imperiali (LS; camera pans left). The Colosseum*
*is in the background.*

*Two tanks loaded with soldiers pass in front of the*     19:93-3″21
*monument to Saint Francis. (FS)*

*Three German motorcycles pass along the New Appian*     20:108-4″12
*Way (FS; camera shoots down from a window whose*
*frame is at left margin of shot).*

*A German tank towing a cannon passes by (FS; camera*     21:44-1″20
*shoots down from a window).*

*Two tanks pass by, one of them towing a cannon. (FS)*     22:88-3″16

*A truck passes by, towing a cannon. Both vehicles are*     23:62-2″14
*loaded with soldiers. There are many passersby in the*
*street. (FS)*

SPEAKER: Miraculously . . .

*German jeeps pass by. (FS from above)* 24:58-2"10

SPEAKER: . . . intact, the city . . .

*Music fades.*

*(Wipe to right)*

*Crowds run along the New Appian Way. (FS)* 25:49-2"1

SPEAKER: . . . hails its liberators.

*An Allied tank (CU) passes (camera pans right).* 26:54-2"6

SPEAKER: June 4, 1944.

*Another Allied tank, loaded with soldiers waving joy-* 27:64-2"16
*fully (FS; camera pans right with tank).*

*A joyful crowd runs along the New Appian Way. (FS)* 28:43-1"19

*An Allied tank passes beneath the arches of the San* 29:130-5"10
*Giovanni Gate (FS; camera pans right).*

*From the San Giovanni Gate into the city, the Allied* 30:85-3"13
*trucks pass between two masses of ecstatic Romans. (LS)*

*Girls toss flowers (TQ) to the American soldiers passing* 31:57-2"9
*in a jeep. (CU)*

*More jeeps pass through the joyful crowd. Everyone* 32:102-4"6
*wants to see and hail the liberators. (WF)*

*An Allied tank on the Vittorio Bridge (LS). Castel* 33:28-1"4
*Sant'Angelo is in the background.*

*Grinning soldiers on an Allied truck (camera pans up-* 34:82-3"10
*ward) answer the cheers of the crowd. (MS)*

*An enormous mass of people and vehicles has filled Piazza* 35:58-2"10
*Venezia. (LS from above)*

*An Allied truck is completely surrounded by the festive*    36:46-1"22
*crowd in Piazza Venezia. (FS)*

*A woman seizes the hand of a soldier in a jeep. (HF)*    37:43-1"19

*A long line of American jeeps has halted in the midst of*    38:60-2"12
*a crowd. (LS from above)*

*An Allied soldier wearing three Italian flags on his*    39:48-2"
*helmet passes down the street in a jeep. (HF)*

*One jeep is loaded with soldiers wearing assorted types*    40:62-2"14
*of peculiar headgear. (WF)*

*A large jeep loaded with soldiers makes its way slowly*    41:97-4"1
*through the crowd. Girls reach out to shake the soldiers'*
*hands. (TQ)*

*A group of Italians come down the street with flags and*    42:91-3"19
*a brass band playing the "Piave Anthem."*

*(The "Piave Anthem" dissolves to . . .*

*A Scottish military band playing a typical Scottish march.*    43:119-4"23

*(Dissolve to . . .*

## SIX MONTHS LATER

*(A crowded street in Rome six months later, FS; camera*    44:558-23"6
*pans left.)*

*It is late in the evening but the shops and the bars are*
*lit up and busy. A carriage goes by. A dance tune echoes*
*through the streets.*

VENDER: . . . American cigarettes, come on, you smokers,
    singles or packs, American cigarettes . . . singles or
    packs. We've got American cigarettes!

*(Dissolve to . . .*

*(A café, HF)*    45:452-18"20

*Two drunken American soldiers are staggering down*

*into the lower room (HF; camera pans left and downward). They make their way (FS) among the tables in the crowded, smoky room, where a small band is playing dance music.*

*Two American soldiers are sitting at a table with several local girls. One of the soldiers is trying unsuccessfully to perform a trick with some matches. The others watch curiously. (HF)*  46:117-4"21

AMERICAN: I know you can't do that! Watch! You see, it ain't gonna work!

*Three Americans and an Italian girl, Francesca, are at a nearby table. One of the soldiers is telling his friends something. (HF)*  47:199-8"7

FIRST AMERICAN: Boy! You should have been here a few months ago when we took this town! It was really exciting! Everybody came out, they kissed us, they threw flowers at us, they gave us . . .

*Bored, Francesca begins to look around, leaning back and forth to have a better look at the other tables. Her attention is caught by something happening at a nearby table.*

*At that table an American soldier is standing and drinking from a glass held only by his teeth; his head is thrown back, and he holds his hands behind his neck. His buddy and two girls watch the exhibition. (HF)*  48:126-5"6

FIRST AMERICAN (*off screen*): . . . anything we wanted to drink!

*The soldier, having successfully completed his stunt, waves broadly at his friends and picks up the money anted up for the bet.*

BUDDY: Ah, that's pretty good, that's pretty good!

*Still looking about, Francesca pays little attention to*  49:110-4"4 *what the soldiers at her table are saying.*

SECOND AMERICAN: Boy! If I'd been here I sure would've got kissed!

THIRD AMERICAN: Aw, hell! I'd have got drunk myself!

*Annoyed by Francesca's stares, one of the two girls at the other table rails at her.*    50:158-6"14

FIRST GIRL: What d'you want? What're you looking for? The whole night long this ugly biddy's looking over here!

*The others at that table look on curiously.*

FRANCESCA, *gesturing insultingly at the first girl*: Some    51:58-2"10
show you're putting on!

BUDDY, *trying to calm them*: Hey, please!

*The soldiers with the two girls try to understand what is going on.*                                                          52:88-3″16

BUDDY, *to Francesca*: Aw, shut up!

SECOND GIRL, *to first*: Who're you yelling at?

FIRST GIRL: At that hillbilly!

FRANCESCA, *reacting promptly*: Who, me? Hillbilly? Why,     53:274-11″10
you slob! You'll be back on the skids when these
guys go! You'll have to forget your little hat! . . .

FIRST AMERICAN, *trying to calm Francesca*: Hey, cut it out,
will you?

FRANCESCA: You'll be back in rags like you always were!

*As Francesca grows more heated, she sets her handbag
on the table and stands up.*

*(MS; resume on Francesca standing up and taking off*     54:114-4″18
*her hat.)*

*As others egg her on, she swoops down on her rival like*     55:39-1″15
*a Fury. The other girl stands too. The whole crowd is
on its feet, yelling. Some of the onlookers try to stop the
fight.*

*The room is filled with noise; some hats fly. Everyone is
on his feet trying to see what is happening. (FS)*

*(RA)*                                                          56:85-3″13
*The street door suddenly opens and a girl runs into
the café and down the stairs to the lower room. (FS)*

GIRL: Girls, girls! The cops, the cops!

*The girls begin to flee through the crowd. (FS)*     57:124-5″4

*Some M.P.s come in from the street. They stop the first*     58:121-5″1

*girls, already at the entrance, and those who now come*
*on screen from right and left.*

*On the street (TQ), one M.P. opens the door of the police*   59:164-6″20
*wagon as other M.P.s drag the girls along.*

*(MS; resume on a woman being thrust into the wagon.)*   60:106-4″10
*Some passersby have gathered to watch.*

*Francesca tries to get free of the M.P. dragging her toward*   61:183-7″15
*the wagon. The other girl is behind her. (HF)*

FIRST GIRL: You creep!

FRANCESCA: Get out of here! *She gestures eloquently, then*
*turns to the M.P.* My papers are in order—they're in
there. Wait a minute.

*The M.P. relaxes his grip slightly. Francesca races away*
*through the crowd, going off screen to left.*

M.P.: Stop her, stop her!

*Francesca comes on screen from right and makes her way*   62:189-7″21
*through the crowd. Throwing her fur over her shoulders,*
*she runs into a movie theater. (MS)*

*(Theater lobby, MS, from the bottom of the stairway)*   63:245-10″5
*Francesca comes forward (WF) and down the stairs among*
*the crowd (camera pans left with her to HF). An usher*
*tries to stop her.*

USHER: Ticket, miss!

FRANCESCA: Just one minute, miss, just one minute.

USHER: Where are you going?

FRANCESCA: Just one minute. *She enters the theater.*

*A policeman comes down the theater stairs (WF), follow-*   64:84-3″12
*ing her, and goes off screen to left. (HF)*

POLICEMAN, *calling usher*: Miss. . . .

*The policeman comes on screen from right and questions*    65:23-0"23
*the usher as she comes toward him. (HF)*

POLICEMAN: Did you see . . .

*Hidden behind a curtain in the theater, Francesca*    66:75-3"3
*nervously twists her handbag as she listens to the con-*
*versation. Another usher is watching her. (TQ)*

POLICEMAN *(off screen)*: . . . a blond girl wearing a fur?

USHER *(off screen)*: No, I didn't.

*The M.P. thanks the usher. He goes off screen to right,*    67:23-0"23
*and she to left.*

POLICEMAN: Thanks.

*As the usher comes on screen from right into the theater,*    68:425-17"17
*Francesca takes some money from her bag as a tip.*

NEWSREEL VOICE: . . . bomber squadrons attack bridges and
     strategic targets in north Italy to prevent supplies
     from reaching the Gothic Line.

FRANCESCA: Thank you.

USHER, *refusing the money*: It was nothing. No thanks,
     you keep that.

*She passes (in CU) and goes off screen to left. Francesca*
*starts for the exit (camera pans right). She nods grate-*
*fully to the usher and goes out.*

*(Dissolve to . . .*

*(Street, MS)*    69:995-41"11

*Francesca walks down a street (toward the camera, which*
*pans left until she is in TQ). She adjusts the fur wrap*
*on her shoulders. A drunken American soldier staggers*
*in her direction. Francesca stops him and pulls him over*
*to the wall.*

FRANCESCA*: Hey, boy, you got a cigarette?

FRED: Sure! *He takes out a pack and offers it to her.*

FRANCESCA*: You got a match?

FRED, *lighting her cigarette with his own*: Sure.

*He starts to go off, but Francesca takes his arm and pulls him along with her (camera tracks sideways with them in HF). They go off screen to left.*

FRANCESCA*: Where are you going?

FRED: Along the street.

FRANCESCA*: Come on with me!

FRED: I don't want to go with you!

FRANCESCA*: Here! Come here!

*Francesca, followed by Fred, comes on screen from right and stops at a doorway. She leans him up against the jamb while she takes the key from her bag, then pushes him inside. (TQ)*     70:465-19"9

FRANCESCA*: Come on, baby!

*She follows him in and slams the door behind her.*

*(Entranceway of the building, TQ)*     71:291-12"3

*Francesca pulls Fred toward the stairway. They come on screen from left (camera pans slightly left with them).*

FRED: Aw, no stairs! *He repeats in Italian*: Niente scale!

FRANCESCA, *in English*: Come on, baby. *In Italian*: It's on the second floor. Come on!

*Fred follows her reluctantly. They go off screen to right.*

*As the doorbell rings, an elderly woman comes on screen from right, from a doorway (WF). Still pulling on her*     72:524-21"20

*robe, she goes to the main door (camera pans slightly left and tracks out in front of her). She opens the door (HF). Francesca enters (camera pulls slightly back), leaving Fred in the doorway.*

WOMAN: Ah, it's you?

FRANCESCA: Good evening. May I? . . .

WOMAN: Good evening. *She glances at the soldier.* But he's drunk!

FRANCESCA: Don't worry, he'll fall asleep right away. *To*

*Fred*: Come in!

WOMAN: Let's hope he keeps quiet at least.

*Francesca takes Fred by the lapel and pulls him along the corridor (camera tracks forward after them, TQ) until they reach a door, which Francesca opens.*

*(WF; resume on door opening)*

73:1658-
1'9"2

*The two enter the bedroom. Francesca kisses Fred mechanically, then turns on the light. The soldier closes the door behind him and, ignoring the girl, drops onto the bed with a sigh, holding his head in his hands (camera tracks out as he sits down).*

FRED: Ah!

*As Francesca takes off her fur, she notices that her dress is ripped.*

FRANCESCA: Dammit, they ripped my dress. Your M.P.s are real stinkers. Why on earth did you bring them along?

*She comes toward Fred (in TQ), takes a scarf from her bag, turns on the night-table lamp, and throws the scarf over it. She tears off a paper tissue and wipes her lips with a coarse gesture. Fred is sitting on the bed, smoking, with an absent air. Francesca takes his head in her hands and kisses him. (TQ)*

FRANCESCA*: What's your name?

FRED: Fred.

FRANCESCA*: Ah, Fred!

*Francesca goes to the dressing table on the other side of the bed and turns out the light (WF; camera pans left and tracks slightly). Fred is lying on the bed, sighing, as she takes off her dress in the background. She sits on the bed (HF) to take off her shoes and stockings, then embraces him. There is a large doll at the foot of the bed.*

FRANCESCA: Is it this cold in America? You come from the front? *She repeats her second question in English.*

*(Closer RA)*                                                   74:963-40″3
*Francesca kisses Fred and slips under the covers. (MCU)*

FRANCESCA: Aren't you going to get undressed, lovey? Your clothes!

FRED: Oh!

FRANCESCA, *embracing him*: What bad manners you have, but you're sweet, you know. *She squeezes close to him.* Ah, warm me up a little.

*Fred continues to smoke and does not react. He unwinds her arms from around his neck.*

FRANCESCA: What's the matter with you?

FRED: Don't bother me!

FRANCESCA: Aren't you ashamed of yourself? A fine young man like you! If you don't like my type you should have thought of it sooner! *She pulls away, sits up, removes her garter belt.* You must have spent the whole day in the bars! *She embraces him again and speaks more seductively.* But isn't a girl better?

FRED: Sure! The bar was full of girls. Rome's full of girls like you!

FRANCESCA: Sure, Rome's full of girls like me. *She moves away from him and leans against the headboard, running her fingers through her hair.*

*Fred is lying with his head on the pillow (CU). Francesca's*      75:951-39″15
*face appears beside his and then is withdrawn again.*

FRED: Yeah! And now you're all alike! Before, it was different somehow. I remember when we first came

into Rome—so long ago it was! You know, when we finally broke through. Girls were all happy and laughing and fresh, full of color, beautiful. Gave us a funny feeling. And now it's all different. You should've seen the one I knew—her name was Francesca. . . .

*(Dissolve to . . .*

*(Street in Rome, MS)*                                          76:262-10″22

*American soldiers are climbing down from a tank halted in the middle of the street, surrounded by a joyful crowd cheering and applauding.*

FRED *(off screen)*: The sun was spread out all over the place. Everything was just like summer air—and for four hours I was shut up in the dirt of that tank!

*Waving at the crowd, Fred climbs out of the tank's turret*   77:198-8″6

*(HF; closer view of preceding shot).*

*(Resume on Fred climbing down from the tank and moving off through the crowd.)*     78:101-4″5

*The crowd tries to touch Fred, to grab his tank-corps goggles. He is almost deafened by the roar of the crowd.*     79:434-18″2

*As he takes out a pack of cigarettes the crowd surges around him, hands outstretched. (HF)*

FRED, *in Italian*: Water, water, please. *In English*: Water. . . . *In Italian*: To wash!

VOICES: A cigarette. Give us a cigarette.

*Among the crowd is Francesca. She says something to him and he follows her away.*

*(Wipe to right)*

*(Francesca's home, TQ)*     80:904-37″16

*Francesca comes on screen from left, followed by Fred. She opens the apartment door. He puts an arm around her waist as they enter (HF; camera tracks forward through the doorway). She goes over to a demijohn set on a chest in the entrance hall and begins to pour water into a pot. Fred kneels down beside her (camera adjusts downward).*

FRANCESCA: Come right in. You know, the pipes are broken, so. . . .

*Noticing that she is having some difficulty balancing the demijohn, Fred stands up and pours the water out himself.*

FRED*: Ah, at last!

FRANCESCA: Thanks.

*She goes off screen to left and returns immediately with a glass.*

FRANCESCA *(off screen)*: It's not very cool, but we've been without water *(on screen)* for two weeks, so. . . .

FRED*, *seeing the glass (TQ)*: Not a glass—a lot of water, to wash . . . to wash my face . . . my face.

FRANCESCA, *setting the glass down and picking up the pot*: Oh, I'm sorry, I didn't understand. Come this way, please.

*She motions to Fred to follow her. They go off screen to right.*

*(Bathroom, TQ)*                                          81:110-4″14

*Coming on screen from left, they enter a modest bathroom. There is a small mirror on the table.*

FRANCESCA, *embarrassed*: Here's the soap. We don't have any other. It's not very good. . . .

*(RA)*                                                    82:264-11″
*As Fred pours the water and begins to wash up (MCU), Francesca, in the background, takes out a towel from a cabinet.*

FRANCESCA: Here's the towel. *She hangs the towel on the handle of the door.*

FRED*, *turning and smiling at her*: Thanks.

*(Corridor and dining room, TQ)*                          83:281-11″17

*Francesca comes out of the bathroom and closes the door behind her.*

FRANCESCA: Take your time.

*She goes toward the dining room at the end of the corridor (camera tracks slightly left; WF). She hesitates, then takes a book from the table and begins to read some English phrases haltingly out loud.*

*(Bathroom, MCU)*                                         84:961-40″1

*Fred is washing up. As he hears Francesca speaking English, he turns instinctively toward the door, smiling.*

FRANCESCA* *(off screen):* The towel is on the door.

FRED: Hey! You speak English! Sorry about the pipes, but it won't last for long. You have to tear down to build something new. Worth all the tearing down to finally get here! Today's a wonderful day! *He resumes his washing.*

FRANCESCA* *(off screen):* I love the Americans and their language.

FRED, *in halting Italian*: I like Italian girls, their . . . language, eyes, hair, bodies.

FRANCESCA*, *reading from the phrase book (off screen):*
"Where is your uncle from?"

*Astonished by the question, Fred takes the towel and comes out of the bathroom.*

FRED: Huh? What's my uncle got to do with it?

*In the corridor (TQ), Fred is drying his hands. Francesca is standing opposite the dining-room door reading from the book.*

85:392-16"8

FRANCESCA*: "Before bedtime I always gargle."

*Fred joins her and begins to read over her shoulder (camera adjusts slightly left).*

FRED, *amused:* "When the robber saw the policeman, he turned the corner and ran."

*They laugh. Fred follows Francesca over to the dining-room door.*

FRANCESCA: I have nothing to offer you. . . .

*(Dining room, HF)*

86:389-16"5

*Francesca enters the dining room. Fred finishes drying his hands (HF). As he enters the dining room he sees a piano.*

FRED: Forget it. Hey, you got a piano!

*He goes over to the piano (camera tracks right with him, TQ). He begins to play the Roman song "Ohi Marì," first standing and then sitting down. Francesca comes over and stands beside him.*

*As he plays, Fred smiles up at Francesca. (MCU)*

87:47-1"23

FRED, *singing:* "Ohi Marì" . . . da-da-da-di-di-da . . . I don't know the words.

*Francesca circles behind Fred to the other end of the key-*

88:353-14"17

*board (HF; camera pans slightly right). Standing, she plays a tune, then puts her arm on the back of his chair. Fred begins to hum.*

FRANCESCA*: You know that song?

FRED, *humming "Stardust"*: Di-di-da-da da-da-di. . . .

*He lays his hand on Francesca's arm. She lowers her eyes, slips her arm away, and goes over to the sofa (camera tracks right with her, TQ.) She sits down. Fred, still humming, comes over and sits down beside her. (HF)*

*(Resume on Fred sitting down)*     89:827-34″11
*Fred lays his arm on the back of the sofa behind her. (HF)*

FRED, *in Italian*: Happy?

FRANCESCA: Yes, very much. Everybody is happy.

FRED: What? *In Italian*: I don't understand.

*He listens patiently, trying to understand Francesca's Italian.*

FRANCESCA: Why did you take so long to get to Rome?

FRED: Huh! Yeah . . . a long time. *In Italian*: Very difficult. *In English again*: Now everything's over— we're here!

*Music begins.*

FRANCESCA, *bowing her head sadly*: Yes, you're here.

*Francesca begins to weep. (MCU)*     90:901-37″13

FRED: What's the matter? *In Italian*: Afraid?

FRANCESCA: Not afraid, happy, so happy. It hardly seems true.

*She stands up and moves to the center of the room (camera tracks out). Fred follows her.*

FRANCESCA: It's been so awful, so awful!

FRED, *in Italian*: Not awful! Lovely, lovely! It's lovely here. Rome's lovely. Everything's lovely! You're lovely!

*She bows her head. Fred lifts her chin and hugs her tightly, patting her gently on the shoulder. Then he takes a bar of chocolate from his pocket and hands it to her.*

FRANCESCA: Chocolate!

FRED, *in Italian*: Yes. . . .

*Fred's companions call to him from outside.*

VOICES *(off screen)*: Get moving, will ya?

*Fred goes off screen to left toward the window.*

*Fred comes on screen from right, pulls the curtain aside, and looks out the window (HF). Francesca follows him.*      91:540-22″12

FRED, *turning toward her*: Gotta go!

*She crosses the dining room (camera tracks left) and stops at the door.*

FRANCESCA: Good-bye!

FRED: I've gotta go, but I'll come back!

*He takes Francesca's arm, and they go down the corridor toward the front door (camera pans left). Music begins.*

*(Wipe to left)*

*(Stairway of Francesca's building, WF)*      92:471-19″15

*Fred goes quickly down the stairs. Francesca goes down a few steps and looks over the banister to say good-bye. Fred stops. (TQ)*

FRANCESCA*: Good-bye! What is your name?

FRED: Fred. What's yours?

FRANCESCA*: Francesca. Good-bye, Fred! *In Italian*: Come back! *She runs back up the stairs.*

FRED: Good-bye, Francesca.

*He goes off screen to right. Music ends.*

*(Dissolve to . . .*

*(Francesca's bedroom in the pension, CU)*                    93:2474-
                                                                1'43"2
*Francesca is leaning against the headboard of the bed in her slip, listening to Fred's story.*

FRED *(off screen)*: Six months . . . I always thought of her. I wanted to find her when I came back. I took Italian so I could talk to her, just to say her name right.

*Music begins.*

FRANCESCA: Francesca . . .

FRED *(off screen)*: Yeah, and what a name!

FRANCESCA: . . . why didn't you look for me, why?

FRED *(off screen)*: Well, how can I find that square and that church?

FRANCESCA: Don't you remember . . .

FRED *(off screen)*: This damn town. . . .

FRANCESCA: . . . the fountain in the middle of the square?

FRED *(off screen)*: Yeah, I've walked all day. On every corner it's the same! Another fountain and another church—all the squares are the same.

*Francesca lies down beside him (camera tracks out until Fred is included).*

FRANCESCA: And Francesca's house was red, and there was a large doorway, larger than the others. *She drops her head, brooding.*

FRED: And maybe she wants to see me too. She said—
*In Italian*: —"Come back." *In English*: What's the
use of talking about it? She's probably like—just like
all the rest. *In Italian*: She's become just like you!

*Francesca is lying face down, her elbows dug into the bed.
She raises her head with a dreamy expression.*

FRANCESCA: No, she hasn't. There are lots of good, fine
girls who work, who've been able to stave off hunger
and poverty, working. She's one of those.

FRED: There was a tree in the courtyard—

FRANCESCA: It's still there. But it hasn't flowered like
that since that day. I know where Francesca's
house is.

FRED: Yeah?

FRANCESCA: In Piazza dei Quiriti, number eight.

FRED: Okay.

*Distraught, Francesca sits up in bed (camera tracks forward). Fred tries to hold her back as she starts to leave.
She calms him and, gently pushing her hand against his
forehead, makes him lie down.*

FRANCESCA: Go to her tomorrow. You'll find her. She's
waiting for you.

FRED: Where are you going?

FRANCESCA: Take it easy, Fred! *In English*: Sleep!
Tomorrow—*In Italian again*:—Francesca and
you. . . .

*(Dissolve to . . .*

*(Pension bedroom and entrance, TQ)*

94:1247-
51"23

*Fred is lying on the bed asleep. He is seen reflected in
the dressing-table mirror. Francesca tiptoes on screen
from left, takes her fur, her bag, and her shoes, and goes*

*to the door, looking back repeatedly at Fred. She goes out (MCU; camera tracks out in front of her) and closes the door. She sits down on a chest (camera tracks forward to TQ) and begins to slip on her shoes.*

FRANCESCA: Signora Amelia!

WOMAN *(off screen)*: I'm coming. Just a minute! *(on screen)* You leaving already?

*Francesca stands up and, leaning against the wall, quickly writes a note (camera pans right). The landlady comes on screen behind Francesca from right. Francesca tears the note from her pad and hands it to the landlady.*

FRANCESCA: Yes. Tomorrow morning, when he wakes up, give him this address.

WOMAN: All right.

FRANCESCA: Please don't forget.

WOMAN: Don't worry.

FRANCESCA: Remind him to go there.

WOMAN: All right.

FRANCESCA, *taking some money from her bag*: Here's the money. *She gathers up her things and goes off screen to left.*

WOMAN: Thanks.

*(Fade-out)*

*(Colosseum, at dawn, MS)*                                     95:147-6"3

*A group of American soldiers, including Fred, are stand-ing in front of the Colosseum with some Italian girls.*

*Fred and another soldier are talking (HF). Fred is very*      96:366-15"6
*downcast and answers his friend with little interest.*

SOLDIER: Give me a light, will ya?

FRED: Here. *He lights the other soldier's cigarette with his own.*

SOLDIER: Have you had a good time in Rome?

FRED: Yeah.

SOLDIER: I've been eating that chow mein all day!

*Fred tosses away his cigarette and takes a slip of paper from his jacket pocket.*

SOLDIER: Hey, what's that you got there?

FRED: Aw, the address of a whore. *He crumples up the note and throws it away.*

*(Entranceway of Francesca's building, WF)*                   97:430-17"22

*Francesca walks impatiently outside. It is raining, and*

*she is suffering from the cold. The concierge comes on screen from right.*

FRANCESCA, *desolately*: Antonio, what time is it?

ANTONIO: It's ten-thirty.

FRANCESCA: No one's come for me?

ANTONIO: No, miss, nobody.

*Francesca continues her vigil, gazing nervously to right and to left, although it is apparent that she realizes it is hopeless.*

*(Colosseum, MS)*  98:548-22″20

*An Allied army truck pulls up. The soldiers get in.*

SOLDIERS, *to the girls*: 'Bye, baby! So long! 'Bye, darling!
'Bye!

*The truck pulls away (camera pans right after it up to
the Arch of Constantine).*

*(Fade-out)*


## EPISODE IV

*(Fade-in)*

*(A mountain road in Tuscany, LS; a long line of trucks*   1:64-2″16
*winding along the rough road.)*[1]

*(The trucks moving along the road toward the camera,*   2:71-2″23
*LS)*

SPEAKER: Pursued by the Allies, the German troops . . .

*(Countryside, MS; men leading a mule train.)*   3:52-2″4

SPEAKER: . . . retreat north from Rome into Tuscany.

*(An Allied tank loaded with soldiers, MS)*   4:85-3″13

SPEAKER: The fighting flares up again . . .

*(LS; a tank stationed on a hillside overlooking a valley)*   5:117-4″21

SPEAKER: . . . on the hills around Florence.

*(A group of tanks maneuvering into shooting position*   6:128-5″8
*on the hillside, MS)*

SPEAKER: But in the beginning of August, Eighth Army
troops liberated the part of the city lying south of
the Arno River.

---

[1] Shots 1–6 are stock shots.

*(Wipe to left)*

*(Street in Florence, MS)*                                              7:121-5″1

*Where the street curves in front of a large gate, a number
of people have stopped to watch the heavy traffic of
trucks and ambulances. A Red Cross sign is on the gate.*

SPEAKER: On the north side of the river, Italian
    partisans . . .

*(A group of Florentines watching outside the hospital,*    8:73-3″1
*HF)*

SPEAKER: . . . were fighting the German troops and the
    Fascist snipers.

*A motorcycle comes past a truck and stops. The motor-*     9:376-15″16
*cycle officer gets off and begins to direct traffic. He stops
a jeep to make way for another car. (MS)*

*(Soldiers in the jeep, HF; a crowd in the background.)*    10:77-3″5
*Sounds of traffic and gunfire are heard.*

*(The onlookers outside the hospital, HF)*                  11:70-2″22

*The jeep is still waiting. Two ambulances drive up and*    12:226-9″10
*enter the gateway. A partisan comes on screen from
right. (LS)*

*(Closer view of previous shot, MS)*                        13:266-11″2

*A group of about ten partisans follows the second
ambulance into the hospital grounds. One of the men
carries a wounded companion on his back. Others transport an improvised stretcher. All of them have bandages
of one sort or another. The jeep moves on.*

*(Dissolve to . . .*

*(Florentine hospital, WF)*                                 14:300-12″12

*The partisans enter one of the rooms in the hospital. A hospital attendant asks the army doctor for instructions for the ambulances. The doctor leads the partisans into the first-aid room (TQ; camera tracks out) as he gives hurried instructions to the nurses.*

ATTENDANT: The ambulances are here. Which cases shall we take first?

DOCTOR: All right, get the three cases down at the end! And you two fellows can ride with the ambulance. What happened here?

PARTISAN: We're wounded, doctor.

DOCTOR: That's all right. Come along! You fellows *(off screen)* can ride down with the ambulance too.

*Two English nurses are helping three slightly wounded English soldiers out of the room. As they speak, the doctor comes on screen from left and picks up something from a table with medical instruments. (TQ)*    15:216-9″

FIRST NURSE: Good-bye, sir!

SECOND NURSE: Good-bye! Have a good time!

DOCTOR: Will you girls come along here and help me?

*He goes off screen to right, followed by the two nurses. A number of people pass back and forth between the camera and the principal characters.*

*The doctor hurries the partisans into a room in which many doctors and nurses are moving about among the wounded (WF; camera tracks forward and pans right).*    16:421-17″13

DOCTOR: All right, hurry along!

*The room is dimly lit by the soft light filtering through the closed shutters of the many windows.*

FIRST PARTISAN, *moaning*: Doctor! Doctor!

SECOND PARTISAN: Tonino! Look at those cute girls!

DOCTOR: Get those men down here!

THIRD PARTISAN: If I'd known the Americans looked like that I'd have got myself shot sooner.

DOCTOR, *giving instructions*: Watch those men there!

*One of the nurses, Harriet, looks first at the partisan who has been carried in, then at another, wounded in an eye.*

FOURTH PARTISAN: My eye hurts, miss.

*A doctor, a nurse, and two partisans are bending down over a partisan lying on the floor. The doctor gives instructions to the nurse beside him, who stands up and goes off screen to left, and to another nurse off screen. (HF)*　17:267-11″3

DOCTOR: Priscilla, you get me those alcohol sponges, and Marsha, get me those dry sponges from up there!

*The nurses come on screen with cotton and gauze. The doctor begins to disinfect the partisan's wound. English and Italian voices are heard.*

*After checking the partisan's eye, Harriet leads him over to a chair (HF; camera pans right and tracks).*　18:381-15″21

HARRIET: Come along!

*She disinfects his eye with cotton, then removes the bandage from his wrist.*

HARRIET, *in heavily accented Italian*: Does that hurt? Let's have a look.

*Harriet continues to unwrap the wrist bandage. The partisan is on left margin of frame. (CU)*　19:142-5″22

HARRIET: Don't worry. *In Italian*: It'll be all right.

FOURTH PARTISAN: You speak Italian?

HARRIET*: Yes, I lived a few years in Florence.[1]

FOURTH PARTISAN, *his wounded left arm slightly raised* (*CU*): They caught us with our pants down. I was up in the woods with nine other fellows. We were really feeling great, we'd had a good long sleep . . .       20:186-7"16

(*Harriet dressing the eye wound of the partisan, CU*)       21:123-5"3

FOURTH PARTISAN (*off screen*): . . . after that fighting on the Arno embankments.

HARRIET, *startled*: On the Arno? Where?

FOURTH PARTISAN (*off screen*): In Florence . . .

(*CU*) . . . sure. We'd waited a good long time for the English to move up. They were in Galluzzo.       22:82-3"10

(*Harriet continues to dress the wound, CU*)       23:224-9"8

HARRIET: Then the English are in the city?

FOURTH PARTISAN (*off screen*): Yes. Why, didn't you know that?

HARRIET: Oh, yes, I know.

FOURTH PARTISAN (*off screen*): But they stopped on this side of the Arno, and since our hands were tied . . .

(*CU*) . . . and there was nothing more we could do, we went down to join them.       24:91-3"19

HARRIET (*CU*): How long ago did you leave Florence?       25:165-6"21

FOURTH PARTISAN (*off screen*): Two days ago.

HARRIET: Oh, by now they'll have occupied the other part of the city too.

FOURTH PARTISAN (*off screen*): I'm afraid . . .

---

[1] Harriet speaks Italian to the partisans hereafter.

*(CU)* . . . not, because the Germans blew up all the   26:92-3″20
bridges. The only one left is the Old Bridge.

*Harriet looks around as if seeking someone. (CU)*   27:181-7″13

FOURTH PARTISAN *(off screen)*: They blew up all the
bridges on both sides of it.

HARRIET: Where do you live, in Florence?

FOURTH PARTISAN *(off screen)*: Me? I'm not from Florence,
I'm from near Lucca . . .

*(CU)* . . . but I joined the Arno Valley brigade,   28:109-4″13
because they needed men badly then.

HARRIET *(CU)*: Yes, but don't you have some friends—   29:549-22″21
don't you know anyone in Florence?

FOURTH PARTISAN *(off screen)*: Why, do you know somebody?

HARRIET: Yes, I had a lot of good friends. . . . *She moves
closer to the partisan.* Tell me, did you ever know a
man named Guido Lombardi, a painter?

FOURTH PARTISAN *(off screen)*: Ah, who doesn't know him
in Florence?

HARRIET: I'd like so much to see him. Do you think it
would be hard to find him?

FOURTH PARTISAN *(off screen)*: Hard? Impossible! He's our
leader, but he's a sort of specter.

*Harriet's hand rests on the partisan's right shoulder. (CU)*   30:120-5″

FOURTH PARTISAN: Everybody talks about him, but not a
soul knows where the famous Wolf is.

HARRIET, *amazed (CU)*: The Wolf?   31:185-7″17

DOCTOR, *appearing from the rear*: I'll take over, Harriet.

You'd better go get set, your transportation's here.

HARRIET: But, doctor, I've asked you before. . . .

DOCTOR: Oh, no! You'd better go! You've been working too hard.

*They are facing each other in profile. The doctor takes Harriet's wrist with an affectionate but firm gesture. The partisan is on left margin of frame.*

*A group of partisans comes in through a doorway (TQ).* 32:79-3″7
*The first to appear whistles and turns to the others. They come into the center of the ward (camera pulls back in front of them).*

FIFTH PARTISAN: Hey, boys, here we are!

*A nurse who is bandaging a partisan's wrist turns sharply* 33:156-6″12 *toward the newcomers. (HF)*

NURSE: Say! Quiet over there! *Silenzio!*

*The doctor meets the newcomers and has them sit down*   34:504-21″
*on a bench. (TQ)*

VOICE *(off screen)*: They got you too?!

DOCTOR: All right! Sit down there!

*A nurse comes on screen from left and begins to examine the partisan who had whistled.*

FIFTH PARTISAN: Oh, they got him good . . .

DOCTOR: Come and help me!

*The nurse looks over the partisan's face wound as he continues to talk. The other men sit down.*

FIFTH PARTISAN: . . . just one shot and he fell like a sack of potatoes.

DOCTOR: Clean out that wound there!

VOICES: Great! That's the way!

FIFTH PARTISAN *(off screen)*: Get a load of these American girls!

*After checking the partisan's wound, the nurse goes off screen to left. The doctor calls for help.*

DOCTOR: Harriet! When you're through there, come and help me!

FIRST PARTISAN: Come on, don't look so glum, you'll see your little wife again!

THIRD PARTISAN: Nobody's heard anything about the Wolf?

FIRST PARTISAN: The Wolf? Some say he's been wounded . . .

*The nurse returns and begins to dress the first partisan's wound.*

*While the nurse dresses his wound, the first partisan talks with the fourth. (HF)*  35:399-16"15

FIRST PARTISAN: . . . some say he hasn't. Some say he's in town, some say he isn't. The one sure thing is that he did a beautiful job in Florence.

FOURTH PARTISAN: He sure did.

FIRST PARTISAN: With my help, of course. I had everything organized very—*slight pause due to the dressing of the wound*—very well in town, especially now. Before the Germans moved in we did everything in broad daylight.

*The partisans are seated or standing (TQ). A nurse is dressing a wound (resume on the nurse's movement).*  36:61-2"13

HARRIET *(off screen)*: Listen, doctor, I don't want to make any trouble for you . . .

*The doctor is again trying to persuade Harriet to prepare for her departure. He puts his hands paternally on her shoulders. (HF)*  37:492-20"12

HARRIET: . . . but you know that if I go to Rome I'll surely be reassigned after my leave, and I'll never get a chance to see Florence again!

DOCTOR: I know, Harriet. I'm sorry for you, but you still have to go to Rome and get some rest!

HARRIET: But I want to stay here! I must get into Florence!

DOCTOR: Now don't get excited, Harriet! Take it easy!

*Increasingly agitated, Harriet looks around nervously. Another nurse adds her advice.*

NURSE: Come on, Harriet, listen to him! I'm sure we'll have a lot of fun in Rome.

*But Harriet has already decided. She runs out of the ward into a corridor. The other nurse follows her.*

NURSE: Harriet!

*(Fade-out)*

*(Courtyard of the Pitti Palace, MS)*       38:128-5"8

*A crowd of women, children, partisans, and English soldiers are milling about.*

*Harriet climbs down from the cab of a truck and heads*       39:223-9"7
*for the entrance to the Pitti Palace (MS; camera pans right with her).*

*(The crowded entranceway of the Pitti Palace, MS)*       40:122-5"2

*Two partisans are standing guard at the entrance. Harriet*       41:378-15"18
*comes in. (MCU)*

HARRIET: Excuse me, have you any news of the Wolf?

FIRST PARTISAN: Nothing very sure. He's fighting up in the Mugnone with some partisans.

SECOND PARTISAN: I heard he was wounded, but you know no one knows what's going on on the other side of the river.

HARRIET: Thanks.

*She enters the courtyard and goes off screen to right. More people come in through the main entrance.*

*The courtyard is crowded with people (MS; camera pans*       42:358-14"22
*slightly left to include a woman with her children, then Harriet moving through the crowd of refugees).*

WOMAN: Only Papa's still home. . . .

*A man with his right arm in a sling walks along the*     43:406-16″22
*arcades looking for someone (HF; camera tracks for-*
*ward and pans right with him).*

MAN'S VOICE: The English trucks are here!

WOMAN' VOICE: Really?!

*The man, Massimo, passes (in MS) among some playing*
*children and heads for the rear of the arcade.*

*A woman sits brooding beside one of the columns in the*     44:653-27″5
*courtyard; the man beside her has his arm around her*
*shoulders. Massimo comes on screen from right and bends*
*down over the woman, shaking her with his good arm to*
*attract her attention. (TQ)*

MASSIMO: Don't you recognize me, ma'am? I live at
     number fifteen, across the street from you—
     remember?

WOMAN, *as if in a state of shock*: Ah, it's the end of the
     world, my boy, the end of the world, for we have
     sinned.

MASSIMO: Can you tell me about my wife and my child—
     have you seen them?

*The man beside her breaks in abruptly, hugging the*
*woman as if to protect her. Massimo straightens up*
*(camera tilts slightly up) and turns to the man.*

MAN: Leave the poor woman alone, will you? Can't you
     seen how she is?

MASSIMO: You're her son, aren't you?

MAN: Yes—what about it?

MASSIMO: Well, you're coming from the other side. You
     really can't tell me anything?

MAN: How could we know anything with what's been

going on here! We have other things to worry about!

*Realizing that he can learn nothing from them, Massimo leaves, going off screen to right.*

*A crowd is gathered around two trucks loaded with sacks and canned goods. Massimo comes on screen from left, looking around. Someone calls him. Harriet runs toward him through the crowd. (MS)*     45:709-29″13

HARRIET: Massimo! Massimo!

MASSIMO: Harriet! What are you doing here? Since when have you been back in Italy?

*Preoccupied with his own problems, Massimo does not show great surprise at seeing Harriet but continues to look around in the crowd.*

HARRIET: I'll tell you later. Can you tell me where Guido is?

MASSIMO: Oh, sure. You don't know that Guido's become a partisan leader, the famous, legendary Wolf?

*A number of people pass between the two of them (in HF) and the camera.*

HARRIET: Yes, I know.

MASSIMO: He's fighting on the other side of the river.

HARRIET, *clutching Massimo's jacket*: I must see him!

MASSIMO: Look, I have to go across to the other side at all costs. My family's there. We can try together if you want.

NEWSBOY *(off screen)*: The first newspaper printed in Florence! The Wolf wounded . . .

*Hearing the newsboy's call, Harriet runs toward him, going off screen to right.*

*A crowd gathers around the newsboy to buy the paper.*  46:703-29"7
*(MCU)*

NEWSBOY *(off screen)*: . . . on the Mugnone front!

VOICES: The paper, give me a paper! The paper, give me
a paper!

NEWSBOY *(off screen)*: The first newspaper printed in
Florence! Paper! The Wolf wounded!

*The crowd gradually thins out, revealing slightly farther
back a man with an open newspaper (HF). His daughter
is on his right, and Harriet on his left.*

GIRL: Look, Papa, then it's true that the Wolf's been
wounded!

*Harriet is leaning over the man's shoulder. She pulls the
newspaper closer to her to see better.*

MAN: The rats! He was the best boy in the world!

HARRIET, *to the man*: Did you know him?

MAN: Of course! We were friends!

GIRL: When I was little he did my portrait—this big! *She
opens her arms to show the size of the picture.*

MAN: He was a good painter too, you know—really an
all right guy.

*Harriet, suddenly realizing that she has left Massimo
behind, leaves the man and girl.*

HARRIET, *calling*: Massimo! Massimo!

*(Dissolve to . . .*

*(Boboli Gardens, LS)*  47:210-8"18

*Followed by Harriet, Massimo comes forward behind a
low wall toward two partisans. They are bending low
in order not to be seen.*

FIRST PARTISAN *(off screen)*: Down! Keep down!

*Massimo and Harriet reach the two armed partisans crouched down behind the wall (camera pans left following them until the partisans are included).*

*Intermittent gunfire is heard from here through shot 61.*

MASSIMO: Where are they shooting from?

FIRST PARTISAN: There's a machine gun in Viale Bardi.

SECOND PARTISAN: Be careful, a grenade just exploded behind there.

*Massimo and Harriet peep furtively from behind the wall. (CU)*     48:91-3"19

*They leave the shelter of the wall and run off screen to right.*     49:61-2"13

*They climb up through the garden (LS; camera tracks right with them).*     50:172-7"4

*They continue up to the top of the slope (WF; camera tracks right with them).*     51:237-9"21

MASSIMO, *pointing*: Look, my house is out there, beyond that boulevard.

*A little further on in the gardens, two English officers are sitting on the grass, looking over the city with a pair of binoculars. Massimo speaks to them in English.*

MASSIMO, *bending over them*: May I have your glasses, please?

*Massimo, behind the Englishmen, repeats his request. (HF)*     52:582-24"6

MASSIMO: Could I have your binoculars, please?

*Without turning, the English officer hands his binoculars to Massimo. He gestures toward the city.*

FIRST OFFICER, *explaining to the second*: The baptistry's the one near the church. It was built at a later date.

SECOND OFFICER: I once saw a picture of the doors of the baptistry—rather like those of Salisbury Cathedral, I thought.

*The first officer turns to Massimo, who returns the binoculars.*

MASSIMO, *to the officer*: What are they waiting for? Why don't they enter the city?

FIRST OFFICER: The situation's not clear yet. They'll probably be here in strength tomorrow.

MASSIMO, *squatting down beside the two officers (MCU)*: But the Germans retreated when you first arrived! 53:52-2″4

FIRST OFFICER: How do you know? That's what we're here to find out. Sir, is the Ponte Vecchio guarded? *He looks through the binoculars again.* 54:186-7″18

MASSIMO: Sorry, I don't know anything. I have no idea. *To the second officer*: But will they destroy all the town? Will they blow up the bridges? All the buildings? 55:191-7″23

*The first officer continues to look through the binoculars.* 56:366-15″6

SECOND OFFICER, *to Massimo*: Why should they stop at Florence? They've destroyed half of Europe already.

*Amused by this remark, the first officer puts down the binoculars.*

FIRST OFFICER: The poor fools! The Jerries always put their foot in it. That's why they're going to lose the war!

SECOND OFFICER, *to Massimo, pointing toward the city*: Can you tell me which bell tower that is, old man?

*(MS; from farther away and at a different angle from the previous shot)*

57:141-5″21

MASSIMO: I'm sorry, I don't know. Thank you.

*Harriet and an Italian policeman are talking near a jeep in the background. Massimo stands up and runs toward Harriet.*

*An English soldier is in the jeep behind Harriet and the policeman, who is facing the camera. (HF)*

58:204-8″12

POLICEMAN: . . . the National Liberation Committee. Maybe they'll be able to tell you something about him there. But on the other side of the river. . . .

*Massimo comes on screen from left.*

MASSIMO, *interrupting:* Any news?

*Massimo and Harriet turn as they hear the sound of gunfire. The policeman is already facing in that direction.*

*(HF; Massimo and Harriet facing the camera, policeman on right margin of frame, gardens in the background; this shot alternates with shot 60 through beginning of shot 70 unless otherwise noted; gunfire is heard inter-mittently.)*

59:213-8″21

POLICEMAN: Believe me, I'd like to go to the other side myself, to chase out those rats that're shooting from the rooftops and the bell towers.

MASSIMO: But who are they shooting at? Are there many partisans in the city?

*(MCU; policeman at right margin of frame, Massimo, back to camera, at left)*

60:292-12″4

POLICEMAN: In some areas. But the Fascists are shooting just out of anger, even at the women going to get water from the fountains. Last night they killed two in Via Guelfa, while these guys—*indicating the two English officers*—are still sitting up here looking at Giotto's bell tower through their binoculars!

HARRIET: But where did you get this news from the city?    61:52-2"4

POLICEMAN: By telephone. . . . Now what have I said? *Though vexed at having let slip this information, he comes closer to Massimo.* There's a telephone cable that joins us—*he hesitates*—that joins us to the city.    62:129-5"9

MASSIMO: And couldn't I—you must help me! You must have a family?!    63:93-3"21

POLICEMAN: What can I do? I could take you there, but they're not letting anybody through.    64:86-3"14

MASSIMO: Take me where, tell me where!    65:49-2"1

*(Harriet, CU; the English soldier in the jeep in the background)*    66:57-2"9

POLICEMAN *(off screen)*: Come, sir, don't make me tell. . . .

Well, the river can be crossed, but I don't know a thing about it. Try it, you can cross like the others.    67:93-3"21

MASSIMO: All right, but how, where? . . .    68:53-2"5

POLICEMAN, *waving toward the Uffizi (MCU)*: A little bit of imagination—it's not hard.    69:137-5"17

MASSIMO: The Uffizi passageway![1]

POLICEMAN: Ah, I don't know anything about it! *He gestures as if to wash his hands of the business.*

MASSIMO, *reassuringly*: You didn't say a word—don't worry. Thanks.    70:214-8"22

---

[1] An elevated passageway runs for about a quarter of a mile from the Pitti Palace on the south side of the river to the Uffizi Museum on the north, across the Old Bridge, the only one not blown up by the Germans.

HARRIET: Thanks.

*Massimo and Harriet starts to go off (camera pans left after them). The policeman starts after them, calling them back.*

POLICEMAN: Hey, listen, don't start from the Pitti Palace because the passageway's broken through in the middle.

MASSIMO: Thanks.

*(Dissolve to . . .*

*(Street in Florence, LS)*                                    71:401-16″17

*Music begins. A mass of rubble; Brunelleschi's cathedral dome appears across the river in the distance, through the skeletons of demolished buildings. Massimo and Harriet come on screen from right, climb over the mass of rubble, and disappear behind it.*

*(Area near the foot of the Old Bridge, FS)*                  72:467-19″11

*Gigi, a partisan, leads Massimo and Harriet through the wreckage of a building. A group of partisans appears from behind a heap of rubble. Music fades.*

GIGI: Hey, what's a guy like you doing around here?

MASSIMO: Gigi! What good luck!

GIGI: Where'd you pop up from?

*The partisans help Massimo and Harriet down the heap of rubble.*

MASSIMO, *laying a friendly hand on Gigi's shoulder (HF):*    73:273-11″9
Listen, I have to get over to the other side.

GIGI, *ironically waving him on:* Step right up! Be my guest!

MASSIMO: Don't kid around, Gigi, please. I know you can get over through the Uffizi passageway.

PARTISAN: So?

MASSIMO: I know that some people have crossed over, and I must too.

*(HF; Massimo at left margin of frame, Gigi and Harriet in the center with the partisan; also shots 76, 78)*     74:86-3"14

*Harriet looks questioningly from one to the other. The partisan wears a National Liberation Committee arm band.*

PARTISAN: Nobody's been through there—they've been feeding you fairy tales!

*(Massimo and Gigi, MCU; also shot 77)*     75:163-6"19

MASSIMO, *sharply*: Look, the passageway's been there for hundreds of years, and that's no fairy tale. I don't care if nobody else's been through. I'm going, friend.

PARTISAN, *snapping forward as if to block his way*: You're not going anywhere, I can tell you that.     76:77-3"5

GIGI, *trying to keep the two men apart, to partisan*: Take it easy, come on!

*Massimo and Gigi have their hands on each other's shoulders.*     77:39-1"15

MASSIMO: I'm free to go wherever I want to.

PARTISAN, *angrily*: Yes, but you're not free to behave like a fool and endanger us all.     78:80-3"8

*(HF; Massimo on left margin, Gigi in the center, and Harriet on the right; also shot 82)*     79:188-7"20

GIGI, *quietly*: Listen, you know people are crossing and you're not the only one that knows, but think what would happen if the Germans found out? It's been a miracle they haven't up to now!

*Harriet watches in silence while the partisan explains*     80:278-11"14 *his reasons. (MCU)*

PARTISAN, *more calmly*: And when you get to the end of the passageway what do you do then? The Germans are in the Palazzo della Signoria, the city's under emergency regulations, and nobody's allowed through the streets. They'd pick you up . . .

*Gigi removes his hand from Massimo's shoulder. (MCU)*    81:75-3″3

PARTISAN *(off screen)*: . . . as soon as you came out.

GIGI: It's hard even for doctors and hospital nurses . . .

*Harriet watches worriedly, perhaps not grasping the*    82:60-2″12
*meaning of the argument. Massimo sits down on the rubble.*

GIGI: . . . to move on the streets, and they have permission.

*(MCU; resume on Massimo sitting down, his eyes are*    83:35-1″11
*downcast.)*

GIGI *(off screen)*: It all depends on how the Germans happen to feel at the moment.

*The sound of gunfire momentarily distracts the men.*    84:36-1″12
*Harriet glances rapidly about (CU), then runs off screen to left.*

*As Massimo calls after her, the partisan runs to catch her.*    85:356-14″20
*She slips by them and begins to scramble up the pile of rubble. (HF)*

MASSIMO: Harriet!

PARTISAN: You don't even know how to find it!

HARRIET: No, but I know I will find it.

*Gigi gives parting instructions to Massimo, who starts after Harriet.*

GIGI: Be careful! The Germans have control of the whole city. Try to get a Red Cross arm band if you can—

understand? The partisans have only the Sant'
Jacopino area.

MASSIMO: All right.

*(Dissolve to . . .*

*(Passageway of the Uffizi Museum, FS)*　　　　　　86:503-20″23

*Music begins. Massimo and Harriet come forward along
the elevated passageway (camera pans slightly left until
they are in TQ, looking out of a window, then tracks
back in front of them, in TQ). Massimo leads the way,
crouching down as he passes each window and signaling
Harriet to do the same. They go off screen to right.*

MASSIMO: Down! Get down!

*(FS; museum full of packing cases and sculpture wrapped*　　87:365-15″5
*up for storage)*

*Massimo and Harriet come on screen from left and
approach a window (camera pans left and tracks sideways with them, in TQ). They peep warily out the
window.*

MASSIMO, *pointing*: Look, that's the way we came.

*(LS; camera pans right over the Old Bridge)*　　　　88:131-5″11
*Above the shops lining the bridge runs the passageway
connecting the Pitti Palace on the south side of the river
to the Uffizi on the north side.*

*Massimo and Harriet go off screen to left, still crouching*　89:49-2″1
*low and moving warily.*

MASSIMO: Come on, let's go!

*They come on screen from right (TQ; camera tracks*　　90:252-10″12
*sideways with them). Massimo stops to look out of a
window. He turns to Harriet, who is somewhat behind
him, takes her hand, and leads her off screen to right.*

MASSIMO: The bastards, they've blown up all the bridges!
Come on, hurry! Come on!

*(LS; camera pans down from the top of the tower of the*   91:448-18″16
*Palazzo della Signoria, next to the Uffizi, which serves as*
*the city hall.)*

*Massimo and Harriet come on screen from left and peep*
*out of a window.*

MASSIMO: Look, the Germans!

*(Camera tracks forward, cutting out the heads of the*
*couple and including, in the square below, a number*
*of German troops and vehicles.)*

*A motorcycle races in from the adjoining square, Piazza della Signoria. The cyclist speaks for a moment with the soldiers and then returns in the direction from which he appeared.*

*(Dissolve to . . .*       92:215-8″23

*(Street, MS)*

*Massimo and Harriet come out of a doorway and run under an archway (camera pans right after them). They pull back into the shadows to hide.*

*(Cathedral square, LS)*      93:324-13″12

*A three-man German patrol moves through the deserted square. A military motorcycle passes by and swings behind the Baptistry.*

*(Street, LS)*                                    94:632-26"8

*Massimo and Harriet dart out from behind a building
(toward the camera) and run toward a doorway (camera
pans right with them). They knock frantically at the door.*

MASSIMO: Open up! Open up, quick!

*Harriet gestures toward the window, Massimo steps over
to the window while Harriet continues to knock at the
door.*

MASSIMO: Ah, the window!

HARRIET: Hurry!

VOICE *(off screen)*: Who is it?

MASSIMO: The Germans are here! Open up!

VOICE *(off screen)*: Just a minute!

MASSIMO: Quick! Quick, open up! Open up!

*The door finally opens, and they enter the building.*

*(Courtyard of the building, LS)*                 95:187-7"19

*(Sound of gunfire)*

*Massimo and Harriet run from the entranceway toward
the end of the garden.*

*(Panorama of Florence, LS; camera pans right over several   96:118-4"22
Florentine buildings.)*

*(Sound of gunfire)*

*(Dissolve to . . .*

*(Rooftops, LS)*                                  97:373-15"13

*Massimo and Harriet climb out of an attic window and
begin to make their way across the rooftops (camera pans
right). There is no sign of life in the streets.*

*A German truck passes slowly along a deserted street   98:108-4"12
(LS). Music fades.*

*(An attic, TQ)*

99:2179-
1'30"19

*A distinguished-looking gentleman is seated at a table with a pair of binoculars hanging around his neck. A boy runs on screen from right (camera pans right after him). Another boy is behind him.*

BOY: Uncle! Listen, Uncle! There are some people who want to cross over the roof.

MAJOR, *to boy*: All right, all right, get moving! *To Massimo and Harriet*: And you keep your heads down!

*(Intermittent gunfire is heard throughout this shot.)*

*Massimo and Harriet come on screen from right. The major takes Massimo's arm and gestures broadly to emphasize his words.*

MAJOR: Listen to that! It's a twenty-caliber machine gun. They've been working that area over for three days. But I think there's no point to it. They're crazy—

MASSIMO, *interrupting brusquely*: Excuse me, which way do I go for Sant' Jacopino?

*The major stands up and points toward an area behind Massimo and Harriet.*

MAJOR: Ah, Sant' Jacopino! Look, there's Borgo Ognissanti. Just go down that way. . . .

*At the sound of firing the major takes his binoculars and looks in that direction.*

MASSIMO, *insistently*: Are the Germans still in the streets?

MAJOR: No. The partisans seem to have gotten control from Borgo Prato to the park two days ago. They're fighting. *He spreads out his arms as if to say that he knows nothing for sure.*

HARRIET: Maybe we can find out about the Wolf there. How long have they been fighting?

MAJOR: For two days. Yes, they started the night before last. *(Sound of cannon firing)* Listen, that's the eighty-eight!

*The sound of the cannon distracts the major's attention, and he again takes up his binoculars.*

BOY *(off screen)*: Sir, your wife said for you to come down, she's worried.

MAJOR, *putting down his binoculars*: No, it's all right. And I can't go now. Tell her to send up my helmet.

*Massimo bends over the maps spread out on the major's table.*

BOY *(off screen)*: All right.

*The Major sits down and turns to Massimo, indicating his own head with broad gestures.*

MAJOR: It's just for the sun, you know, because I can tell you to the millimeter just where the bullets will pass. *To Harriet*: I went through the other war, from beginning to end—the real war, the 1915 one.

*A man comes on screen from right with a topographic map.*

MAN: Renato, here's another map.

MAJOR, *checking the map rapidly*: Oh, good, good! Let's see, hm—here, here—they're at Galluzzo. Send word on right away. *To boy*: Send the latest position on right away.

BOY, *going immediately off screen to right*: Sure, yes, sir.

*The major examines the new map.*

MASSIMO, *to man*: You live in this building—tell me how

to get down.

MAN, *pointing to the rooftops*: Try over the rooftops, but be careful. A lot of tiles are broken, and it's dangerous.

*The major looks up at the sound of firing as Massimo and Harriet are going off.*

MAJOR: That's the twenty-caliber machine gun again.

MASSIMO: Good-bye. Thanks, Major.

MAN: Good luck.

*Massimo and Harriet leave the terrace (camera pans right). They go up a stairway (camera pans upward) and off screen to right on the rooftop (in WF). Music begins.*

*(Deserted boulevard, LS from above)* 100:436-18"4

*A German motorcycle and a military truck meet. The cyclist points out a direction to the truck, which then proceeds slowly until the boulevard is again deserted.*

*(Stairway in another building, MS from below)* 101:1235-<br>51"11

MAN, *appearing at the head of the stairs*: Hey, these two've come from the Pitti Palace. The English are there, and they've brought loads of white flour.

WOMAN: Really? White flour! How much did they bring? Will there be enough for everybody?

*Massimo and Harriet come on screen from left, from the top floor (camera pans left). Holding hands, they start down the stairs (WF; camera tilts slightly downward).*

MASSIMO, *to the woman*: Yes, yes, lots of sacks. I saw them myself, and they'll be bringing even more too.

*They continue on down (camera pans left with them).*

MAN: Well, why did they stop? Why aren't they pushing forward?

MASSIMO: Why aren't they pushing forward? They're having a time of it, because—because the Germans blew up all the bridges the night before last.

*The stairway is full of women, children, and old people. Massimo and Harriet continue down (camera pans left from above). A woman stops them.*

WOMAN: All the bridges? My God! My aunt lives near the Santa Trinità Bridge. Did the buildings nearby go down too?

MASSIMO: No, no, just the ones at the Old Bridge.

*They are about to start on down again when a man calls from the floor above.*

MAN *(off screen)*: But what are they waiting for? The partisans have occupied Sant' Jacopino. They're in command there. What are the English dragging their feet for?

*Massimo looks at him but does not answer. As Massimo and Harriet start down again a woman picks up the theme.*

WOMAN: Look, that woman over there with those bottles comes from there. The partisans have liberated the whole area. People can go out on the streets there.

MASSIMO: Ah, that's just the place I have to get to. What's the best way to go?

*The woman accompanies them down the stairs (camera pans left, tilts down, and pans right).*

WOMAN: You go from our courtyard into the Rucellai Gardens, and from there it's very close—just a few minutes away. But you have to be careful. The Fascists are shooting from the rooftops.

MASSIMO: Oh, I'm not afraid of them. So long, and thanks!

*(Street, MS)*                                                        102:305-
                                                                                        12"17

*Massimo and Harriet come out from a doorway and, hugging the wall of the building, reach the street corner. They hurry across (camera tracks sideways with them) and slip under an archway (camera pans right).*

*Massimo and Harriet enter a garden from the inner*      103:284-
*doorway of a building (WF). Hearing gunfire, they stop*          11"20
*(TQ), trying to identify the direction of the firing. Then*
*they begin to run again (camera tracks with them, in HF,*
*and pans right into MS).*

*(Dissolve to . . .*

*(Gardens, MS)*                                                                                      104:359-

                                                                                                                   14"23

*They scramble over the garden wall, using some debris
and a tree to help them over (camera tilts up). Massimo
is impeded by his wounded arm.*

*(Street, MS from above)*                                                                    105:297-12"9

*Two men pull a wagon along as another man pushes from
behind. One of the men wears a Red Cross arm band. A
man's body lies on the wagon. A woman in tears follows
them (camera pans upward into LS).*

MAN: Red Cross, Red Cross, Red Cross.

*(Sound of gunfire)*

*(LS; camera pans left across a deserted intersection,*        106'266-11"2
*following a cart, carrying a demijohn, that is being pulled
with a rope.) Two small groups of people are hiding
behind the buildings at the two corners.*

*(Sound of gunfire)*

*A partisan pulls the cart toward the corner. (WF)*            107:295-12"7

WOMAN: Be careful, will you? Don't let it bump against
the curb.

PARTISAN: Don't worry.

*He unloads the demijohn. The four women who are wait-
ing begin immediately to fill their containers with the
water, while a partisan on the other corner pulls the
wagon back by the rope.*

*(The other end of the "ferry," WF)*                               108:423-

                                                                                                                   17"15

*A partisan pulls the wagon up to the curb. Another
partisan, lying beside a water spout, fills another demijohn. Some women are waiting beside him. Massimo
and Harriet come on screen from right and are immediately stopped and questioned by the partisan.*

PARTISAN: Keep back, keep back! Where are you coming from?

MASSIMO: From downtown. I have to get to the Mosse Bridge—my family lives there.

FIRST WOMAN: That's just where I'd like to go—I have relatives there. But they're not letting anyone through.

PARTISAN: Of course not, there are Fascists and Germans there.

*Massimo excitedly moves toward the partisan to ask for more information but is brusquely pushed back.*

MASSIMO: Have they blown up any buildings?

PARTISAN: Keep back!

*Massimo turns to the woman. Several Fascist posters* 109:227-9″11
*can be seen on the wall behind them. (TQ)*

MASSIMO: Do you know?

FIRST WOMAN: No.

MASSIMO: Have they blown up the buildings?

FIRST WOMAN: I really don't know a thing.

SECOND WOMAN: There was a lot of smoke over that way this morning.

MASSIMO: Thanks. *He takes Harriet's hand and they go off screen to right.*

*(Wipe to left)*

*(Street, LS)* 110:802-
33″10

*Massimo leads the way. They hurry along almost at a run (camera pans right, tracks sideways, and pans right again with them). Heaps of rubble are scattered here and there in the street (pan stops in LS). Two partisans sud-*

*denly pop out from the ruins of a building with rifles at the ready.*

PARTISAN: Halt! Stop! You can't go there!

*Massimo raises his good arm in surrender. As he approaches the partisan he recognizes him as a friend.*

MASSIMO: Carlo, is that you? Don't you recognize me? I live right over there.

CARLO: Yes, I recognize you, but I can't let you through.

*The partisans are high up on the rubble (in LS), Massimo is below.*

MASSIMO: But I have to go!

CARLO: But there's fighting!

MASSIMO: My family's there.

CARLO: But it's dangerous. The Fascists are up on the roofs, shooting on the street.

MASSIMO: But I told you, I have to see my family.

CARLO: You want to get yourself killed?

*Harriet comes up.*

CARLO: All right, all right, we'll ask the boss. Come on up.

*He gestures for them to follow him. The other partisan remains on guard.*

MASSIMO, *to Harriet*: Be careful.

*The partisan, Massimo, and Harriet come out from behind a pile of rubble. (LS)*                    111:44-1"20

CARLO: Hey, Marco. . . .

*A group of partisans is crouching down behind some piles of rubble. Marco turns as he hears his name called. (MS)*                    112:30-1"6

MARCO: What?

*Massimo and Harriet have stopped on top of the pile of rubble. (LS)*    113:44-1″20

CARLO: Hey, these people want to go across. . . .    114:87-3″15

*Marco, the partisan leader, moves away from his men and beckons for them to come forward (MS). He turns as he hears a whistle.*

MARCO: All right, let them come across. Come on! Come on!

*On the street (WF) a partisan gestures from a doorway.*    115:29-1″5

MARCO, *to the partisan hiding in the doorway*: All right.    116:129-5″9
   *To his men*: On your toes, boys, they're moving out there! *To Massimo and Harriet*: Come on!

*Massimo and Harriet run down from the pile of rubble.*    117:130-5″10
*Massimo reaches the ground first and helps Harriet down.*

CARLO: Marco, I know this guy.

MARCO, *stopping Massimo and Harriet (MS)*: Halt!    118:27-1″3

*As Massimo removes his glasses, Marco searches him. (HF)*    119:250-
                                   10″10
MARCO: Where are you going?

MASSIMO: Right near here.

MARCO: You crazy or something? You can't cross the street now.

*Marco continues searching Massimo, who, with both hands raised, gestures with his head.*

MASSIMO: Look, let me go! My wife and my kid are in that building right across from here. It'll just take a minute. Let me go, please!

*Marco steps back into position as gunfire is heard (MS).*    120:37-1″13
*Massimo seizes the moment to race away, going off screen to right. A partisan stops Harriet from following.*

HARRIET: Massimo, no! Stop!

*Harriet is held back by the partisan. (MCU)*    121:22-0″22

HARRIET: Stop!

*Massimo races across the tree-lined boulevard as bullets*    122:53-2″5
*whistle around him. (LS)*

*The partisan who has been hiding in the doorway steps*    123:40-1″16
*out. (MS)*

PARTISAN: They're coming! They're coming!

*He is hit amid a cloud of smoke.*

*Harriet is horrified as she sees the partisan hit. (CU)*    124:24-1″

HARRIET, *in English*: My God!

*(Street, LS)*    125:56-2″8
*Massimo steps out from the shelter of a recess in the wall*
*and runs along the wall, going off screen to right. In*
*the distance the body of the wounded partisan is lying*
*on the pavement of the street.*

*From the ruins (MS) a partisan runs toward his wounded companion. Harriet follows him.* 126:51-2"3

*On the street (MS), the wounded partisan is lying in a pool of blood (WF). His companion appears on screen from left, picks up the gun, and, with Harriet's help, drags the body into the doorway. He takes the rifle and gets into position.* 127:442-18"10

WOUNDED PARTISAN: Marco, Marco, Marco, oh baby. . . .

*The partisan is ready to leave the doorway. (HF)* 128:22-0"22

*The deserted boulevard is suddenly filled with activity. In the background a group of partisans appear from around a corner with several captured Fascists. A partisan runs along a wall. Other partisans run up from various directions. (LS)* 129:405-16"21

WOUNDED PARTISAN *(off screen)*: Marco, Marco, they got me!

*(Closer view of preceding shot, MS)* 130:457-19"1

*The partisans push and pull three Fascists. A few on-lookers appear at the windows (camera tracks right). The partisans kick the Fascists. (WF)*

*The partisans push the Fascists along. As they pass the doorway with Harriet and the wounded man, they force the prisoners to look. Then they bring the prisoners into the middle of the boulevard (camera tracks out) and throw them to the ground off screen to left. The doorway can still be seen in the background. (WF)* 131:221-9"5

PARTISANS: Look, you dogs! Look what you've done! Get over there!

*The Fascists are lying on the ground (WF from above). The partisans are standing over them with rifles aimed at them. Other partisans move away, and they all shoot* 132:90-3"18 *at once.*

*In the doorway (TQ) Harriet is seated on the ground
with the wounded partisan's head in her lap. She is looking outside (camera tracks slightly onto them, very
slowly).*

133:474-<br>19"18

WOUNDED PARTISAN: My God, Marco, go tell my family
what's happened to me, so they don't worry. Oh,
Mama, I feel so cold down here! Marco, oh Marco . . .

*(Harriet and the partisan, CU)*   134:794-33"2

WOUNDED PARTISAN: . . . everything's gone bad today since
the Wolf died.

HARRIET, *lifting her eyes to the sky, in anguish*: The Wolf,
Guido!

WOUNDED PARTISAN: You won't be breaking my back any
more, Wolf, we're in the same boat now.

HARRIET, *in English*: I wanted to see him!

WOUNDED PARTISAN: My God! *He dies.*

*Music ends.*

*(Fade-out)*

## EPISODE V

*(Fade-in)*

*(Apennine mountain landscape, LS)*[1]   1:97-4"1

SPEAKER: The Gothic Line is a natural . . .

*(Countryside, MS)*   2:49-2"1

SPEAKER: . . . mountain barrier.

---

[1] Shots 1–6 are stock shots.

*(Three Allied soldiers firing a machine gun from behind an outcrop of rock, MS)*  3:57-2"9

*(An American soldier firing a machine gun from behind a stone wall, MS)*  4:48-2"

SPEAKER: Every village and hamlet . . .

*(A tank firing, MS)*  5:62-2"14

SPEAKER: . . . must be captured with bitter fighting. The enemy . . .

*(Columns of smoke rise where the gunfire has hit, LS)*  6:65-2"17

SPEAKER: . . . battles desperately to maintain his positions.

*(Dissolve to . . .*

*(Mountains, ELS; a monastery is perched atop a mountain ridge.)*  7:84-3"12

*(Dissolve to . . .*

*(Closer view of the monastery, LS)*  8:153-6"9

*(Dissolve to . . .*

*(Monastery, TQ)*  9:93-3"21

*A friar, the organist, looks out of one of the windows.*

*(Monastery chapel, FS)*  10:47-1"23

*A friar sweeps the steps of the main altar. He stops for a moment to listen to the gunfire.*

*(Cell of the Father Superior, MCU)*  11:59-2"11

*The young Father Superior meditates over a book.*

*(Monastery kitchen, TQ)*  12:111-4"15

*Two friars listen to the sounds of the raging battle.*

*(Dissolve to . . .*

*(View of monastery, LS) Church bells are heard.*          13:256-10"16

*(Dissolve to . . .*

*(Monastery bell tower, TQ)*          14:94-3"12

*A friar rings the bells.*

*(Dissolve to . . .*

*(Corridor in monastery, MS)*          15:220-9"4

*The friars come out of their cells, embrace, and kiss one
another.*

*(Dissolve to . . .*

*(Another corridor, MS)*          16:186-7"18

*A friar lets some chickens out of the building. The other
friars file slowly out into the courtyard.*

*(Courtyard, MS)*          17:129-5"9

*Some friars stand around. Another is shooing the chickens
out of the building.*

*Other friars file out from the corridor into the courtyard.*          18:97-4"1

*The chickens scurry among the friars in the courtyard.*          19:141-5"21

*The Father Superior, with the organist at his left, joins
his hands in prayer and, lowering his eyes, kneels down.
The other friars do the same.*          20:104-4"8

FATHER SUPERIOR: Brothers, let us thank the Lord Who
    has delivered us from all danger.

*(Resume on the friars kneeling.)*          21:629-26"5

*Music begins. Another friar appears from the left and
joins the group of five. A young peasant runs toward them
from the rear.*

*(Dissolve to . . .*

*(Courtyard, HF)*            22:173-7″5

*Two friars are speaking with a peasant couple at the monastery door.*

PEASANT: If my wife had listened to me and we'd brought the pigs up here, the Germans wouldn't have gotten them!

FRIAR, *pointing to something on the ground*: So take your chickens, anyway.

*(Insert—from above: three baskets crammed with live chickens and rabbits)*      23:132-5″12

*Hands reach in several times to take out some of the chickens.*

PEASANT *(off screen)*: These are mine.

*(Dissolve to . . .*

*(Chapel, FS)*                                                    24:97-4″1

*A friar sweeps the steps of the main altar.*

*In his cell (MCU), the Father Superior is writing a letter.*    25:156-6″12
*He stops for a moment to think.*

*(Insert: the Father Superior's letter)*                          26:378-15″18

*"Savignano di Romagna, September. Very Reverend*
*Provincial Father. With the assistance of Divine*
*Providence, we are safe and sound. Our monastery has*
*not suffered much. . . ." The last two words are being*
*penned by the Father Superior's hand.*

*Fra' Pacifico is walking along the corridor (MS). As the*       27:160-6″16
*monastery doorbell rings, he hurries (toward the camera)*
*and goes off screen to left.*

*(Dissolve to . . .*

*(Stairway, MS; camera shoots down from the stairs, across*      28:561-23″9
*the courtyard, to the doors of the monastery; also shot 62.)*
*Fra' Pacifico is opening the door. Several boys enter.*

FRA' PACIFICO: What is it?

FIRST BOY: The Americans are here!

SECOND BOY: They've come in cars!

THIRD BOY: Little tiny cars!

FOURTH BOY: There's a whole lot of them! The town's full
     of them.

*(Music begins)*

*As the boys go out again to call the Americans, the*
*friar starts back toward the stairway, going off screen to*
*right.*

BOYS, *to the Americans*: Come on, come on! Come in!

*(Courtyard, HF)*                                               29:1226-51"2

*Three American military chaplains—Jones, Martin, and Feldman—enter, accompanied by the four boys.*

BOY: Fra' Pacifico'll be right here.

JONES, *bending down toward the boy*: What? Five hundred years old, eh? Well, it doesn't show its age, *bambino!*

*As Martin, the Catholic chaplain, begins to talk, the three Americans come forward in the courtyard (camera tracks out in front of them). They look about in admiration. The boys pester Jones, touching his woolen hood.*

MARTIN: You know, I can't help thinking that by the time this monastery was built, why, America hadn't even been discovered yet . . . an immense wilderness! These walls, these olive trees, that church bell, were already here. This time—this time of the evening five hundred years ago—everything had the same soft color.

FELDMAN: Is that from Shakespeare?

MARTIN: No—Captain Bill Martin!

JONES: I'm deeply moved, Chappie, but I—I hope these monks are more up to date! *He laughs.*

*Sound of birds singing. The chaplains look around. Martin is smoking. Fra' Pacifico comes on screen from right.*

FRA' PACIFICO: Praised be Jesus Christ.

*The chaplains salute the friar.*

MARTIN*: Hello . . . forever and ever.

FRA' PACIFICO: The Father Superior's waiting for you. *To the boys*: All right, boys, run along now.

*As the boys go out, the chaplains, who are following Fra'
Pacifico, wave good-bye.*

MARTIN\*, *to boys*: So long!

*(Dissolve to . . .*

*(Stairway, MS from above)*                                    30:236-9″20

*Music begins. The three chaplains follow Fra' Pacifico up
the stairs.*

MARTIN, *to companions*: See how these stairs are worn?
 The footsteps of monks for five hundred years!

*He salutes upon seeing the Father Superior at the head
of the stairs.*

*(Corridor at the head of the stairs, MS)*                     31:45-1″21

*The Father Superior and other friars await the guests.
The Father Superior bows his head slightly in greeting.*

*The chaplains remove their helmets as they continue up*       32:83-3″11
*the stairs. (MS from above)*

*The chaplains (backs to camera) follow Fra' Pacifico on*      33:1003-
*screen from left. The friar steps aside, and the Americans*          41″19
*come up to the Father Superior. (MS)*

FATHER SUPERIOR: Peace be with you, brothers! May Saint
 Francis bless you!

*Martin embraces the Father Superior, kissing him on
both cheeks. He steps aside to his left and introduces his
companions.*

MARTIN, *in Italian*: We're three American chaplains. *In
 English*: Captain Jones . . .

JONES: Pleased to meet you.

MARTIN: . . . Captain Feldman . . .

FELDMAN: How do you do?

MARTIN: . . . me, Captain Martin. *In Italian*: Could we
spend the night here?

FATHER SUPERIOR: The doors of our monastery are open
to all. *To Fra' Pacifico*: Fra' Pacifico, will you prepare three rooms for these gentlemen?

*Fra' Pacifico goes off screen to left as the Father Superior
introduces the other friars.*

FATHER SUPERIOR: These are our other brothers—the
vicar, the substitute, the organist. Please come with
me. *He leads them toward a door behind them, on*

*the left margin of frame.*

*(A room, WF)* 34:97-4"1

*The door opens. The Father Superior stepping aside, invites the chaplains to enter. Martin enters first and looks around.*

FATHER SUPERIOR: Please come in.

*The other chaplains and the friars enter the room.* 35:130-5"10

*(Camera pans left as they enter the room.)* 36:775-32"7

*The Father Superior does the honors as a gracious, modest host. The Americans cross to the far wall of the room.*

JONES: Nice, very nice!

MARTIN: My, it's very nice here!

FATHER SUPERIOR: Please sit down.

MARTIN: Thank you.

*Music ends.*

FATHER SUPERIOR: A chair, Father Claudio.

*A chair is immediately brought for Feldman.*

FELDMAN: Thank you.

JONES, *to Feldman*: Sit down.

FATHER SUPERIOR: Take their helmets.

*As one friar takes their helmets, the vicar comes up to the Father Superior, standing at left of frame.*

VICAR, *quietly*: I'd like to ask about my town, San Leo.

FATHER SUPERIOR: I'll ask them.

VICAR: Thank you. *He steps back as the other friar passes by with the helmets.*

FATHER SUPERIOR: Father, may I. . . .

*Martin stands to offer a cigarette to the Father Superior.*

FATHER SUPERIOR: You are very kind, but no, thank you.

*Martin then offers cigarettes to the other friars.*

*The four friars (lined up diagonally to camera) all graciously refuse Martin's cigarettes. (HF)*    37:124-5″4

FRIAR: No!

FRIAR: No, thank you.

FRIAR: No, thank you.

*Slightly bewildered and embarrassed, Martin takes his seat again. Jones stands up and, opening his haversack, moves toward the friars.*    38:247-10″7

JONES: Maybe they'd like some candy. Father?

*The Father Superior, leaning against the table, turns to Martin. (HF)*    39:34-1″10

FATHER SUPERIOR: Father, perhaps you can give me news . . .

*The two seated chaplains listen; they try to get the gist of the conversation. (HF; also shot 42)*    40:148-6″4

FATHER SUPERIOR *(off screen)*: . . . of San Leo?

*Hearing the name of the town, the chaplains glance at each other.*

FELDMAN: San Leo? There was a German in every single hole!

MARTIN: They were hiding everywhere like rats.

FATHER SUPERIOR: Is it badly damaged?    41:46-1″22

MARTIN*: Not badly.    42:40-1″16

*Jones hands out chocolate to the friars. (HF)* 43:475-19″19

FRIAR: Thank you.

JONES, *to Fra' Raffaele*: For you, Father?

*Fra' Raffaele hesitates, but Jones insists.*

JONES: There we are.

FRA' RAFFAELE, *warmly*: Thank you, thank you, a thousand thanks. I'll say a special prayer to the Holy Mother for you, for spiritual and temporal aid throughout. . . .

FATHER SUPERIOR, *cutting him off gently (off screen)*: That's all right . . .

*The Father Superior moves to the back of the room (TQ;* 44:53-2″5 *camera pans left). Another friar stands at left margin of frame. (HF)*

FATHER SUPERIOR: . . . Fra' Raffaele. We understand.

FRA' RAFFAELE *(off screen)*: Yes, Father.

*Silenced, Fra' Raffaele clasps his hands around a bar of* 45:33-1″19 *chocolate.*

*The Father Superior carries a tray with three glasses* 46:485-20″5 *toward the Americans (camera pans right to HF). Setting the tray down on the table, he begins to pour a liqueur.*

FATHER SUPERIOR: This is a liqueur we make from our own apples, Fathers.

*After filling the glasses, he corks the bottle and sets it down, then comes up to them with the tray.*

FATHER SUPERIOR: Will you have some?

*Martin and Feldman stand up and take glasses; Jones* 47:384-16″ *does not. (TQ)*

FATHER SUPERIOR *(off screen)*: Please help yourselves.

MARTIN, *in Italian*: Thanks, thanks, Father.

FELDMAN, *in Italian*: Thank you.

JONES, *in Italian*: No, thank you. *In English*: I never touch the stuff.

MARTIN: *A la santé!*

*Martin and Feldman touch glasses and begin to drink. Someone knocks at the door. The chaplains turn to watch.*

FATHER SUPERIOR *(off screen)*: Ave Maria. . . .

*Fra' Pacifico opens the door behind the line of friars. (HF)*     48:74-3″2

FRA' PACIFICO: Gratia plaena. The rooms are ready, Father Superior.

*The Father Superior motions to the chaplains to follow*     49:378-15″18
*him. (TQ)*

FATHER SUPERIOR: Fathers, will you come? . . .

JONES: Thank you.

FELDMAN: Good!

*Martin finishes his drink, sets down his glass, and goes out with the friars. Feldman picks up his helmet and follows him out. The vicar remains alone in the room. He goes over to the table, picks up a helmet, examines it curiously.*

*With childish delight, the vicar touches the helmet, turns*     50:153-6″9
*it, and starts to try it on, then abruptly checks himself.*
*(HF)*

*The vicar starts to leave the room. (TQ)*     51:50-2″2

*(Corridor, WF)*     52:377-15″17

*The friars are just outside the door, grouped around the*

*Father Superior.*

ORGANIST: Father, what people those three chaplains are! *The vicar comes out carrying the helmet, which he hands to the Father Superior.*

VICAR: Father, they forgot this helmet!

FATHER SUPERIOR: Don't worry. They're just in the other corridor. *He gestures down the corridor.*

ORGANIST: Are they staying here tonight?

SUBSTITUTE: Are they going to have dinner here?

ORGANIST: Umm. . . .

FATHER SUPERIOR: Certainly. We'll share whatever there is with them.

*The friars disperse.*

*(Dissolve to . . .*

*(Kitchen, TQ)*                                            53:258-10"18

*Fra' Felice, the cook, is cleaning vegetables with the help of a boy.*

FATHER SUPERIOR *(off screen)*: Jesus Christ be praised!

FRA' FELICE: Forever and ever.

FATHER SUPERIOR *(off screen)*: What are you giving us for supper?

FRA' FELICE: Broccoli.

*He stands up and approaches the Father Superior (camera tracks right with him until the Father Superior appears in HF). Fra' Pacifico and another friar are in the doorway to the rear.*

FATHER SUPERIOR: Will there be enough for three very welcome guests . . .

*The cook shakes his head. (MCU)*　　　　　54:66-2″18

FATHER SUPERIOR *(off screen)*: . . . we have with us this
　　evening?

FRA' FELICE: No, there's very little.

FATHER SUPERIOR *(MCU)*: We could mix in some　55:46-1″22
　　potatoes. . . .

FRA' FELICE *(MCU)*: There's not many potatoes either!　56:45-1″21

FATHER SUPERIOR *(MCU)*: A few days ago I saw that the　57:141-5″21
　　pear tree in the garden was beginning to bear fruit.

FRA' FELICE *(MCU)*: They won't be ripe for another　58:92-3″20
　　month, and anyway they're wild. They're no good
　　to eat.

FATHER SUPERIOR *(MCU)*: Try to do your best. I know I　59:214-8″22
　　can count on you. Divine Providence will help us.
　　Jesus Christ be praised. *He goes off screen to left.*

*Fra' Felice returns to the fireplace, where the boy is still*　60:28-1″4
*at work. (MCU)*

FRA' FELICE: Forever and ever.

*(Stairway, MS from below)*　　　　　61:446-18″14

*Music begins. Followed by two friars, the Father Superior*
*is going up the stairs when he hears the doorbell ring.*
*He stops.*

FATHER SUPERIOR, *to Fra' Pacifico, just behind him*: Go
　　open the door.

*Fra' Pacifico turns and goes off screen to left, while the*
*Father Superior continues up the stairs, glancing back*
*several times. At the top of the stairs he turns to have a*
*better look.*

*Fra' Pacifico goes down the stairs, crosses the courtyard,*      62:204-8"12
*and opens the monastery door for a peasant couple carry-*
*ing bundles.*

*Astonished, the Father Superior goes back down a few*      63:96-4"
*steps, while the other friar continues on up. (MS from*
*below)*

FRA' PACIFICO *(off screen)*: Well, what is it?

PEASANT WOMAN *(off screen)*: An offering for the
     monastery!

PEASANT MAN *(off screen)*: Because you saved our animals!

FRA' PACIFICO *(off screen)*: Thank you, thank you.

*(Courtyard, TQ)*      64:144-6"

*The two peasants, accompanied by a boy, are carrying*
*large bundles, a basket, and some chickens.*

FRA' PACIFICO: Saint Francis bless you!

PEASANT WOMAN: Take this one!

FRA' PACIFICO, *to the boy*: Help me bring this stuff in,
     will you? Thanks.

*The boy helps Fra' Pacifico bring the offerings inside.*
*They go off screen to right.*

*(A friar's cell, TQ)*      65:182-7"14

*Jones is emptying his haversack onto the bed. He turns*
*to look around as if he is hearing someone.*

*(Another cell, TQ)*      66:122-5"2

*Standing at the window with a book in his hand, Feldman*
*is saying his prayers.*

FELDMAN: Praised be the Lord Who hath given us the
     evening for rest and for prayer. Blessed be the Lord
     our God . . .

*(Another cell, TQ)*  67:802-33"10

*Martin, the Catholic chaplain, empties his haversack onto the bed, then steps to the door, opens it, and looks up and down the corridor for someone.*

MARTIN\*, *calling*: Please. . . .

*Fra' Pacifico comes in, and Martin hands him his provisions.*

MARTIN\*: Meat and vegetables—good! Chocolate, butter, more meat—all very good food! Go. . . .

*Martin loads up Fra' Pacifico, then indicates that he should come back for the rest. The friar goes to the door, but Martin calls him back and hands him another package.*

MARTIN: Ah, toothpicks!

*Fra' Pacifico goes off screen to right. Music ends.*

*Fra' Pacifico rushes excitedly down the stairs (MS from*  68:163-6"19
*below), coming on screen and going off to left.*

*(Kitchen, WF)*  69:842-35"2

*Fra' Pacifico comes on screen from left and goes to the center (camera pans left and tracks along with him), where Fra' Felice sits working (TQ). Fra' Pacifico excitedly hands the cook one of the cans. Two other friars come up to them.*

FRA' PACIFICO: Look here, Fra' Felice, look what they gave me! There's eggs and butter and chocolate!

*Fra' Felice stands up, looks incredulously at the can, and passes it to Fra' Salvatore.*

FRA' FELICE: What? Eggs in cans? In here?

FRA' SALVATORE: How can that be?

ANOTHER FRIAR: Let me see the chocolate!

FRA' SALVATORE: These Americans! They think of everything! Give me the thingumajig. . . .

*Fra' Salvatore goes to the fireplace, where the boy is stirring up the fire (camera tracks forward with him to HF). He starts to open the can, but Fra' Felice comes up to him from right and takes possession of it himself.*

FRA' FELICE: Careful, Father Salvatore, you might cut your fingers. This isn't your line! Ah!

*Fra' Felice moves to his left (camera tracks left with him). Fra' Salvatore follows him. Fra' Felice sets the can on the sink and prepares to open it, while the others gather around to watch.*

*A friar watches Fra' Felice attentively. (CU)*      70:35-1″11

*Fra' Salvatore, in profile, watches too. (CU)*      71:26-1″2

*Fra' Felice is intent on opening the can. (MCU)*      72:37-1″13

*One friar is at the cook's left, with Fra' Salvatore behind him. Fra' Felice lifts the lid off the can, which he passes to Fra' Salvatore. (TQ)*      73:747-31″3

*Fra' Salvatore sniffs at the open can, then passes it to another friar. (CU)*      74:64-2″16

FRA' SALVATORE: It's milk!

*The friar sniffs at the can, then hands it back to the cook. (CU)*      75:70-2″22

FRIAR: Mm, good!

*Fra' Felice takes the can, dips a finger into it, and tastes. He lays his finger on his cheek in the traditional gesture of appreciation. (MCU)*      76:149-6″5

FRA' FELICE: Fantastic!

*(Garden, TQ)*                                                       77:2570-
                                                                        1'47"2

*Martin and the organist stroll along the monastery wall.*
*Another friar is working in the background.*

ORGANIST: Nothing would ever grow here. Now it's
    become the most fertile part of our garden. A miracle
    of our Fra' Raffaele's.

*Martin gazes about admiringly (as they come forward to*
*HF, camera tracks slightly sideways). The friar goes off*
*screen. Martin (MCU) breathes deeply.*

MARTIN*: Mm, good smell.

*(Camera pans right to pick up the organist again in*
*MCU; Martin is on margin of frame.) The organist in*
*turn breathes deeply.*

ORGANIST: Mint.

MARTIN*: Yes?

*They reach the doorway to the corridor (camera tracks*
*sideways with them and pans right), from which the other*
*two chaplains (HF) are now coming out.*

MARTIN*, *to chaplains*: Hello.

FELDMAN*: Hello.

JONES*: Oh, a very beautiful garden!

MARTIN: We've just been talking about miracles.

*Jones joins them; the organist is between them (all face*
*the camera).*

JONES: I'm inclined to believe you. Where else could they
    happen but here?

MARTIN: They're really fine fellows! *To organist, in*
    *Italian, indicating Jones*: He's very bad!

ORGANIST, *slapping Jones on the shoulder*: No! He's good!

JONES: I only wish I could speak their language well. So I could talk to them—ask them a few questions.

MARTIN: No need to ask any questions. You'll find everything very clear and simple here.

*The organist looks from one to the other, trying to follow the conversation. Then he makes a small bow, returned by the chaplains.*

ORGANIST: Excuse me, I must go now. *He goes off screen to left.*

MARTIN*: Yes, Father.

*Jones and Martin continue their conversation.*

JONES: He—he's very young.

MARTIN: He's twenty-five.

JONES: Don't you think he's too young to be in here?

*Feldman, who has been smoking his pipe in the doorway, steps down into the garden and joins the others. Martin and Jones begin to stroll in the garden, then turn back after a few steps (camera pans left and tracks with them, then pans left to MCU).*

MARTIN: No. He told me he always wanted this vocation, that since he was ten he always wanted to enter this monastery.

JONES: I think one can really be in peace with his Lord without removing himself from the world. *They stop for a moment (HF).* After all, it was created for us. The world is our parish.

FELDMAN, *coming on screen from right, pensively*: How can they judge us and life if they don't know what it's all about?

*The Christian chaplains begin to stroll again (camera pans left). The church bells ring. Fra' Pacifico enters from the rear, carrying a pail. At the sound of the "Ave Maria" he sets down the pail, kneels, and begins to pray out loud.*

JONES\*, *to Fra' Pacifico*: Hello.

*Martin tosses away his cigarette, crosses himself, and joins his hands in prayer. The other two chaplains, amused, watch Fra' Pacifico's broad gestures and listen to his singsong. As he prays the friar casts questioning glances at them.*

FRA' PACIFICO: In the name of the Father, of the Son, and of the Holy Ghost. Ave Maria, gratia plena, Dominus tecum, benedictus fructus ventris tui, Jesus, Sancta Maria, mater Dei, ora pro nobis. . . .

*Seeing that two of the chaplains are not praying, he stops, stands up (in TQ), and questions Martin.*

FRA' PACIFICO: Why aren't they praying?

MARTIN\*, *taking his arm and indicating his companions*: Those two are very bad. He's Protestant—and he's a Jew.

*Jones laughs at Martin's joke. Shocked, Fra' Pacifico clasps his hands in astonishment and abruptly departs, going off screen to right. Music begins.*

JONES, *amused*: I'm Martin Luther!

MARTIN: Sh! *He shakes his head at Jones.*

*(Dissolve to . . .*

*(Stairway, MS)*                                       78:340-14″4

*Fra' Salvatore is coming down the stairs. Fra' Pacifico rushes upstairs, telling his news as he goes, almost without breaking stride.*

FRA' PACIFICO: Father Salvatore, Father Salvatore, one of the chaplains is a Jew!

*Fra' Salvatore absorbs the news slowly. He goes back up a few steps, calling to Fra' Pacifico, but the latter has already disappeared around the corner.*

FRA' SALVATORE: Hey! Come here! Come here!

*Meanwhile Fra' Felice has come on screen from below and reaches Fra' Salvatore.*

FRA' FELICE: What's up, what's up?

FRA' SALVATORE, *whispering in his ear*: One of the chaplains is a Jew!

FRA' FELICE: Oh, merciful Saint Francis!

*Extremely excited, he turns back down the stairs.*

*Two friars are walking along the corridor (MS). Fra' Pacifico comes on screen from left, tells them the news, and still on the run, goes off screen to left into a room giving onto the corridor.*     79:185-7″17

FRA' PACIFICO: Father Claudio! Father Claudio! One of the chaplains is a Jew!

*(Another stairway, MS)*     80:249-10″9

*Fra' Raffaele is climbing the stairs when Fra' Pacifico rounds the corner on his way down, coming on screen from right. He tells Fra' Raffaele the news and continues on down, going off screen to left.*

FRA' PACIFICO: One of the chaplains is a Jew!

*Fra' Raffaele stops in his tracks, joins his hands, kneels, and begins to pray.*

FRA' RAFFAELE: Jesus, Jesus . . .

   *(CU)* . . . protect us, help us. . . .     81:101-4″5

*Fra' Raffaele is still kneeling in prayer when the vicar appears, lost in meditation. He does not notice Fra'*     82:450-18″18

*Raffaele at first, but then comes up to him. (TQ)*

VICAR: What is it?

FRA' RAFFAELE: Oh, one of the priests is a Jew!

VICAR: No, don't worry about it, don't worry about it!

*He helps Fra' Raffaele to his feet, calming him. Music ends.*

*(Dissolve to . . .*

*(A room, MS)*                                        83:871-36"7
*Some friars are discussing the news.*

FRA' FELICE, *to Fra' Salvatore*: A Jew in our monastery!

FRA' PACIFICO, *to Fra' Salvatore*: The short one's a Protestant!

FRA' RAFFAELE: Luther—the heresy of Luther, the worst Protestant!

*The Father Superior enters the upper part of the room (camera tilts up toward him).*

FATHER SUPERIOR: What's going on, my sons?

FRA' PACIFICO: One of the chaplains is a Jew, and another one's a Protestant.

FRA' RAFFAELE: Two lost souls, Father Superior!

*As the Father Superior comes down the few steps to join them (camera pans slightly downward), he reassures the friars in a clear, calm voice.*

FATHER SUPERIOR: No, no soul is lost as long as it lives and has the will to save itself. *He passes through the group.* There are always opportunities for redemption. We can do something for them, brothers.

*The other friars move in the opposite direction.*

*(Dissolve to . . .*

*(Chapel, TQ)* 84:438-18″6

*The Father Superior and Martin leave the main altar (camera pans left). They stop in the middle of the chapel.*

FATHER SUPERIOR: Forgive me if I ask you something, Father.

MARTIN*: Of course, Father.

*They begin to walk again (camera tracks left with them).*

FATHER SUPERIOR: You and the other two chaplains have lived together for quite a while?

*They stop (Martin's back is to the camera).*

MARTIN*: We've been together for the whole Italian campaign—twenty or twenty-one months.

*(Martin and the Father Superior at right margin of* 85:239-9″23 *frame, MCU)*

*Several friars begin to come into the chapel at the rear for evening prayers.*

MARTIN: Sicily, Salerno, Rome, Florence. They're my good friends, my dear friends. I admire them very much.

*(The Father Superior, his eyes lowered, and Martin, at* 86:99-4″3 *the left margin of frame, MCU)*

FATHER SUPERIOR: You've never tried to lead them to the true religion?

*The friars gather around Martin. (MCU)* 87:304-12″16

FATHER SUPERIOR: You never tried—

MARTIN*, *after a moment's hesitation*: But, Father, the Protestant and the Jew are just as convinced they are in the true path.

*(The Father Superior with the vicar and another friar,* 88:304-12″16

*and Martin on the left margin, MCU)*

FATHER SUPERIOR: But we know they're in error.

VICAR: We know it.

MARTIN*: Oh, yes, yes, of course.

FATHER SUPERIOR: But we must use every means to try to save those two souls, which might be lost.

*(Martin and Fra' Salvatore, MCU)*                                89:162-6"18

MARTIN*: I'm a Catholic, Father, and I'm a priest, and I humbly believe I'm a good Catholic.

FATHER SUPERIOR: Excuse me, Father, I didn't mean to remind you of your duties. I meant—you're military chaplains.                                90:219-9"3

*(Martin, surrounded by the friars, MCU; also shot 93)*      91:578-24"2

FATHER SUPERIOR: In your mission you expose yourselves to the same risks, to the same dangers, as the soldiers. Haven't you ever thought that your two companions might perish any day?

FRA' SALVATORE: Saint Paul says, "Omnes quidem resurgemus, sed non omnes mutabimur in gloria."

*Feldman and Jones appear in the doorway of the chapel.*

MARTIN*: But for those in good faith, "In novissima tuba surget in gloria."

*(The Father Superior, his hand on his chin, listening attentively, MCU)*                                92:196-8"4

VICAR: That's true, but have you ever examined their consciences?

ORGANIST: Are you sure they're in good faith?

FATHER SUPERIOR: Have you ever discussed these things

with them?

MARTIN*: No, I've never examined their consciences. I've never discussed this with them. I've never asked them anything, because I've never thought I could judge them. I know them too well. They're very good friends.[1] Perhaps you, in this peaceful world, in this atmosphere of—untroubled meditation, you consider me guilty. I don't feel guilty. My conscience . . .

93:779-32″11

*(The Father Superior and other friars, MCU)*

94:100-4″4

MARTIN *(off screen)*: . . . is perfectly clear.

[1] Here Feldman and Jones disappear from the scene, which has been edited from two different negatives.

*A bell rings.*

*Martin turns and sees other friars entering. (MCU)*     95:101-4"5

*The friars enter the pews, kneel, and begin to pray. (MS)*     96:666-27"18

*(Wipe to right)*

*(The empty refectory, MS)*     97:71-2"23

FRIAR *(off screen)*: Benedicite. Tristis est anima . . .

*(Martin's empty cell, MS)*     98:65-2"17

FRIAR *(off screen)*: . . . mea usque ad mortem. My soul . . .

*(The empty corridor, MS)*     99:53-2"5

FRIAR *(off screen)*: . . . is sad unto death.

*(Kitchen, HF)*     100:535-22"7

*Fra' Felice (back to camera) opens the oven with the help of the boy and takes out a pan, which he brings over to the sink and sets down (camera tracks out and pans left to TQ). Music begins. Fra' Felice takes a sausage from the pan over to the table (camera pans right) and begins to slice it under Fra' Pacifico's hungry eyes.*

*Fra' Felice slices the sausage under Fra' Pacifico's watch-ful eyes. (TQ)*     101:170-7"2

*(Insert: CU of a friar bending down to sniff at the pan)*     102:98-4"2

*(Dissolve to . . .*

*(Corridor, TQ)*     103:675-28"3

*The Father Superior and the guests come on screen from left, going toward the refectory door. The Father Superior, who is carrying a camera, opens the door.*

FATHER SUPERIOR, *to Martin*: Our rule, Father, asks us to remain silent during meals. I'm sorry I cannot make an exception for you.

MARTIN, *translating for his companions*: The Father
says to keep silent during the meals. It's a rule.

*(Camera tracks behind them into the refectory.) The
chaplains look around curiously.*

*The friars enter the refectory (MS) in double file, each
carrying a lighted candle and saying prayers. They go
off screen to right.*

104:223-9"7

*(RA of shot 102)*
*The friars (backs to camera) stand at their places, then
kneel in prayer. After the Father Superior has made the
sign of the cross, they respond with an "Amen" and take
their seats (FS). While the reader reads, Fra' Felice comes
on screen from left bearing a large tray, which he takes
to the Father Superior. He serves the three chaplains with
the help of the Father Superior and another friar, then
goes off screen to left.*

105:1444-
1'0"4

READER: Benedicite. On this day the following brothers passed on to a better life: in 1722 Father Salvatore of San Leo; in 1743 Father Giambattista of Rimini; in 1744 Father Teodoro of San Marino. Requiem aeternam dona eis, Domine, et lux perpetua luceat eis. Requiescant in pace.

FRIARS: Amen!

*The three chaplains open their napkins. They are somewhat ill at ease. (HF)*     106:177-7″9

*(Martin and the Father Superior sitting near each other at the head of separate tables, HF; also shot 108)*     107:193-8″1

FATHER SUPERIOR, *leaning toward Martin*: Start right in.

MARTIN*: We'll wait for you, all of you.

FATHER SUPERIOR: We . . .

*(Three friars sitting at a table on which there is no food, HF)*     108:51-2″3

FATHER SUPERIOR *(off screen)*: . . . are fasting.

MARTIN*: Why?     109:251-
    10″11

FATHER SUPERIOR: Because Divine Providence has sent to our refuge two souls on which the light of truth must descend.

FATHER SUPERIOR, *staring straight ahead (MCU)*: Our human presumption makes us hope that with this most humble—*he turns to Martin*—offering we may obtain a great gift from Heaven.     110:182-7″14

*The three chaplains begin to eat. (HF)*     111:149-6″5

*Martin raises his spoon to his lips, then hesitates and sets it down again. (MCU)*     112:561-23″9

MARTIN*, *looking at the Father Superior*: Forgive me if

I don't observe your rule, but I want to talk to you.
I want to tell you . . . *He stands up.*

*(Resume on Martin standing up; the others listening to him, MS)* 113:273-11"9

MARTIN\*: . . . that what you've given me is such a great
gift *(music begins)* that I feel I'll always be in your
debt.

*The other two chaplains glance at each other, realizing what has happened. (HF)* 114:104-4"8

MARTIN\* *(off screen)*: I've found here that peace of
mind . . .

*(Two friars listening, HF)* 115:54-2"6

MARTIN\* *(off screen)*: . . . I'd lost . . .

*(The other two chaplains trying to understand what Martin is saying, HF)* 116:92-3"20

MARTIN\* *(off screen):* . . . in the horrors and the trials of
the war . . .

*(A corner of the refectory, friars seated at an empty table,* 117:51-2″3
*MS)*

MARTIN\* *(CU):* . . . a beautiful, moving lesson of humility, 118:211-8″19
simplicity, and pure faith . . .

. . . Pax hominibus bonae voluntatis. 119:210-8″18

*(Fade-out)*


EPISODE VI

*(Fade-in)*

*(Delta of the Po River, near Venice, ELS)* 1:540-22″12

*(Music begins)*

*An object is floating slowly downstream (toward the
camera, which pans slightly left). It turns over slowly,
and a sign appears briefly (in CU), reading "Partisan."
Then the sign, nailed to a pole that has been thrust into
a life preserver along with a dead body, floats off screen
to left.*

SPEAKER: Behind the lines, Italian partisans and American
OSS officers join forces in a struggle which, although
not mentioned in the war bulletins, is perhaps even
tougher and more desperate.

*Music and sounds of water lapping against the banks are
heard after each shot.*

*Carried along by the current, the partisan's body comes* 2:160-6″16
*on screen from right, passes by a village on the far shore,
and goes off screen to left. (LS)*

*On the bank, Italian peasants and German soldiers watch* 3:126-5″6
*the body float past (LS; camera tracks right past the
people from the river).*

*Wrapped in heavy black shawls, some women silently*   4:67-2"19
*watch the corpse float by (HF; camera tracks and pans*
*right).*

*The partisan is carried along by the current, more slowly*   5:40-1"16
*now. (LS; camera pans left).*

*A German soldier, standing among the local people*   6:38-1"14
*(in WF), points out the body to another soldier. (TQ)*

GERMAN: Partizanen, Banditen!

*The body of the partisan is carried along by the current.*   7:37-1"13
*(LS)*

*A group of women and children follow the drifting corpse*   8:165-6"21
*from the bank (WF; camera tracks left in front of them).*

*(Dissolve to . . .*

*(The partisan's corpse floating downstream, LS; the*     9:124-5″4
*other bank of the river recedes gradually in the back-*
*ground.)*

*(Dissolve to . . .*

*(Canebrake along the Po, TQ)*     10:69-2″21

*The bank of the river is concealed by the canebrake.*
*Two men, an American soldier and a partisan wearing a*
*woolen hood, make their way through the cane. The*
*partisan points out the body in the river.*

CIGOLANI: Another partisan . . .

*(Corpse continuing to drift downstream, LS)*     11:46-1″22

CIGOLANI *(off screen):* . . . killed. I'll get him!

DALE: You'd better be careful of that German tower down     12:331-13″19
there—*in Italian*—Germans!

CIGOLANI: I don't care. I'm going anyway.

DALE: All right. I'll go around to the beach and explode
that mine to distract their attention.

CIGOLANI: All right, go on, but be sure to do it right.

DALE: Okay.

*The partisan pushes Dale's skiff out of the cane into the*
*river. As soon as he is free of the cane, Dale (in CU)*
*begins to row.*

*(Wipe to left)*

*Dale (back to camera) reaches the bank with the last*     13:363-15″3
*stroke of his oars. Taking his submachine gun, he climbs*
*out of the bow of the skiff and pushes it into the cane-*
*brake. (WF)*

*Cigolani, seen through the cane, poles his skiff along with*     14:53-2″5 *an oar. (MS)*

*(The corpse of the partisan, almost immobile in the middle of the river, LS; the far shore of the Po is in the background.)* 15:58-2″10

*Hunched over and carrying his gun, Dale runs behind a large mine washed up on the beach (MS; camera pans slightly left with him).* 16:106-4″10

*Crouched down and half-hidden by the mine (at right margin of frame), Dale attaches a fuse, then unrolls the fuse along the sand. (HF)* 17:244-10″4

*(Two Germans with submachine guns standing watch on a tower rising above the canebrake in foreground, WF) One German indicates something in the river to the other.* 18:84-3″12

GERMAN: Schau! [Look!]

*(The corpse of the partisan afloat in the middle of the river, LS; camera pans slightly left; the far shore of the Po is in the background.)* 19:37-1″13

*One of the German soldiers takes a cigarette, offers one to his companion, then lights his own.* 20:184-7″16

*Cigolani rows quickly and expertly (toward the camera) across the river. (WF)* 21:134-5″14

*Dale lights the fuse with his cigarette, waits a moment to make sure it has caught, then moves away. (HF)* 22:217-9″1

*(Dale crouching down behind a small dune, ELS)* 23:99-4″3

*The mine explodes in the distance, releasing a huge cloud of smoke.*

*The two soldiers on the tower whirl around as they hear the explosion. (LS)* 24:81-3″9

*(The partisan's body coming to rest near the bank, LS)*     25:325-13″13
*Cigolani appears on screen from left, rowing quickly up*
*to the corpse. He rests his oars, removes the sign, and*
*begins to pull the body into his skiff.*

*The two Germans notice Cigolani and open fire. (WF)*     26:67-2″19

GERMAN: Schau! Feuer! [Look! Shoot!]

*Cigolani is now out of the skiff and up to his knees in the*     27:33-1″9
*water, trying to get the body out of the life preserver. The*
*Germans' shots scatter around him. (WF)*

*Dale stands up in his skiff, so that his head appears above*     28:42-1″18
*the cane. He shoots toward the German watchtower. (WF)*

*(Shorter view of the watchtower, seen from below, HF)*     29:118-4″22
*Dale's shots hit the tower. The Germans turn in his*
*direction. (HF)*

GERMAN: Verfluchte Schweinerei! [Damned bastards!]

*The Germans' submachine-gun fire tears into the cane-*     30:62-2″14
*break near Dale, who cannot be seen. (LS)*

*Dale straightens up again in his skiff to fire another*     31:58-2″10
*shot at the Germans, then crouches down among the cane*
*stalks. (WF)*

*The Germans continue to fire toward Dale. (HF)*     32:57-2″9

*Cigolani has gotten the corpse and the life preserver into*     33:196-8″4
*the skiff. He climbs aboard and begins to row. (WF)*

*(Dissolve to . . .*

*(Cigolani rowing upstream to left, trying to reach the*     34:343-14″7
*shore, FS)*

*He enters a short, narrow branch of water, where the*
*cane grows so thickly that he cannot row. He hunches*

*down to pole with an oar.*

*(Dissolve to . . .*

*(A narrow branch of the river, bordered by canebrakes*    35:897-37"9
*and divided down the middle by a sandbar, MS)*

*Cigolani poles his skiff over to the sandbar (camera pans
left after him). Dale approaches from the other side, pulls
his skiff up on the sand, and then helps Cigolani to do
the same.*

*Keeping low, the two men pull Cigolani's skiff over the*    36:574-23"22
*sandbar. Dale indicates the direction they are to take,
then helps Cigolani back into the skiff and pushes it off
on the other side of the sandbar. Dale then follows
(camera pans left) with his own skiff. (WF)*

*Cigolani's skiff passes through the cane, going off screen*    37:156-6"12
*to left. (MS)*

*Dale, seen intermittently through the wind-blown cane*    38:271-11"7
*(MS), continues rowing (camera pans left over to a long,
uninterrupted stretch of cane).*

*(Dissolve to . . .*

*(Two skiffs appearing on screen from left, HF)*    39:696-29"

*A partisan sentinel is hidden among the cane stalks.*

PARTISAN: What's up?

CIGOLANI: Another partisan in the Po.

*(Camera pans slightly right.) Three partisans are on the
riverbank, heading toward the skiffs. Two Allied soldiers,
Alan and Dan, and other partisans come forward from
farther away. (LS)*

*(Dissolve to . . .*

*("Canary" area, WF)*             40:167-6″23

*A large group of partisans meets the two skiffs on the shore. They begin to lift the body of their dead companion out of Cigolani's skiff.*

PARTISAN: Boys, another partisan in the Po.

DALE, *to Alan*: What've you heard from Fifth Army . . .

*Dale and Alan walk along the beach (HF; camera pans*     41:527-21″23
*right). Dan appears.*

DALE *(off screen)*: . . . Headquarters?

ALAN: General Alexander's Headquarters says to cease all operations and for all partisans to return immediately to their homes.

DALE: There's another partisan in the Po.

*The music fades out in the sound of the wind, which is heard in the following shots along with the sounds of water. The three Americans stop to watch the partisans carrying the corpse.*

DAN: These people aren't fighting for the British Empire. They're fighting for their lives.

*The Americans start walking again (camera pans right after them).*

DALE: What else did Headquarters have to say?

ALAN: I told them we were completely cut off, and that any minute now—

DALE: What the devil do they expect us to do?

*Shotguns slung over their shoulders, the partisans carry*     42:809-33″17
*the corpse (HF; camera tracks along with them and pans right up to LS). They set the body down gently. The three Americans (TQ) come on screen from left and*

*stop (in CU). In the background the partisans kneel down and begin to dig a grave.*

DALE *(off screen)*: Have you told them we have no ammunition, no food, and no possible means of defense?

ALAN *(off screen)*: I told them our entire situation. Their answer is still "Cease all activity!"

DALE *(off screen)*: What do they expect us to do? We're entirely surrounded by Germans!

ALAN: I'm expecting a confirmation of my last message. There's supposed to be a plane coming over tonight to make a food and ammo drop over at Canary. *To Dan*: So that there will be no mistakes, we'll light three-second signal fires on the beach.

DALE: But don't you understand? If we light those fires, the whole German Army'll be down on our necks!

DAN: Well, we'll all die one way or another—but that's a small matter for Headquarters.

ALAN: I didn't want to get our food supplies by sea because it'd take too long, so I made arrangements for a plane . . .

*(Dale watching the partisans, CU)* 43:141-5″21

ALAN *(off screen)*: . . . tonight.

DALE: All right, all right. Nothing can hurt us now anyway!

*(The face of the dead partisan, CU)* 44:110-4″14

*Hands appear on screen to pick him up.*

*(Dissolve to . . .*

*(The partisans burying the body, throwing dirt over it with their hands, HF)* 45:276-11″12

*Cigolani comes on screen from right and places the life preserver and the "Partisan" sign at the head of the grave. He rises (camera tilts up) and slowly removes his hood. All the other partisans do the same.*

*(RA; resume on partisans rising, MS)* 46:476-19″20

*They stand in silence. In the background, the three Americans appear from the left, remove their helmets, and join the partisans in silence. Music begins. The men all start toward the boats (camera pans left with them up to LS).*

*The men appear on screen from right on their way to the shore. They climb into their skiffs two by two and push off (camera pans left). They pole along the first shallow stretch of water. (WF)*  47:448-18″16

DALE\*, *to partisans*: Take guns.

*(Dissolve to . . .*

*(Three skiffs coming along the middle of the river at a short distance from each other, LS)*  48:770-32″2

DALE\*, *calling from the skiff*: "San Marco!" Where are you? Where's the radio set?

"SAN MARCO": Here!

*(Camera pans left with the first boat until it includes a man who is climbing out of a completely submerged cask.) Dale's skiff approaches the Italian marine from the San Marco division, who passes over the radio and his gun and then climbs aboard (the camera, mounted on a boat, pulls back). The other boats file by (in CU and in background) until all have gone off screen to left.*

*("Riva Grande" area, ELS; the boats in the distance, hugging the edge of the canebrake)*  49:143-5″23

*(Dissolve to . . .*

*(The skiffs closer to the shore, LS)*  50:141-5″21

*(Dissolve to . . .*

*(Partisans and Americans jumping out of the skiffs even before they touch shore, LS)*  51:388-16″4

*They run along the sand (toward the camera, which pans left with them) until they go off screen to left. The men who have beached the boats come last. Music ends.*

DALE, *to one of the partisans (TQ)*: I want you to get those boats over here in the canal and set up the radio over here. Take all the men and disperse them around into trench position. Is that clear?    52:313-13"1

PARTISAN, *in English*: Yes.

DALE: Okay, take over!

*The partisan goes off screen to left and repeats the instructions to his companions.*

PARTISAN: Take the boats right over to the canal.

*Dale and Dan step aside to let the boats pass.*

*The partisan (HF) tells his companions to keep low as they push the boats along. (MS)*    53:244-10"4

PARTISAN: Keep low, boys, keep low!

*He goes off screen to left as those pushing the boats come on screen from right, slip the boats into the water, and jump in.*

*(Dale and Dan coming toward the camera, HF)*    54:323-13"11

DALE: How do you feel?

DAN: It's all right. I'm feeling better.

DALE: Okay. Then I want you to take two of these men, go back over to those houses, and set up signal fires for the plane tonight. I'll try to get something over to eat a little bit later on. Okay?

DAN: All right. I'll take over. *He goes off screen to left.*

*Dan comes on screen from left toward two of the partisans. He motions to them to go with him. (HF)*    55:128-5"8

DAN*: You, and you, come with me. *They all go off screen*

*to left.*

DALE, *to Dan and the two partisans (MS)*: Don't forget     56:110-4″14
about that ammunition!

DAN: I'll take over!

*Cigolani comes on screen from right carrying his gun
in one hand and a weeding hook in the other. As Dale
comes up to him, Cigolani points to a farmhouse with
the hook.*

CIGOLANI: That place there's . . .

*(A farmhouse, "Casal Madalena," lying low on the*     57:41-1″17
*horizon over a sea of cane, LS)*

CIGOLANI *(off screen)*: . . . Casal Madalena.

*Dale motions to Cigolani to follow him. They go off*     58:59-2″11
*screen to left. In the background Dan and the two
partisans start for the house.*

*Armed with shotguns, the partisans take up positions*     59:108-4″12
*around a natural hollow in the earth (MS). Music begins.*

*Some partisans are around the radio set. The radio man*     60:101-4″5
*is trying to make contact. (WF)*

*(Casal Madalena, LS)*     61:130-5″10

*Dale and Cigolani (WF) are heading toward the farm-
house. (LS)*

*(Dissolve to . . .*

*(Dale and Cigolani making their way through the water,*     62:380-15″20
*TQ)*

DALE\*, *stopping*: The guns!

*Cigolani hands Dale his shotgun. Dale hands Cigolani his
pistol, which the Italian puts in his pocket, keeping only*

*the weeding hook in his hand.*

CIGOLANI: You'll see, we'll find something to eat there.

*Cigolani goes off screen to right while Dale covers him with the submachine gun.*

*(Wipe to right)*

*Cigolani walks along the bank of a canal toward Casal Madalena (LS). Music fades.*   63:109-4"13

*(Dissolve to . . .*

*(Inside Casal Madalena, TQ)*   64:147-6"3

*Some peasants are sitting around the table. Looking through the glass door, one of the men sees Cigolani approaching and gets up to open the door (camera adjusts slightly left).*

PEASANT: Here's Cigolani.

OTHERS: Oh, Cigolani, come on in!

*Cigolani enters, looks around to see who is there, then takes the pistol from his pants pocket and lays it on the table.*

PEASANTS: Hello!

CIGOLANI: Hello, folks, what's new?

*(A peasant seated at the table with a bottle of wine in front of him, CU; also shot 68)*   65:34-1"10

PEASANT: The Germans were here yesterday.

*(Cigolani standing by the table, MCU; a woman is behind him.)*   66:132-5"12

CIGOLANI: Let them look. I'm not afraid of them. You
    people know I've got the Americans hidden?

*(Cigolani leaning against the table, TQ; the seated*   67:255-10″15
*peasant is at margin of frame, with three others beside*
*him.)*

PEASANT: Yes, yes.

CIGOLANI: It's been three days since we've lit a fire. The
    Germans would've seen the smoke.

PEASANT: They've got sentinels all over the place!

CIGOLANI, *gesturing broadly to emphasize his words*: And
    they're hunting us hard out there.

PEASANT: Hmm, hmm . . .

CIGOLANI: Would you have something for me to eat?

PEASANT: Just what we've got—a little polenta.    68:51-2″3

WOMAN: We could cook up a couple of eels.    69:238-9″22

CIGOLANI, *turning to the woman*: That'd be good. *He*
    *points outside.* I've got a friend outside, a good
    fellow, an American. Can I call him in?

PEASANT: Sure, call him in.

*The peasant stands up, and everyone goes to the door to*
*welcome the newcomer (camera pans left with them).*

*Cigolani comes outside the farmhouse, followed by the*   70:64-2″16
*others (TQ; camera pans right).*

CIGOLANI, *shouting and motioning to Dale*: Hey! Hey!

*Music begins.*

*In the distance, Dale climbs onto the canal bank and*   71:119-4″23
*starts toward the house. (ELS)*

*(Dissolve to . . .*

*(Cigolani and Dale going toward the house, MS; camera*   72:264-11″
*tracks out in front of them and then pans left.)*

*They come up to the group of peasants in front of the house. Music fades.*

CIGOLANI: We can go in and eat.

PEASANT, *to another peasant*: Go get some eels.

*Dale and Cigolani enter the house as the peasant goes off to the left.*

*(Dissolve to . . .*

*(Inside Casal Madalena, TQ)*                    73:703-29"7

*Cigolani sits down and is served by the woman, who is carrying a crying baby. Dale puts his gun down by the fireplace, takes off his jacket, and looks at the child.*

DALE: You've got a lot of mosquito bites there, youngster. I've got something for that.

*He gets up to put his jacket on a chair as a peasant serves him. Dale takes a small bottle from his pants and hands it to the peasant woman, warning her to hide it.*

DALE, *in Italian*: On his face. . . . *In English*: You ought to be careful with it though. *In Italian*: Hide it! Hide it!

*Dale sits down opposite Cigolani at the table (camera pans slightly right) and begins to eat.*

*(Outside Casal Madalena, HF)*                    74:197-8"5

*A peasant is standing on a bridge over a canal. He turns to another peasant.*

FIRST PEASANT: How many?

SECOND PEASANT: Take eight or ten—as many as you want.

*The peasant dips a fish net into a straw basket anchored in the water.*

*The net scoops up some small eels and deposits them in a small basket. (CU)*     75:136-5″16

*(Inside Casal Madalena, TQ)*     76:336-14″

*Dale eats heartily. The peasant enters and places the basket on the table (camera adjusts slightly left toward him). He takes out an eel and cuts off its head.*

*(Dissolve to . . .*

*(Riva Grande, MS)*     77:321-13″9

*Two partisan sentries, lying in the grass, notify the others of Dale's and Cigolani's return.*

FIRST PARTISAN: Here they are!

SECOND PARTISAN: They're coming!

*Dale and Cigolani make their way up the small slope and down into the hollow where the other partisans are stationed with the radio (camera pans downward with them). They are carrying bags and bottles of wine. (WF)*

*Dale joins the others. (HF)*     78:57-2″9

RADIOMAN, *to Dale:* I've gotten confirmation for the drop.

*Dale and Cigolani finish setting down their supplies.*     79:60-2″12

DALE*: Ah, that's good!

*(Fade-out)*

*(The lagoon at night, LS; several shadowy figures can be glimpsed through the darkness.) Sound of airplane engines is heard through shot 83.*     80:127-5″7

*(The clear night sky, LS)*     81:68-2″20

*(The lagoon, LS)*     82:284-11″20

DALE: What time is it?

PARTISANS: Cigolani, Cigolani, the signals!

CIGOLANI: Light the fires, boys! The signals!

*Two fires flare up in the dark.*

PARTISAN: Hey, there, the signals!

*Sound of a plane is heard in the clear night sky (LS).*     83:77-3″5
*Something falls into the sea.*

CIGOLANI: Put out the fires!

*A shadowy figure runs toward the fire and begins to*     84:181-7″13
*throw water on it. (LS)*

PARTISAN: Douse the fire! Tell him to douse the fire!

*Coming on screen from left and going off on right, a*     85:204-8″12
*shadowy figure runs through the shallow water, searching*
*for the supplies dropped by the plane. (MS)*

*(Several shadowy figures near the lagoon, LS; the fires*     86:158-6″14
*are out.)*

DALE: Did you pick up anything?

ALAN *(off screen):* Not a damn thing!

DALE: Well, look around!

*A shadowy figure runs toward the left through the*     87:283-11″19
*shallow water. He stops to answer, gesturing broadly.*
*(MS)*

CIGOLANI *(off screen):* You didn't find anything?

PARTISAN: Nothing, nothing!

CIGOLANI *(off screen):* Look better! *Gunfire is heard.*
    Douse the fire!

*(The partisans huddling around the dead fire, LS)*     88:222-9″6

DALE: Alan! Alan!

CIGOLANI: Damn! They're shooting at Casal Madalena!

*(Shorter view of previous shot, MS)*  89:161-6"17

PARTISAN: Casal Madalena?

CIGOLANI: You think they found out we went there?

DALE: Damn! The Jerries figured we were there!

*(The lagoon, LS)*  90:122-5"2

ALAN *(off screen)*: Cigolani! Cigolani!

CIGOLANI: What is it?

ALAN* *(off screen)*: All of you go to Pancirli and wait there!

CIGOLANI: To Pancirli, boys!

*(The empty lagoon, LS)*  91:282-11"18

PARTISAN: Back to the houses! Keep your eyes open! Let's go!

*Coming on screen from left, Dale calls Alan softly. Both run off screen to left.*

DALE: Alan, Alan, come with me!

*(Dissolve to . . .*

*(Casal Madalena, WF)*  92:62-2"14

*Dale and Alan make their way along the canal bank toward the farmhouse. They stop as they hear the sound of a child crying.*

*Weeping, a child wanders among the dead bodies of his family, scattered along the bank in front of the farmhouse. A dog is also wandering from corpse to corpse. (LS)*  93:185-7"17

*Dale and Alan stop in horror as they see what has happened (TQ; then toward the camera, to HF).* 94:123-5″3

*(The dog and the child wandering among the corpses, LS; camera tracks slowly with the child as he comes closer.)* 95:212-8″20

CHILD, *crying*: Mama . . . Mama. . . .

*Dale and Alan go forward and off screen to left. (HF)* 96:70-2″22

*(Camera tracks along bank until crying child is cut off, MS)* 97:194-8″2

*(Fade-out)*

*(Pancirli area the next day, WF)* 98:48-2″

*A group of partisans and the three Americans, in their skiffs, watch a dogfight among planes in the air above.*

*(Two planes swooping low over the lagoon, strafing, then veering upward, ELS)* 99:177-7″9

PARTISAN: Look, boys, the English planes are strafing Scardovari!

*(One plane twisting through the sky, ELS)* 100:54-2″6

*(Another plane twisting through the sky, ELS)* 101:48-2″

DAN, *pointing up*: Hey! That plane up there! It's on fire! It's falling! 102:115-4″19

*Dale shades his eyes to see better.*

*(A plane sweeping low over the canebrake, falling, ELS; camera pans left, following the plane almost into CU.)* 103:164-6″20

*Seeing that the plane is going to crash nearby, Dale decides to move.* 104:196-8″4

DALE: It crashed over there! *In Italian*: Quick, let's go! Come on, hurry!

*The three boats with the partisans and the American soldiers push off from the bank and go off screen to left. Music begins.*

*(Wipe to left)*

*The men disembark near a farmhouse, on a bank divid-ing the canal from the open sea. While some pull the skiffs up onto the bank, the others run along the sea side (camera pans left with them) toward the fallen plane. (LS)*    105:149-6″5

*The partisans run along the bank waving their arms, whistling, and shouting to the fliers (camera pans left with them).*    106:60-2″12

*The plane is still afloat but starting to burn. Two fliers perched atop it answer the partisans' shouts. (LS)*    107:54-2″6

*(RA; the farmhouse seen from the sea, with the partisans on the bank waving their arms at the two fliers, LS)*    108:52-2″4

*Dale, Cigolani, and a few other partisans separate from the main group (camera pans right). Dale gives orders to Alan and Dan, who remain behind.*    109:326-13″14

DALE: Get back to the houses and tell the radioman to arrange for another drop tonight!

*Dale goes to the boats and boards one, which immediately pulls away from the bank.*

*(Dissolve to . . .*

*(Dale's boat coming on screen from left and approaching the two fliers on the floating wreck, MS)*    110:688-28″16

DALE: Hello! Hello! Anybody get hurt? Are you all right?

ENGLISH FLIER: Yes, yes! Are you American?

DALE: Yes, I'm an American.

ENGLISH FLIER: Who are these fellows?

DALE: Italian partisans. We're with the OSS.

ENGLISH FLIER: Where are the Jerries?

DALE: They're all over the place!

ENGLISH FLIER: Any chance to get out of here?

DALE: Not a chance! Not a chance to get out of here!

*The two fliers board a boat manned by one partisan. The boats immediately turn about and head back to the shore.*

*(Dissolve to . . .*

*(The two boats returning to shore, LS; camera pans down-* 111:762-
31″18

*ward and to right.)*

ALAN *(off screen)*: Hi!

DAN *(off screen)*: Hello!

ENGLISH FLIER, *to Dale*: Who are all these people here?

DALE: They're Italian partisans too.

PARTISAN *(off screen)*: Cigolani, were there just those two?

CIGOLANI: Yes, just those two. But they're English, not American.

PARTISAN *(off screen)*: Better than nothing. They're all wet.

CIGOLANI: We'll have to get them something warm.

*The two boats touch the shore. The Englishmen (WF) and Dale get out (camera pans upward and to right, following them) and climb onto the bank, aided by the partisans.*

PARTISANS: Come on, give me your hand, up you go!

ENGLISHMEN: How are you?

PARTISAN: Come on, there's one more.

*The two fliers head toward the farmhouse, going off screen to left. Dale follows them. Music ends.*

*Cigolani and the partisan pull their skiffs away from the shore, circle around the bank on which the Pancirli farmhouse stands, and enter the cove in front of it. (MS)* 112:168-7″

PARTISAN *(off screen)*: Did the plane sink, Cigolani?

CIGOLANI: Yes, it sank.

PARTISAN *(off screen)*: Could you get anything?

CIGOLANI: Not a thing!

PARTISAN *(off screen)*: Nothing at all?

CIGOLANI: Nothing! Nothing!

*The two fliers, flanked by Dan and Alan, are followed by*     113:664-27″16
*the partisans (WF; toward the camera). They turn the*
*corner of the house (camera pans right and tracks after*
*them).*

DAN: How are you feeling now? All right?

FIRST ENGLISH FLIER: A bit wet!

SECOND ENGLISH FLIER: Say, how were you fellows hit?

*As they are about to enter the house, Dale comes up (TQ)*
*and stops them.*

DALE: Hold it up! Hold it up! You can't stay here! I've got
to get you some blankets and some warm clothes!
*To Alan*: You take care of that, will you? Blankets,
oilskins, and raincoats for them.

ALAN*, *to partisans*: Go get them some oilskins.

*Some partisans come on screen from right with large*
*blankets, which they throw over the fliers' shoulders.*

DALE: Get these boats ready! We'd better get out of here
in a hurry! Tell you why we can't stay here—we had
a plane come in for a food and ammo drop last
night, but the Germans spotted it and we lost
everything.

ENGLISH FLIERS: Have you got some fresh supplies in,
then?

DALE: Not a thing! Not a thing! Everything went to sea.
*Dale looks in through the farmhouse doorway.*
*He asks, in Italian,* Transmitted?

*In the farmhouse (TQ) two partisans are at the radio set*     114:64-2″16
*on the table.*

RADIOMAN: Already transmitted.

DALE *(off screen)*: Let's go in these boats right away!

PARTISAN *(off screen)*: Already transmitted.

*The radioman removes his earphones and, with the other man's help, begins to take the radio apart.*

*The Englishmen, the three Americans, and several partisans clamber down the bank and board the skiffs (camera tracks right and pans downward).*

115:802-
33″10

FIRST ENGLISH FLIER: Where are we going? What are we going to do?

SECOND ENGLISH FLIER: If you get us some civvies I'll get back on my own!

DALE: You know if you get caught in civvies you'll get shot, don't you?

SECOND ENGLISH FLIER: Well, that's better than staying in this place, isn't it?

DALE: All right, then I'll send you over to Popsky's private army and you can stay over there if you don't like it here!

FIRST ENGLISH FLIER: Where are the Germans concentrated?

DALE: Oh, they're all over! Come on, let's get out!

*The boats pull away from the bank and head for the mouth of the inlet formed by the bank on which the farmhouse stands (camera pans downward). The two radiomen run out of the house with their equipment and call to the remaining partisans.*

RADIOMAN: Quick, boys, or the Germans'll get us!

*(Dissolve to . . .*

*(Skiffs moving along a canal bordered by high cane, LS;*    116:281-
*camera panning right with them up to the entrance to*    11″17
*another canal; music begins)*

PARTISAN, *signaling to the others*: Ssh!

CIGOLANI: Who's there?

ENGLISH SOLDIER *(off screen)*: Popsky.

CIGOLANI: It's all right.

DALE: Who's that over there?

ENGLISH SOLDIER *(off screen)*: Who are you anyway?

DALE: I'm Dale, OSS.

*(Two skiffs from Popsky's band moving toward Dale's*    117:98-4″2
*along another canal, LS)*

ENGLISH SOLDIER: I'm one of the Popsky men. The
    Germans are coming up the river now in a gunboat!

DALE *(off screen)*: How are you fixed for . . .

*Dale stops to talk with the English soldier while the boats*    118:36-1″12
*file along behind him. (WF)*

DALE: . . . ammunition?

*The English soldier has two partisans with him. (MCU)*    119:54-2″6

ENGLISH SOLDIER: Not much. I've only a couple of mags
    left.

DALE *(CU)*: So it's better if we take off for the beach down    120:103-4″7
    there. On the sand there's a better setup for defense.

ENGLISH SOLDIER *(MCU)*: Okay, I'll come with you.    121:30-1″6

DALE, *jerking his head (CU)*: Okay, let's go!    122:37-1″13

*The boats of the two groups move gently to and fro with*    123:525-
    21″21

*the weak currents. The oarsmen try to stay as low as possible. The others are lying low in the boats. (MS)*

PARTISAN: Boys, the Germans are on the Po.

CIGOLANI: Boys, we've got to scatter and get to the sea quick.

VOICES: Quick, boys! Keep down! Keep down!

*The boats begin to scatter, going off screen to left and to right.*

*(Dissolve to . . .*

*(Three large German boats coming slowly up the river in single file, ELS)*     124:71-2″23

*(The prow of the first German boat, with several manned machine guns, MS; camera pans left.)*     125:69-2″21

*(The second German boat, LS)*     126:65-2″17

*(The third German boat, slightly smaller than the others, LS)*     127:65-2″17

*(Beach, LS)*     128:221-9″5

*The partisans draw their skiffs up into a cove, jump out, and scatter among the sand dunes (camera pans right with them). Gunfire is heard.*

*(Lagoon, LS; the last two German boats seen from the stern of the first, where a machine gun has opened fire)*     129:55-2″7

*On the beach (MS) the partisans, led by Dale, come on screen from left, stop, and return the fire.*     130:66-2″18

*The surface of the water in the lagoon is raked by the German machine-gun fire. (LS)*     131:130-5″10

*(The last two German boats seen from the stern of the*

*first, LS)*

A German officer *(TQ)* directs the fire of the two gunners    132:46-1″22
in the stern of the first boat.

The shore where the partisans landed is raked by the    133:64-2″16
German fire. *(ELS)*

One German gunner inserts a fresh magazine. *(TQ)*    134:65-2″17

The partisans leave their skiffs behind and disappear    135:44-1″20
behind the dunes.

The two German machine gunners, seen from behind,    136:45-1″21
continue to fire. *(WF)*

The dune concealing the partisans is raked by German    137:66-2″18
fire. *(LS)*

A gunner reloads his machine gun. *(WF)*    138:31-1″7

The partisans answer the German fire from behind the    139:63-2″15
dune. *(LS)*

Dale *(CU)* fires another shot, then begins to retreat.    140:56-2″8

A group of German soldiers runs down the beach. *(LS)*    141:66-2″18

Another group of Germans advances at a run, skirting a    142:159-6″15
marshy area *(ELS)*. A partisan appears on screen from
right *(CU)*. He fires and kills a German.

Two German soldiers fire a machine gun from atop a    143:17-0″17
dune. *(WF)*

Two partisans in a skiff are felled by German fire. *(MS)*    144:29-1″5

Three partisans retreat while continuing to fire. One is    145:94-3″22
hit and falls into a puddle of water. *(MS)*

A German *(CU)* appears on screen (from bottom margin    146:26-1″2 *of frame), firing his rifle.*

*A partisan, hit from behind, falls to the ground. (MS)*     147:31-1″7

*The machine gunners cease fire and motion to other German soldiers to advance. The soldiers pass them by and go off screen to left. (WF)*     148:120-5″

*The partisans flee, scattering in all directions. (MS)*     149:165-6″21

*Two Germans fire a mortar. (WF)*     150:75-3″3

*A German hurls a grenade. (WF)*     151:26-1″2

*A German fires his rifle (MCU) and goes off screen to left.*     152:33-1″9

*A German officer throws a grenade (CU), then shouts to the partisans to surrender.*     153:46-1″22

GERMAN OFFICER: Hände hoch! [Hands up!]

*A partisan sits down beside a fallen comrade, reloads his rifle, and sets the muzzle under his chin. (WF)*     154:175-7″7

*Another German officer (CU) comes on screen from right,*   155:54-2"6
*calls on the partisans to surrender, and then goes off*
*screen to left.*

GERMAN OFFICER: Hände hoch! [Hands up!]

*The partisan pulls the trigger and kills himself. (WF)*   156:29-1"5

*Dale starts to reload his gun but finds he is out of*   157:201-8"9
*ammunition and angrily hurls it to the ground behind*
*him. (TQ)*

*The English soldier starts to reload his tommy gun but*   158:172-7"4
*finds he is out of ammunition. Behind him, the partisans*
*are fleeing. Resigned, the Englishman lays down his gun*
*and waits. (TQ)*

*Dale, hanging his head, comes on screen (TQ; toward the*   159:72-3"
*camera).*

*The English soldier lights a cigarette. (TQ)*   160:94-3"22

*A German officer congratulates his troops. (TQ)*   161:214-8"22

GERMAN OFFICER: Gut! Gehe ihr! [Good! Let's go!] *He*
     *goes off screen to left.*

*In the background (LS) the prisoners come forward.*

*The Allied soldiers are brought forward by German*   162:186-7"18
*soldiers. (MS)*

*German soldiers bring forward the partisans in a separate*   163:157-6"13
*group. (LS)*

*(Dissolve to . . .*

*(Outside the Pancirli farmhouse at night, MS)*   164:137-5"17

*Cigolani's body hangs from a roof beam. The other*
*partisans are tied and huddled together beneath his feet,*

*guarded by German soldiers.*

*(Music ends)*

*(Inside Pancirli, MS)*                                    165:1380-
57"12

*A German soldier (TQ) paces in front of the group of Allied prisoners. A German officer enters the room (camera pans left to him), removes his hat, and sets it down on the table, on which there are two bottles and a glass. He speaks English to the Allied prisoners.*

GERMAN OFFICER: Do you want to have a drink?

*He serves one of the English fliers, then returns to the table, takes another of the cups that a soldier has brought in the meantime, and offers a drink to the Englishman from Popsky's band.*

GERMAN OFFICER: Have a little drink?

*He returns to the table and pours himself a drink, then sits down (back to camera at right margin of frame). The prisoners ignore his attempts at conversation; they smoke silently, heads lowered. Even the two who have accepted drinks are lost in thought and seem to have forgotten the glasses in their hands.*

GERMAN OFFICER: It is cold. In my country it's even colder. We have big stoves. I suppose you have them too. *Skol!* In my country most of the houses are made out of wood. They are warmer but they burn! They burn easily!

*Unnerved by the prisoners' silence, the German officer begins to pace up and down the room, then returns to the table.*

GERMAN OFFICER: Do you think you can make me feel uneasy? We Germans are not afraid. Nor are we worried. The war we are fighting means life or death for us.

*(Dan and one of the fliers listening in amazement, TQ)* 166:219-9″3

GERMAN OFFICER *(off screen)*: We are building a new civilization to last a thousand years. But to do that it is necessary to destroy . . .

*(Dale, Alan, the English soldier, and the second English flier listening, TQ)* 167:275-11″11

GERMAN OFFICER *(off screen)*: . . . everything before us! The Germans will do this! We will keep our promise to the world, at any cost, because this is our mission!

DALE, *interrupting him brusquely (CU)*: What are you going to do with these partisans you've got tied up like animals out there? 168:65-2″17

GERMAN OFFICER *(CU)*: No international law protects the partisans. They are not considered soldiers. They are just outlaws! 169:114-4″18

DALE *(CU)*: What about the two San Marco men? They're from the regular Italian Army! 170:65-2″17

GERMAN OFFICER *(CU)*: No, we don't recognize Badoglio's government. 171:56-2″8

DALE *(CU)*: Well, what are you going to do with them? 172:26-1″2

GERMAN OFFICER *(CU)*: I'm expecting orders from my headquarters. 173:51-2″3

*(Outside Pancirli, MS; camera pans from Cigolani's body to the partisans lying on the ground.)* 174:1085-45″5

*A German guard paces back and forth in front of them.*

PARTISAN: What'll they do to us?

PARTISAN: They'll kill us!

PARTISAN: You think they'd kill Cigolani and not us?

PARTISAN: They'll kill us too.

PARTISAN, *singing softly*: "Poor Giulia, you're dead

now. . . ."

PARTISAN: My folks'll never know what happened to me.

PARTISAN: He pissed on me like a whore!

*(Dissolve to . . .*

*(The shore near Pancirli, MS)*                    175:164-6"20

*Six partisans, hands bound behind their backs, are lined up on board one of the German boats, facing the water.*

*A German soldier checks their ropes one by one.*

*The Allied soldiers are on shore, guarded by the Germans*    176:41-1"17
*(MS). The German officer waves an order to the soldier on the boat.*

*The German soldier pushes the first partisan into the*    177:50-2"2
*water.*

*Hearing the partisan's scream, Dale and one of the*    178:153-6"9

*English fliers turn to see what the Germans are doing.
They run toward the boat to try to stop them (camera
pans left).*

DALE: Stop!

*The German officer gives another order, and the two men
are shot down.*

*The German soldier pushes another partisan off the boat.*   179:50-2″2

*The bodies of the partisans break the calm surface of*   180:656-27″8
*the water for a moment, then disappear beneath it. (MS)*

SPEAKER: This happened in the winter of 1944. At the
    beginning of spring, the war was over.

*(Music)*

*(Fade-out)*

## THE END

# Germany—Year Zero

This film is dedicated to the memory of Romano
Roberto Rossellini, Roberto Rossellini's son

# Credits

Presented by La Cineteca Nazionale

Written, produced, and directed by Roberto Rossellini for Tevere Film, in collaboration with Salvo d'Angelo Productions

Screenplay by Roberto Rossellini in collaboration with Max Colpet

Photography by Robert Julliard

Music by Renzo Rossellini, conducted by Edoardo Micucci

Sound by Kurt Doubrawsky

*Cast:*

| | |
|---|---|
| *Edmund Koeler* | Edmund Meschke |
| *His father* | Ernst Pittschau |
| *His sister Eva* | Ingetraud Hinzf |
| *His brother Karl Heinz* | Franz Grüger |
| *Herr Enning* | Erich Gühne |

*(Fade-in; music begins)*

*(A devastated Berlin street, MS; pan tilts up along a*   1
*telephone pole from wet street to bombed-out building.)*

*(Dissolve to . . .*

*(MS; pan right and down along bombed-out buildings,*   2
*FS)*

*(LS, continuing the previous shot; camera tracks right*   3
*along bombed-out buildings; credit titles appear and*
*disappear with wipes.)*

*(Music ends; fade-out)*

*(Legend)*   4

*When an ideology strays*
*from the eternal laws of morality and of Christian charity,*
*which form the basis of men's lives,*
*it must end as criminal madness.*

*It contaminates even the natural prudence*
*of a child, who is swept along from one*
*horrendous crime to another, equally grave,*
*in which, with the ingenuousness of innocence,*
*he thinks to find release from guilt.*

*(Fade-out)*

*(Bombed-out buildings, LS; camera tracks right)*   5
*Music begins.*

SPEAKER *(off screen)*: This film was shot in Berlin in the
summer of 1947. It is intended to be simply an objec-
tive, true-to-life picture of this enormous, half-
destroyed city, in which three and a half million

people are carrying on a frightful, desperate existence almost without realizing it. They live in tragedy as if it were their natural element, but out of exhaustion, not through strength of mind or faith. This film is not an act of accusation against the German people, nor yet a defense of them. It is simply a presentation of the facts. But if anyone who has seen the story of Edmund Koeler comes to realize that something must be done . . .

*(Wipe to right)*

*(LS; camera pans almost 360° to right over bombed-out*    6
*buildings, ending with the ruins of the Chancellery in the foreground.)*

SPEAKER *(off screen)*: . . . that German children must be taught to love life again, then the efforts of those who made this film will have been amply rewarded.

*(Fade-out)*

*(LS; camera pans to right continuing the previous shot*    7
*and showing a part of the city less devastated by bombing, and ending with a park in the foreground; tilt down to show a cemetery among the trees of the park.)*

*(Dissolve to . . .*

*(Cemetery, MS; camera pans right.)*    8

*Three old women (WF) are digging a grave. Two other women carrying tools pass by (TQ; camera pans right to follow them).*

FIRST WOMAN: If you work for the Americans you get fifty grams of margarine too.

SECOND WOMAN: What good is that? We'll all die anyway.

THIRD WOMAN: I'm worn out! When'll they give us our hour off?

FIRST WOMAN: If you're tired of living, go jump in that hole there.

*(Pan continues until it includes the foreman, TQ)*

*The foreman is heading for the grave that Edmund and a man are digging. (LS)*

FOREMAN: What's going on, everybody's worn out this morning? You've been working three hours and you're already dead on your feet! *(Pan ends) He takes out a tape measure and turns to the man excavating the grave.* Can't you get it through your head that the hole has to be two and a half meters by seventy-five?

MAN: It looks all right to me.

FOREMAN: If you don't want to work, get out of here!

MAN: You bawl me out, but I'm the one that's doing the work here. The kid hasn't done a thing.

FIRST WOMAN: What's that kid doing here?

*The foreman lays his hand on Edmund's shoulder but the boy, pretending not to notice, continues to dig.*

FOREMAN: How old are you?

EDMUND, *turning to the foreman (MCU)*: I'm fifteen!       9

FIRST WOMAN *(off screen)*: No, he isn't!

*The man climbs out of the grave and points to Edmund.*

MAN: If he's more than thirteen, I'll hang.

*The first woman comes on from left and lays her hand on Edmund's head to see him better.*

FIRST WOMAN: You liar! I know you! You went to school with my son! You're only twelve!

FOREMAN, *clutching Edmund's shoulder*: So that's the way it is, is it?

*Edmund pulls away and steps to the left away from the adults (camera tracks with him).*

EDMUND: Leave me alone! What's it to you if I work?

FOREMAN: Let's see your work permit.

EDMUND: I've got a permit . . .

FOREMAN: Where is it?

EDMUND: . . . but I forgot it at home. *He picks up the bag he has left on a tombstone and runs away toward the rear.*

FIRST WOMAN *(off screen)*: It's not true! These kids are all crooks and liars.

SECOND WOMAN *(off screen)*: They take food out of the mouths of people who have a right to work.

MAN *(off screen)*: Then they go sell their ration cards on the black market.

FOREMAN *(off screen)*: Get back to work now!

SECOND WOMAN *(off screen)*: Fine business!

*(Dissolve to . . .*

*(Street, MS)*                                                          10

*Edmund runs along a half-destroyed street, then stops (in TQ; another rubble-filled street is in the background). He places the bag between his legs in order to pull on his sweater, meanwhile gazing intently to the left.*

*(As seen by Edmund, a group of people in the middle of*    11
*the street, MS, speaking in several languages)*

*Without putting on the sweater, Edmund runs off screen*    12
*to right. (TQ)*

*The people are gathered around the carcass of a horse*    13
*Some leave while others come up. Edmund comes on*

*from left just as a man with a knife bends over the horse to quarter it. (MS)*

*(Insert: man cutting around the animal's hoof)* 14

*Several hands touch the amateur butcher as if to pull* 15
*him away. A policeman steps in and pulls the man to his feet. Edmund makes his way through the crowd, pulls the policeman's arm. (MS)*

EDMUND: What is it? Let me see too.

POLICEMAN: What're you doing here? Go on home, kid.

*He leads the boy out of the group (TQ; pan follows them to right).*

*Another policeman comes up, and the two officers break* 16
*up the crowd, using force in some cases. (MS)*

*Edmund walks on screen from left (LS; camera pans with* 17
*him to right, the devastated city in the background). He stops in front of a policeman directing traffic, just as a tractor passes by hauling a load of coal.*

*Edmund stands on tiptoe to see better. (Wide HF)* 18

*Some coal slips off as the vehicle joggles over the pocked* 19
*road. Edmund rushes to pick up some lumps, behind the policeman's back, then runs off screen to right (camera pans briefly to right).*

POLICEMAN: Don't you touch that coal, hear? Get out of
here!

*Edmund makes his way through a mass of rubble (LS;* 20
*track and pan to left). He stops (in TQ) and looks around to get his bearings, then starts off again (pan and track with him to left, in HF, down along a street, LS).*

*(Dissolve to . . .*

*(Edmund walking along, HF; camera tracks out in front* 21

*of him and then pans to right)*

*He nears his own building, waits for a tractor to roll by, then runs across the street (short tilt up to take in the building, LS).*

*(Dissolve to . . .*

*(Hall and stairway of Edmund's building, LS)*    22

*Edmund runs into the building, crosses the devastated hallway, and goes up the stairs (HF; the camera, on the landing, shoots down and slightly left, then tilts up as it pans to right). He goes up another flight of stairs and rings a doorbell. (MS)*

*(Entrance to the apartment where the Koelers and others*    23
*live, TQ)*

*The numerous occupants of the apartment have all gathered around the inspector from the electric company, who is up on a stool, having just read the meter.*

INSPECTOR: Well, you've run up ten kilowatt-hours more than last month.

*As the bell rings, Fräulein Rademaker, the daughter of the owner of the apartment, crosses to open the door (TQ; track to right). Edmund enters.*

EDMUND: What's up?

FRÄULEIN RADEMAKER: They're checking the electric meter.

*Edmund comes inside and makes his way through the group toward his sister Eva (camera tracks forward). Meanwhile the inspector steps down from the stool (CU, his back to camera).*

INSPECTOR: You've gone over your quota. You'll have to pay the fine.

RADEMAKER *(off screen)*: I told you so!

*(Camera pulls back to take in the whole group.)*

BLANKE, *one of the women tenants, to inspector*: But look, we're twelve people living here!

RADEMAKER: And five different families, understand?

INSPECTOR: The law can make no exceptions. I'm sorry, but I have to fine you.

*He goes off screen to right, followed by several of the tenants, while Rademaker goes over to Eva.*

RADEMAKER: Have you got any cigarettes?

EVA: No, I've given them all away.

RADEMAKER: Damn it!

BLANKE: I still have three.

RADEMAKER, *to Edmund*: What about you?

EDMUND: I don't have any more.

RADEMAKER: Didn't you bring anything home?

EDMUND: Just some coal.

*As the inspector is about to leave, Rademaker approaches him (camera tracks to right). He hands over the cigarettes he has collected and opens the door for the inspector.*

INSPECTOR: Well, I'll mark the extra amount down on next month's reading.

RADEMAKER: Thanks. Good-bye.

*Rademaker closes the door and comes back to the others (camera tracks left after him, to HF).*

RADEMAKER: That's what I get for having taken you all in! Last month the gas, now the electricity!

TILGHER *(off screen)*: When the law forces you to take so many people in, it's no wonder!

RADEMAKER: I warn you all that from now on things are going to be different around here, starting with no hot water. It's a luxury.

BLANKE: You don't expect us to go around like pigs, do you?

FRAU RADEMAKER: I always wash in cold water, and I defy anyone to say I'm not clean!

FRÄULEIN RADEMAKER: I warn you, Papa, that I'm not giving up my hair drier!

RADEMAKER, *to his daughter*: Keep quiet, stupid!

*Eva pulls Edmund away. They go off screen to left.*

TILGHER *(off screen)*: It's the Koelers' fault.

*Edmund goes into a room, followed by Eva (TQ; camera pans and tracks to left). Upon hearing Rademaker's words, he starts back out again.*          24

RADEMAKER *(off screen)*: That old mummy, I'll put him away myself if he doesn't kick the bucket soon.

*Eva holds her brother back and pulls him away.*

EVA: Let him talk, Edmund, don't answer him. Come on, let's go!

*Two women come up to her. One, Thilde, is pregnant; the other is a former expatriate.*

THILDE: What's going on?

EVA, *reassuringly*: Nothing, nothing.

*Without leaving the room, Thilde moves toward the group in the hall, which can be seen through the doorway (WF; camera pans and tracks back to right).*

TILGHER *(off screen)*: He stays up all night with the light on.

RADEMAKER *(off screen)*: Five families have to suffer on account of one useless old man. Poultices, hot-water bottles, *(on screen)* all kinds of problems. This place has gotten to be impossible to live in.

*(The group continues its discussion, TQ)*  25

THILDE: But look, have some heart. He's very sick.

RADEMAKER: One's sick, another's pregnant. But I've got my own troubles.

EXPATRIATE: But I—I know that when—

FRAU RADEMAKER: What do you know? You were abroad when hell broke loose here.

*The expatriate turns away and goes off while Frau Rademaker is still talking.*

*The group breaks up (resume on expatriate turning).*  26
*The Rademakers head toward the rear. The expatriate comes back to Thilde, who has been watching from the doorway (camera pans slightly to left). They both go off screen to left.*

THILDE: Is he mad at me?

EXPATRIATE: No, don't pay any attention to him.

*(The Koelers' room, CU)*  27

KOELER: What's going on, children?

*Edmund kisses his father (camera pulls back) and sits down beside him.*

EVA *(off screen)*: The electricity man was here. We've run up too much.

KOELER: Ah, they'll cut off our light too now.

EVA *(off screen)*: No, we persuaded him to overlook it.

KOELER: Ah!

*Eva takes Edmund's arm and pulls him away (camera tracks sideways with pan into CU).*

EVA *(off screen)*: You're filthy, as usual. *(on screen)* Did you get the Number Two Card?

EDMUND: No. They chased me away because I'm not fifteen yet.

*Eva takes Edmund's bag and goes off screen to left.*

KOELER *(off screen)*: I knew that would happen! *(on screen)* But you know, I'm glad you won't be going there any more. It wasn't any kind of work for a boy your age.

*Edmund returns to his father, who takes his hand (camera tracks with him until it reveals a cot behind the headboard of Koeler's bed). Karl Heinz is sitting on the cot. Eva is working in the background.*

EDMUND: But it would have given us something more to eat, for Karl Heinz too. *He goes toward his brother.* (WF)

KOELER: Did you hear that, Karl Heinz?

*At his father's veiled reproof, Karl Heinz stands up. Music begins.*

*Karl Heinz goes to sit at the foot of the father's bed (MCU; camera tilts slightly upward and tracks right). He seems indifferent and skeptical.*    28

KOELER *(off screen)*: My boy, you can see that poor Edmund, at his age, can't possibly provide for us all . . .

*(Koeler, MCU from slightly above; also shots 31, 33, 35, 37)*    29

KOELER: . . . he's still a child. *He takes off his glasses.* But what do you do? You hide out here, and don't report in, and so you don't even get the starvation rations we do. How can four people live with only three ration cards? What can it cost you? If you report in, you can . . .

*(Karl Heinz at the foot of his father's bed, MCU)*    30

KOELER *(off screen)*: . . . work and you'll get the Number Two Card . . .

*Edmund comes on screen and looks at his brother.*

KOELER *(off screen)*: . . . and we won't have to turn to this damned black market.

KOELER: I've sacrificed everything. I've sold everything. I   31
don't feel up to it any more, it's up to you now. What
you're doing is foolish. What are you afraid of?

*(Karl Heinz and Edmund, MCU; also shots 34, 36, 38)*   32

KARL HEINZ: I don't want to end up in a concentration
camp. I've had enough! What do you want from
me anyway?

KOELER: Haven't you read the papers? They've even   33
announced it on the radio.

*Edmund sits on the edge of the bed. (CU)*

KOELER: Veterans just have to report in to the police.
You go . . .

*(off screen)* . . . to the police station like everybody   34
else, and they won't do a thing to you.

KARL HEINZ: Sure, and when I tell them what regiment I
was in and that I fought in the streets right up to
this building, you think that . . .

*(off screen)* . . . they'll just let me go?   35

*Edmund turns toward his brother.*

KOELER: But the war was still on then. Nobody could
blame you for that. You just did your duty as a
soldier.

KARL HEINZ: It's easy to talk, it's not your skin.   36

EDMUND, *moving closer to his father on the bed*: Suppose   37
that what the papers say is just a trap?

KOELER: But what are you all afraid of? Have we had
any . . .

*(off screen)* . . . trouble up to now?   38

KARL HEINZ: All right. *He rises (camera tilts slightly up).* I'll go report in. But I warn you, if they try anything on me I don't know how it'll end. *He throws himself down on his bed again (camera pans right and tracks forward).*

*Edmund gets up and approaches his brother (camera tracks with him and pans right, to TQ).*   39

EDMUND: No, Karl Heinz! You mustn't go! Stay here! We'll take care of you. I'll find another job, and Eva too. You'll see! *He goes toward Eva (camera tracks and pans right, to MCU).* Listen, Eva, we have to find some money.

EVA: Don't worry, dear, we'll do all we can to save Karl Heinz.

EDMUND, *going toward the door*: I'm going to see Herr Rademaker now. He said he had something for me to do. I'll be right back.

*Edmund goes out while Eva (MCU) goes to straighten her father's bed (CU; camera pulls back and pans left with her).*

EVA: And we've always managed so far, haven't we? Rest a bit now, Papa!

*The father lies down. Eva goes over to Karl Heinz (camera pans right and tracks with her). She kneels down to talk to him (camera tilts slightly down and tracks forward, to MCU).*

EVA: Listen, I have to talk to you alone.

KARL HEINZ: What is it?

EVA: Not here. Come into my room.

KARL HEINZ: Ah, then that informer'll see me and turn me in.

EVA: Thilde's a friend. Don't be afraid.

KARL HEINZ: Hah! These so-called victims of Nazism. We know their type.

EVA: Then come into the bathroom. No one'll see us there.

*They get up and go toward the door. Eva goes off screen to right. Karl Heinz follows and reaches her at the door (MCU; camera tracks and pans to right).*

KARL HEINZ, *whispering*: See if anybody's out there.

EVA: Come on, no one's there. Quietly!

*They go out and close the door behind them.*

*(The bathroom, MCU)* 40

*The bathroom door opens and Eva comes in, followed by Karl Heinz, who looks warily about (camera pans right and pulls back).*

EVA: Listen, Karl Heinz, I haven't said anything for so long because I didn't want to talk in front of Papa. You know he's very sick and mustn't be upset at all.

*Eva and Karl Heinz cross back and forth (from MCU to CU), sometimes together and sometimes alone, seen from front and from back. The camera follows them, picking up the one and then the other during their heated discussion. Karl Heinz leans against the wall, then sits down on the edge of the bathtub as Eva moves to his former position against the wall.*

KARL HEINZ: I didn't start it. I want to be let alone, understand?

EVA: Because you're a coward . . .

KARL HEINZ: Maybe so.

EVA: . . . and a terrible egotist. You don't care where we get our food just as long as it's there.

KARL HEINZ: Was I the one who sent Edmund out to work?

EVA: Ah, you don't talk! You're just hiding out! But you want to eat, you want to drink, and you don't even ask yourself where I go every evening. The important thing is that I come back home with a couple of cigarettes for you.

KARL HEINZ: Just because I smoke them every now and then!

EVA: No, but you know very well that cigarettes are used to buy things with.

KARL HEINZ: And I should thank you for this? All the women are doing it these days!

EVA: Oh, as far as that goes, they do even worse things!

KARL HEINZ: You see?

EVA: So tell me to be a prostitute!

KARL HEINZ: Get out of here!

EVA, *regretting her words*: No, forgive me! I shouldn't have said that. *She embraces her brother.* We've both got our nerves on edge, but the situation is getting desperate. Life gets harder every day.

KARL HEINZ: You don't have to tell me that.

EVA *(off screen)*: But you understand, that child can't possibly—

KARL HEINZ: I know that too. You think I don't think about it too? You! You only talk about your own selves. All my sufferings in these years don't count?

EVA *(off screen)*: You shouldn't say that—*(on screen)*—

that's not fair. When you were dying of thirst in Africa, and dying of cold in Russia, our thoughts were always with you.

KARL HEINZ: I don't want to suffer any more, understand? I want to end it all.

EVA, *embracing him*: Don't talk like that! Maybe the worst is over. Help us to have a little hope.

*Music ends.*

*(Dissolve to . . .*

*(Eva and Thilde's room, at night, MS)*          41

*Thilde is working at a sewing machine. A little girl is in front of her. Both turn as the door, as seen in the mirror, opens.*

EXPATRIATE *(off screen)*: Gina, what are you doing here? Come in the other room.

GINA: No, Mama, I like it here.

THILDE: Let her stay, she doesn't bother me.

*The expatriate comes on screen from left and picks up Thilde's work (TQ; camera adjusts slightly right toward her).*

EXPATRIATE: But how can you work with so little light?

THILDE: We have to save electricity.

*The expatriate goes to turn on the bedside light (WF; camera tracks left with her and pans right).*

EXPATRIATE: The excess, but not the necessary. . . . You want me to give you a little help?

THILDE: No, thanks, I can do it by myself.

EXPATRIATE: I know, you're suspicious of me too, just like the rest of them!

THILDE: No I'm not!

EXPATRIATE: Here they all think I'm an informer. . . .

*The expatriate moves to the center, between Thilde and the girl (camera pans right with her). She leans against the wall.*

EXPATRIATE: But why? Because I was abroad during the war and now I've come back.

THILDE: Well, maybe because your political ideas are a little—

EXPATRIATE: No, that's not why! I'm convinced the Rade-makers hate me just because I occupy one of their rooms.

GINA: Then they'll send us away from here too, Mama?

EXPATRIATE: No, darling, we'll stay here, but keep still. *She comes over to Thilde at the sewing machine.* You sleep in Fräulein Koeler's room. I have the feeling they're good people, but they don't like me either, do they?

THILDE: It's because they're afraid someone'll turn their son in.

*Eva opens the door. She enters and approaches the bed (camera pans after her and tracks left). She watches the expatriate, who is going out of the room.*

EXPATRIATE: Come, Gina. Oh, by the way, I'll give you some of my old linens *(off screen)* that you can make into baby clothes.

THILDE: Thanks! . . . *To Eva*: Why are you against her? She's always ready to help everybody.

*Eva gathers up some clothing on the bed and starts out again (followed by pan to right).*

EVA: I don't believe in being helped by other people. Everybody has to help themselves these days.

*(The Rademakers' room, MCU)*      42
*Edmund is at left margin of frame (CU). Rademaker is sitting at a table (MCU). His daughter is combing her hair at a mirror in the background. Music begins.*

RADEMAKER: I'm certainly no monster, my boy, but keeping you people here . . .

*Edmund moves thoughtfully through the room (followed by pan to right). He stops (wide MCU). In the background, to the left, Frau Rademaker is sitting on the bed, sewing.*

RADEMAKER *(off screen)*: . . . has been quite a burden for me and you know it. And I don't see how you could help me even if you wanted to.

EDMUND: Look, couldn't I get stuff for you?

RADEMAKER *(off screen)*: What stuff? You know I'm against the black market.

*Edmund (wide MCU) walks toward Frau Rademaker (camera tracks forward with him, HF).*

EDMUND: I could trade something for you.

RADEMAKER *(off screen)*: Oh, there's the exchange center for that.

FRAU RADEMAKER *(MCU)*: But they're a bunch of crooks there. Why don't you give him the scale to sell?

FRÄULEIN RADEMAKER *(coming on screen from left, TQ)*: What?! My scale? How can I weigh myself?

RADEMAKER *(off screen)*: You keep quiet!

FRAU RADEMAKER: We've made do without more important things, dear. You can lose weight even without the scale.

FRÄULEIN RADEMAKER: This too!

*She goes off screen as Edmund and the wife approach Rademaker (camera tracks left with them).*

EDMUND *(HF)*: How much should I ask?

RADEMAKER, *to his wife (MCU)*: How much do you think we can get for it?

FRAU RADEMAKER: Oh, not less than two hundred marks.

RADEMAKER: That's too little. I want three hundred, not a bit less.

FRAU RADEMAKER: Then I could buy three sticks of butter.

EVA *(off screen)*: Edmund. . . .

*They all turn as Eva enters.*

*(Music begins)*

EVA *(TQ)*: Oh, excuse me! Edmund, dinner's getting cold, and I have to go out afterward, so hurry up.    43

*Eva comes forward (HF), then goes out, closing the door behind her.*

EDMUND *(off screen)*: All right, I'm coming.

EVA: Good night.

EDMUND: Fräulein Rademaker . . .    44

FRÄULEIN RADEMAKER: What?!

EDMUND: . . . then will you show me this scale?

FRÄULEIN RADEMAKER: Here it is.

*In her room she picks up the scale and places it on a chair. Edmund goes in (camera pans left) and begins to examine the scale (HF). Meanwhile the two adults continue their conversation, although they are aware that Edmund can hear them.*

FRAU RADEMAKER *(CU)*: Did you hear that? That sister of his goes out every night. She has no sense of shame! She's up to the same thing as all those other girls. You shouldn't allow our daughter to come into contact with such people!

RADEMAKER *(CU)*: Someday I'm going to throw all these whores right out of here!

EDMUND, *coming out of the daughter's room (CU)*: What have you got to say against my sister? And what have you got against all of us?

RADEMAKER: You shut up! And get out of here! Take the scale and don't come back here until you have the three hundred marks, hear?

EDMUND: All right, Herr Rademaker. I'll come get it tomorrow morning.

*Edmund goes off screen to left as the daughter comes toward her parents. Music ends.*

*(Entryway of apartment, MCU)*                                    45
*The door opens, and Edmund comes out (camera tracks out in front of him).*

EDMUND: Eva!

EVA *(off screen)*: What?

EDMUND: Where're you going?

*Eva is turning on the light (camera pans left to pick her up). She stops, facing her brother.*

EVA: I'm going out.

EDMUND: Tell me why you're going out.

EVA: What's the matter with you? I go out every evening. *(Camera pulls back and pans to include Blanke, as she comes forward, all dressed up.)*

EDMUND: But why do you go out every evening?

EVA: What a question! To have a little fun.

BLANKE: Come on, we have to go.

EVA: All right, I'm coming.

BLANKE: You know they're annoyed if we show up late.

*Vexed, Eva steps away from her brother, waves her friend out, then comes back to Edmund (camera tracks forward).*

EVA, *to Blanke*: Go on! Go on, I'll catch up with you.

EDMUND: Eva, I don't want you to go out every night.

EVA: But, Edmund, what's got into you? What are you

thinking of? What is it, my baby? Look into my eyes—*(she embraces him and kisses his forehead)*—come, you go to bed now, yes, and don't think of ugly things.

*She goes out, leaving Edmund alone (camera adjusts slightly onto him). Music begins. Edmund turns thoughtfully toward the camera for a few moments.*

*(Dissolve to . . .*

*(Night club, MS)*                                                                      46
*The music fades into a dance tune being played by the band. The dance floor is packed. Only one man is at the bar. A bar girl approaches him (from CU) and touches the man's glass with her own.*

BAR GIRL *(off screen)*: Cin-cin.

FRENCHMAN: A la santé mademoiselle! C'est très bon ce champagne!

*The Frenchman remains in the dim light (camera remains behind the bar).*

FRENCHMAN: Vous voulez une cigarette, mademoiselle?

BAR GIRL *(off screen)*: Oui, monsieur.

FRENCHMAN: Oui, je vous en prie. C'est drôle, à Berlin everybody accepts cigarettes but nobody ever smokes.

*(Camera shifts slightly to right to take in the room.) The band stops playing, and the dancers go back to their seats. An American and a young women come toward the bar. The band strikes up again; voices and applause for the band.*

AMERICAN: Now, miss, I'll buy you a whisky. *In English*: Do you like it? We Americans like whisky a lot. Do you?

YOUNG WOMAN: Yes, thanks.

AMERICAN: Two whiskies, I'm paying.

*Eva and her companion, Georges, come to the bar too.*

*Eva sits down as Georges offers her a cigarette (MCU;*  47
*resume on Eva sitting down).*

GEORGES: Vous fumez, mademoiselle? Une cigarette?

EVA: Thanks.

GEORGES: Deux cognacs, garçon!

*He flicks on his cigarette lighter, but Eva puts the ciga-*
*rette in her handbag.*

EVA: No, I'm going to smoke it later, thanks.

GEORGES: Deux cognacs, garçon!

BAR GIRL: Et voilà, monsieur.

ANOTHER MAN: Allo, Georges. Toujours à Berlin!?

GEORGES: Oui, mon vieux. *To Eva*: Vous m'excusez, mademoiselle?

EVA: Certainly.

*Georges goes off screen to right with the newcomer. A young woman comes over to Eva.*

YOUNG WOMAN: You know, that little Frenchie's really cute!

EVA: Yes, he's very nice.

YOUNG WOMAN: You're lucky.

BAR GIRL: But look, sweetie, you should be a little more on the ball. You let some beautiful chances pass by. If I were you—

EVA, *checking her makeup*: Oh, I don't care. I just come here to have a little fun.

BAR GIRL: But what're you waiting for, anyway? You'd better learn how to handle men while you're still young.

EVA: I don't want to.

BAR GIRL: That's stupid. I've seen so many girls come here just to have a little fun. Then they found fellows to marry them.

EVA: I may be stupid, but if I were looking for a husband I wouldn't look here.

*The bar girl goes off screen to left. Two other women come on screen from left and greet Eva.*

FIRST FRIEND: Hi, Eva, having a good time?

EVA: Yes, pretty good.

SECOND FRIEND: Why don't you come to the Piccadilly Club with us?

EVA: No, I can't. I'm going home, but I'll walk part of the way with you.

*She gets off the bar stool and all three go off screen to left. Music fades.*

*(Fade-out)*

*(Berlin street during the day, MS)* 48

*Women are lined up in front of a doorway, which they enter one at a time as others come out. A postman comes out of a doorway. (CU)*

*(RA) Some of the women converse as they move slowly forward in line. (WF)* 49

FIRST WOMAN: Lines are for dumb people. The black market's for smart ones.

SECOND WOMAN: You know the Mayer kid?

THIRD WOMAN: The mason's son?

SECOND WOMAN: He's only ten, and he makes more money on the black market than the whole family put together.

EVA *(coming on screen from left)*: Come on!

*(Resume on Eva as she appears, urging her girl friend on, HF)* 50

EVA: Hurry up, or there'll be nothing left.

FRIEND: For what they give us there's no point in rushing.

EVA: Sure, that's easy to say, but at home they want to eat every day.

*The women already in line protest loudly as the two girls do not immediately take their places at the end of the line (camera pans right).*

VOICES: Look at that! You two! What are you, pregnant, you can't wait your turn?

*Eva and her friend go to the end of the line (MCU;* 51
*resume on their movement).*

EVA: Some days I'm just beat. Three men in the house and never a thing to feed them.

FRIEND: Say, they've offered me butter at four hundred marks a kilo.

EVA: Some buy! My father's pension's seventy-four marks, when they decide to pay it.

FRIEND: And you waste your evenings to bring home a couple of cigarettes?

EVA: I get twenty marks for them.

FRIEND: What do you buy with that? A couple of kilos of potatoes? I told you, you're a fool.

EVA: Maybe you're right, but I just can't do anything else.

FRIEND: You're waiting for Wolf?

EVA: Yes.

FRIEND: Don't you think he'd understand what kind of situation you're in? A lot of fellows have come back from POW camps and accepted these things. He'll understand too.

EVA: But that's not the point! Of course, the thought of him helps me go on, resist . . .

*Eva and her friend move slowly forward in line (camera pans left, HF).*

EVA, *(CU):* . . . but that's not the only thing that's holding 52
me back. I waste my evenings for a few cigarettes, but

even if I let myself go, you think I'd be better off? What do you get out of the kind of life you're leading? Hunger and poverty, like me, like everybody else. Can't you understand?

*The line moves forward (HF). The friend shakes her head skeptically.* 53

EVA: So I might as well resist and keep on hoping he'll come back someday.

FRIEND: You don't think of your family?

EVA: I'm doing all I can.

FRIEND: It takes very little to satisfy you, dear.

EVA: I know, but I haven't the courage to do anything more.

FRIEND: I used to think the same thing, but when you've downed a couple of drinks you find the courage to do anything, even that.

*Again the line moves slightly forward, and the girls with it.*

*(Street, LS; camera pans right)* 54
*Edmund (HF), his bag over his shoulder, is talking to a boy.*

FIRST BOY *(off screen)*: Hey, what're you up to? *(on screen)* This is our territory.

EDMUND: None of your business. Keep away from me, understand?

*The two move toward the center of the sidewalk (WF) where Edmund has left his scale. A second boy is weighing himself.*

SECOND BOY: Where'd you get this scale?

EDMUND: What're you doing? Leave . . .

*Hearing the quarreling, a well-dressed gentleman comes* 55
*up to the boys (HF; camera pans left after him).*

EDMUND *(off screen)*: . . . my scale alone!

SECOND BOY *(off screen)*: Some nerve!

FIRST BOY *(off screen)*: This is our place! You go find yourself *(on screen)* another place.

GENTLEMAN, *intervening in the argument (MS)*: What's    56
all this? How much do you want for this scale?

EDMUND *(TQ)*: Three hundred marks.

*The gentleman laughs heartily. He picks up the scale,*
*examines it, then puts it down again.*

GENTLEMAN: You're crazy. For a rusty old piece of junk!

EDMUND: What're you doing? Junk? It's almost new. It
works perfectly.

GENTLEMAN: All right. I'll trade you. *He picks the scale*
*up and turns to look for someone.*

EDMUND, *stopping him*: Where're you going?

GENTLEMAN: Hold it! . . . Let's see, wait a minute, take it
easy, what're you scared of? Heavens, I'm not going
to run away! Come over here. Kurt, take this.

*He signals to a friend at the wheel of a waiting car, hands*
*him the scale, and takes a tin can out of the car to show*
*to Edmund.*

GENTLEMAN: Here, look, I'll give you this.

EDMUND: What's in it?

GENTLEMAN: Meat. It's American.

EDMUND: That's all you're giving me for the scale?

GENTLEMAN: Come on, it's even too much.

EDMUND: It's not enough! I have to have three hundred marks.

GENTLEMAN: Well, I'll give you another can. I'm feeling generous today! *Condescendingly, he takes another tin can out of the car.*

EDMUND: I don't want it! I don't want it!

GENTLEMAN: That'll do! Run along! Thank God you've gotten more than it was worth.

EDMUND: No, I don't want it! Give me back the scale!

GENTLEMAN: Cut it out! Get out of here! *He gets into the front seat of the car.*

*(Edmund and the gentleman, LS)*                    57

EDMUNDS *(WF)*: Give me back my scale!

GENTLEMAN: Let's go, Kurt!

EDMUND: Wait, give me back my scale!

*The car drives off. Edmund runs across the street and away. Behind him, the boys shout threats.*

FIRST BOY: And you'll get what for if you come around here any more!

*(Dissolve to . . .*

*(A square with a large baroque fountain, LS; a large,*    58
*half-ruined building is at the margin of the frame.)*
*Edmund goes toward the fountain, where there are some*
*children.*

*(Children playing Indians, inside and outside the dry*    59
*fountain, MS)*

*Edmund comes on screen from right and goes over to the*    60
*broken edge of the fountain (TQ; camera tracks forward*

*after him and pans left, HF). He steps into the fountain
and sits down. A man approaches him from the background.*

*The man (MS) comes forward (up to HF) and looks* 61
*curiously at Edmund (camera pans slightly left to follow
the man).*

*Edmund recognizes the man as his former schoolteacher.* 62
*He stands up deferentially to greet him. (TQ)*

EDMUND: Hello, Herr Enning.

ENNING: Weren't you in my class?

*The teacher steps into the fountain and sits down (HF;
camera tracks right and pans left). The children continue their game, chasing each other around the fountain.*

EDMUND: Yes, Herr Enning.

ENNING: See what a good memory I have? Now tell me, what's your name?

EDMUND: Edmund, Edmund Koeler.

ENNING: That's right, Edmund Koeler, first desk on the left. How you've grown! *He claps his hand on the boy's neck, pulls him closer, and begins to fondle Edmund's ear with his thumb.* You're a handsome young fellow now. How's your father?·

EDMUND: He's sick. He's sick pretty bad now.

ENNING: Oh. And didn't you have a brother in the Wehrmacht?

EDMUND: Yes, Karl Heinz. He was a soldier, and now he's home.

ENNING: I see. Then he's out of a job like me. *He drops his head.*

EDMUND: But why? Aren't you a teacher any more?

ENNING: No. The authorities and I don't see eye-to-eye any more on—*he caresses the whole length of the boy's arm up to his neck, then under the chin*—educational policy. Well, let's skip that. Dear Edmund, and what are you doing here?

EDMUND: Oh, nothing special.

ENNING: Then you can come along with me for a bit, if you like. *As he gets up he lays his hand on Edmund's neck.*

EDMUND: Yes, Herr Enning, with pleasure.

ENNING: I'm always happy to run into my old boys.

*They go off screen to right.*

*(Wipe to right)*

*(Street, MS)* 63

*Enning and Edmund come up to a bus stop (HF) where a small group of people are waiting. Enning looks around as if trying to spot a bus coming.*

*A group of men and women are excavating close by (TQ).* 64
*Seeing Enning, one of the men stops work.*

MAN: Hey, Enning!

*Enning turns and, followed by Edmund, goes off screen* 65
*to left.*

ENNING *(off screen)*: Oh, it's you!

*Enning and Edmund come on screen from right.* 66

MAN: You didn't recognize me, did you?

ENNING: Yes, yes. Labor Corps.

MAN: Labor? *He leans on his shovel.* Slave labor's what
  it is!

*Edmund looks around, not paying attention to them.*

ENNING: We've had some dirty deal.

MAN: First they called us National Socialists. Now, now
  we're Nazis.

ENNING: You're right there.

EDMUND: Herr Enning, here comes the bus.

MAN: Well, so long.

ENNING, *to Edmund*: I'll be right there. *To man*: Good-
  bye.

*Enning and Edmund go off screen to left while the man
goes back to work.*

*The streetcar pulls up. The ticket collector steps down,* 67
*followed by some passengers. Edmund and Enning come*

*on screen from left, wait their turn, then get on the bus.*
*(MS)*

TICKET COLLECTOR *(off screen)*: All aboard!

*The streetcar starts off, passing in front of the camera*
*and revealing behind it a large rubble-filled square.*

*(Dissolve to . . .*

*(Square, LS)*                                                    68

*The streetcar approaches from the center of another*
*large square and stops (CU). Edmund and Enning (MCU)*
*step down (camera adjusts slightly to right).*

*(Wipe to right)*

*(Street where Enning lives, TQ)*                             69

*Edmund and Enning walk along (camera tracks out in front of them). Enning's hand, on the boy's neck, caresses it from time to time.*

EDMUND: Is that friend of yours in the Labor Corps?

ENNING: You saw—they're clearing rubble.

EDMUND: You don't have to do that?

ENNING: No, thank goodness!

EDMUND: My brother was afraid they'd make him, so he hasn't reported in.

ENNING: He's perfectly right. Everybody who thinks our way should do the same thing! *He caresses Edmund.* Remember, Edmund, your father once handed in a forged certificate so you wouldn't have to join the Hitler Jungend, but you told me right away it was forged, because you knew what your duty was. *He touches Edmund's cheek.* And I ought to have reported him to the Party *(as they cross the street, camera pans right, to MS)* and the reason I didn't was because I'm fond of you.

*In front of Enning's building, the teacher looks up toward the windows of his apartment.*

ENNING: Ah, here we are.

EDMUND: Have you always lived here?

ENNING: No.

EDMUND: Then you haven't been here very long.

*(Camera stops panning and tracking.)*

ENNING: That's right. A friend of mine's putting me up. Come on up, Edmund, and we'll see if I can't help you.

*They go up the outer steps of the building.*

## 70

*(Entrance to Enning's building, WF)*

*They enter the building. Enning opens the gate, lets Edmund pass through first, and closes the gate behind him. Laying his hand on the boy's shoulder, he gently pushes Edmund on. Enning enters cautiously, trying not to make any noise. Edmund trips (camera tracks right alongside them). They reach a parlor, where a woman is lying on a couch and a man is sitting on a chaise lounge. A girl is doing exercises nearby. Enning is forced to stop.*

WOMAN: Oh, Herr Enning!

MAN: Ah, at last.

*Enning enters the parlor, removing his hat. Edmund remains in the doorway.*

ENNING: Hello, ma'am.

WOMAN: Hello.

MAN: Did you go there?

ENNING: Yes, sir.

MAN: Who's that boy?

ENNING, *turning*: He's a . . .

## 71

*(RA; WF)*

ENNING: . . . former pupil of mine.

MAN: He's cute! Did you get those papers?

*Edmund enters the room and, looking around, comes toward the man.*

ENNING: No, sir.

MAN: Why not?

EDMUND: Hello.

*Edmund (in TQ) comes up to the man, who caresses his*

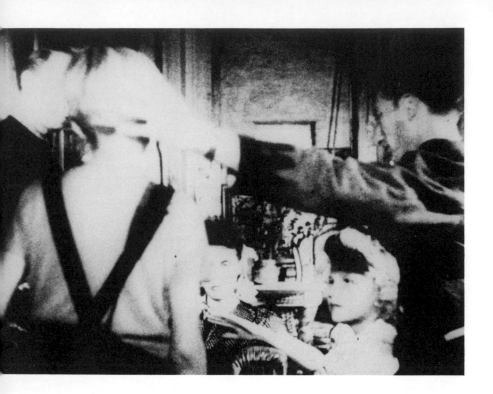

*arm repeatedly.*

ENNING: They told me I'd have to go back to the office tomorrow to get the permit.

WOMAN *(off screen)*: Did you bring me nail polish?

*They all turn toward her. Enning goes over to her (camera pans and tracks right). He opens his briefcase and takes out a small bottle, which he hands to her.*

ENNING: Here you are, ma'am. I hope you like the color.

WOMAN: Very nice. *To her husband:* How do you like this, "Tango Boubi"?

*She holds the bottle up to the light to see it better, then shows it to her husband. He has risen and comes on screen from left to sit down near her. The girl is now between them.*

ENNING: Edmund, say good-bye.

EDMUND, *coming on screen from left*: Good-bye.

*The woman begins to apply the nail polish, while the husband shakes Edmund's hand and pats his head.*

MAN: Good-bye.

WOMAN, *paying scarce attention*: Good-bye.

*Edmund and Enning go off screen to left.*

WOMAN: Pretty color, isn't it?

MAN: It's a little garish.

WOMAN: Of course there's no point in asking your opinion about feminine things. *Still polishing her nails, she glances at the girl.*

*(Stairway, MS)* 72

*Edmund and Enning start up the stairs, the man's hand on the boy's shoulder. Another man passes them on the way down.*

MAN: What a nice boy! Who is he?

ENNING: A former pupil of mine.

MAN: Oh, I see.

ENNING, *coming close to the man*: Is *he* in?

MAN: Yes, he's on the terrace.

*Enning and the boy continue up the stairs (camera pans right and upward).*

*Enning passes furtively in front of an open door, smiling* 73 *with a conspiratorial air at Edmund, who is following him (WF). Continuing along the railing they (MCU)*

*reach Enning's door (HF; camera pans right and tracks
with them). Enning opens the door and lets Edmund in.*

ENNING: Come on in.

*(Enning's room, TQ; resume on Enning letting Edmund* 74
*into the room; camera pulls back)*

*Enning closes the door behind the boy.*

ENNING: Ah, here we are.

*He takes Edmund's bag and places it on a dresser (WF),
then returns to the boy, who is still standing in the center
of the room.*

ENNING: Let's put your bag over here. And now tell me
what you've been up to all this time.

*He sits down on the bed (camera pans left and adjusts
slightly down) and draws Edmund over to him. (MCU)*

EDMUND: Nothing special.

*Enning adjusts the boy's suspenders and begins to caress
his neck, cheeks, and chin.*

ENNING, *persuasively*: Come, come over here to me. Tell
me about what they're telling you in school these
days, about democracy—

EDMUND: I don't know, because I haven't been able to go
to school for quite a while now.

ENNING: Why not? Don't you like the new teachers?

EDMUND: No, that's not it. I have to work now.

ENNING: How come?

EDMUND: Well, there are four of us at home now, and we
have only three ration cards.

ENNING, *putting his face beside the boy's*: Poor Edmund!

Why doesn't your brother have a card?

EDMUND: Because he hasn't reported to the police. He was fighting in the streets until the Allied troops came, and now he's afraid.

ENNING: Don't worry, we'll help him.

EDMUND: That's just what I wanted to ask you. Couldn't you get me some kind of job? I've done everything. I even went to dig graves at the cemetery, but they wouldn't give me the Number Two Card.

ENNING: Oh, dear boy!

*Enning suddenly realizes that someone is opening his door (at the right margin of frame). He jumps to his feet, and Edmund does the same.*

*A man in a white suit comes in and immediately closes the door behind him. Edmund and Enning come on screen from left and stand on either side of the newcomer. (TQ)*

75

GENERAL: Back already?

ENNING: Yes, sir, Herr von Laubniz. This is a former pupil of mine.

*The general caresses Edmund's face gently, looking intently at him. Then he turns back to Enning.*

GENERAL: The orders have been carried out?

ENNING: No, sir. I'll try again tomorrow.

GENERAL: You still haven't gotten anywhere?

ENNING: No, sir.

GENERAL: Remember, you must succeed.

ENNING: Yes, sir, Herr von Laubniz.

*The general leaves. Enning closes the door (TQ), then*

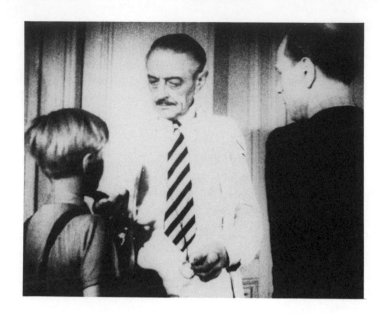

*turns to Edmund and, after a moment's hesitation, takes*
*the boy's arm and leads him over to the dresser (camera*
*tracks right and pans slightly).*

ENNING: So, my dear little Edmund, I intend to help you,
but remember this: you mustn't tell a soul, understand?

EDMUND: No.

ENNING: You see—not that there's anything wrong about
it, but I just wouldn't want it known. *(He moves to*
*Edmund's left; camera pans slightly right, HF)*

EDMUND: Yes.

ENNING: Now look, I'm going to give you something to
sell, but if anyone asks you, even in this building,
you must say it's yours, understand?

EDMUND: Yes, sir.

ENNING: You'll go to the Chancellory, understand? There

you'll find a lot of English and Americans. They're stupid. You try to get them to buy this record—let's have your bag.

*Edmund turns to take the bag, and Enning puts the recording into it. As Edmund closes the bag, Enning hands him a wind-up phonograph, which Edmund takes after slinging the bag over his shoulder.*

ENNING: It's one of the Führer's speeches. Here, take the phonograph too, but don't tell anybody I gave you this either.

EDMUND: Yes.

ENNING: Now, let's see if you do me proud, eh?

*He accompanies Edmund to the door (camera tracks and pans to right). They go out together.*

*(Street, TQ)* 76

*Joe, a boy about seventeen, and Christel, a girl about thirteen, are talking outside the building.*

JOE: How much did you get?

CHRISTEL: A million.

JOE: Who d'you think you're kidding, stupid?

CHRISTEL: Then mind your own business.

JOE: I did well for myself. I'm like one of the family now.

*Enning and Edmund, coming down the steps, appear on screen from right. The two youngsters turn and come up to Enning. (WF)*

ENNING: Christel, Joe, come here a minute!

JOE: What d'you want?

ENNING: Take this boy to the Chancellory. He's got something he has to sell.

JOE: All right.

ENNING: And see he doesn't get taken, eh? You watch out for him.

JOE: I get it.

ENNING, *to Edmund, laying a hand affectionately on his head*: You go with them.

JOE: Come on, let's go!

*The three youngsters go off toward the left as Enning goes back into the building.*

*(Dissolve to . . .*

*(Square, LS; camera pans left across the square, which is*       77
*bordered by bombed-out buildings.)*

*(Dissolve to . . .*

*(Chancellory, WF)*                                              78

*Three American soldiers come up to a guide (TQ), who is showing the sights. Other soldiers arrive simultaneously from another direction (camera pans right). The soldiers follow the guide's patter attentively.*

GUIDE, *in English (off screen)*: Come along, boys. Now that, over there, *(on screen)* that white building is Hitler's bunker, and that one in front is where they burned the bodies of Hitler and Eva Braun. If any of you want to go and take a picture of it, I'll take a picture of you first.

*he group breaks up. The soldiers arrange themselves*
*the souvenir photograph as the guide steps back into*
*on (camera adjusts slightly to right).*

*ricans (MCU) look around and walk toward the*        79
*f the building (camera pans downward; TQ).*

FIRST SOLDIER: That's the place Hitler was burned.

SECOND SOLDIER: What? To death?

FIRST SOLDIER: Yes.

*They stroll through the courtyard (camera pans right), then stop for a last look (HF) before going off screen to right.*

*(Edmund and Christel chatting as they sit on chunks of rubble, WF)* 80

EDMUND: Wouldn't you like to see foreign countries?

CHRISTEL: What for? They must all be the same.

JOE *(off screen)*: Edmund! Run!

*Edmund jumps to his feet, picks up the phonograph, and goes off screen to right.*

JOE *(off screen)*: Quick! Hurry up! 81

*Joe appears in the doorway at the top of the steps leading into the Chancellory. He motions to Edmund to hurry. Edmund runs up the steps, and both boys disappear through the doorway (camera tilts up).*

*(Inside the Chancellory, WF)* 82

*Joe and Edmund appear at a run and race down a stairway at the foot of which are the two American soldiers, waiting for them.*

JOE: Here he is!

SOLDIER: We're wasting too much time.

*Joe takes the phonograph from Edmund and, with the latter's help, gets it ready to play.*

JOE: Quick, now we'll put on the record. You don't know
    a thing about doing business, do you?

EDMUND: Here it is.

JOE: You good-for-nothing!

*Edmund puts the record on. Then he sits down on the steps as the Americans and Joe gaze curiously at each other.*

HITLER'S VOICE: . . . Bade, Sonnenschein, gerade dadurch stürmt . . . und wenn es wettert . . . und ich bin stolz darauf, der Führer dieser Nation zu sein . . .

*In a very long, very wide corridor of the building a man    83
with a child looks around as he hears the voice. (LS)*

HITLER'S VOICE: . . . und ich bin glücklich darüber, besonders in schweren . . . und ich bin glücklich, dass in Sonnentagen einer Nation vor mir aus . . .

*(Camera pans right and tilts up from a bombed-out build-    84
ing to a view of caved-in rooftops, LS)*

HITLER'S VOICE: . . . wieder graut . . . und Vertrauen geben kann, dass ich das ganze Deutsche Volk wieder aufrichten darf und aufrichten kann, dass ich ihm kann, Deutsches Volk, sei voll beruhigt . . .

*The man motions to the child, who is pulling along a toy,    85
and they go off screen to left.*

HITLER'S VOICE: . . . das werden wir alles meistern, auf, eingestellter Sieg. [. . . gone forward in rain and in sunshine, and above all in time of storm, and I am proud to be the Führer of this nation, and I am particularly happy to be so in difficult times, and I am happy that in this country's days of glory, for which I am responsible, it can again put its faith in me, that I can again rouse the entire German people and say: Germans, do not fear, we will overcome all with a victory which has only just begun.]

*(Wipe to left)*

(Street, HF)

*Enning watches from behind a pile of rubble. Then he walks (camera pans left and tracks) toward Edmund, Christel, and Joe crossing the street. (MS)*

ENNING: Hey, kids! Where're you going? You were supposed to come back to my place.

*The youngsters go toward him. (WF)*

JOE: You scared we'll run away?

*Enning lays his hands on Edmund's neck as they walk (toward the camera, which pulls back and pans right).*

ENNING: Tell me, it went all right, did it?

EDMUND: Very well, Herr Enning!

ENNING: How much did you get for the record?

EDMUND: They gave me two hundred marks.

*Edmund and Enning return to the sidewalk (camera still tracks out in front of them) and stroll up and down (TQ) at a slight distance from Joe and Christel, who have stopped at the edge of the sidewalk.*

ENNING: Where's the money?

EDMUND: Here you are.

ENNING: Ah, here it is—and here's ten marks for you. See how I keep my promises? And come back to see me again, will you? So long.

*Enning takes the phonograph from Edmund and goes off screen to left. Joe and Christel go off in the opposite direction. Stunned by the brusqueness of the teacher's departure, Edmund starts to follow him.*

JOE: Come on, Christel!

*Edmund hesitates, then turns and runs after Joe and Christel, going off screen to right.*

EDMUND: Hey, kids!

*(Dissolve to . . .*

*(Street, LS)*                                            87

*The three youngsters walk along an alley (toward the camera; to HF), bordered on one side by a low row of houses, and on the other by a long stretch of rubble.*

JOE: You two wait here for me.

EDMUND: Why do we have to wait here for him?

CHRISTEL: When he's doing business he wants to be alone.

EDMUND: What business?

CHRISTEL: Don't be a dope! You think we just go down to the bank when we need money?

EDMUND: I want to see what he's up to.

*Christel follows Edmund off screen to right.*

*(Wipe to right)*

*(Intersection with pedestrian underpass and subway station, LS)* 88

*Joe (HF) looks around, then strides down into the underpass just as Edmund, followed by Christel, comes on screen from left. The street is filled with a steady stream of traffic and pedestrians.*

EDMUND, *to Christel*: Come on.

*They follow Joe down into the subway.*

*(Subway station, MS)* 89

*Joe walks along, then turns casually and sees Edmund following him. Edmund appears on screen from left. (HF)*

EDMUND: What're you up to?

JOE, *annoyed, punching Edmund's shoulder*: Stupid! Why didn't you wait back there for me?

EDMUND: But what are you doing?

*Christel catches up with them, coming on screen from left. Joe seizes Edmund by the shirt and pulls him closer, whispering in his ear.*

JOE: I'm selling stuff.

EDMUND: What stuff?

JOE: This. *He points to something in his pocket.*

EDMUND: What's that?

JOE: Soap.

EDMUND: You said you had a job for me, but instead we come here just to sell a few cakes of soap?

JOE: Leave it to me, I'll show you what you can get for a cake of soap. Go wait outside for me. *To Christel*: Hey, stupid, take him out of here!

*He hurries Edmund and Christel away. They go off screen to left. The subway train comes in immediately afterward. The station fills with people.*

*(RA) Edmund and Christel go off, with frequent back-* 90 *ward glances. (MS)*

*Joe has singled out, from among the passengers leaving* 91 *the train, a well-dressed woman wearing a hat. (MS)*

JOE: You want to buy some soap, ma'am?

WOMAN: How much it is?

JOE: Well, I'll give it to you for fifty marks.

WOMAN: Let me see it first.

JOE: Come over this way.

*Joe and the woman (coming into HF; camera pans left) move toward the exit and stop. Joe takes out his cake of soap.*

JOE: Have a smell. It's American.

WOMAN: It looks good, but it's expensive.

JOE: It's not expensive, but you can have it for forty.

WOMAN: All right.

*She takes the money out of her handbag. Joe grabs the money out of her hand and races away, passing under the turnstile (camera pans rapidly left).*

WOMAN: Oh, you crook! Thief, thief! Help, thief!

*Shouting, the lady tries to follow Joe. She passes around the ticket booth. Christel and Edmund, watching from the bottom of the stairs, run away.*

*The three youngsters run out of the underpass. Joe*    92
*races off screen to right. Edmund and Christel, after a moment's hesitation, follow him.*

*(Dissolve to . . .*

*(Square, LS; a streetcar crosses the square, coming for-*    93
*ward toward the camera, which pans right.)*

*The three youngsters get off at the stop.*

JOE: Hurry up! Follow me, kids!

*They hurry along (camera pans left after them, WF) and cross a bridge (camera tracks with them, MS).*

JOE, *to Edmund*: See how you handle dopes like that?

*Joe, followed by Edmund and Christel, walks along*    94
*(camera pans left). He stops and looks around, evidently expecting to see someone. (TQ)*

JOE: Nobody's here yet. I told them all to come here! You wait here, I'll go look for Ali Baba. *He goes off screen to left.*

EDMUND: Is he your brother?

CHRISTEL, *looking disgusted*: Who, Joe? Hell no!

EDMUND: You always go around together!

CHRISTEL: What's so strange about that?

EDMUND: Wherever he goes, you trail after him.

CHRISTEL: That makes him my brother? Hey, Joe!

*Christel runs toward Joe (camera pans after her to left, WF). A friend of Joe's, Frank, comes on screen from left and greets Christel with a slap on the behind.*

FRANK: Hi, monkey!

CHRISTEL: Hands off!

*She slaps his hand as Joe and another boy come on screen from left.*

BOY: You're getting stuck up, eh?

*He too gives her a slap on the behind, then escapes off screen to right as she chases after him.*

CHRISTEL: You stupid!

FRANK: Who's she think she is, that dumbbell?

*Joe and Frank come over to Edmund (camera pans right, to TQ).*

JOE: By the way, Frank, I've lined up another terrific girl. I'll introduce you tonight.

*They reach Edmund just as another boy suddenly comes on screen from left, crossing over to Joe and laying a hand on his shoulder.*

BOY: Hey, on your toes, fellows! There's another train coming in tonight with a load of potatoes.

FRANK: Potatoes? Fine, we'll go pick up a few.

EDMUND: Where?

JOE: Run!

*They all go off screen to left; Edmund is with Joe, Christel is still chasing the boy.*

FRANK: The cops'll be there.

JOE: So what?

CHRISTEL: Hey you! Where're you going?

*(Dissolve to . . .*

*(Street, at night, LS)* 95

*Several boys cross the street from right to left, pulling small wagons.*

*(Bridge over railway, LS; camera shoots down from the* 96
*bridge.)*

*As a train passes slowly down the tracks, several boys run toward it from one side of the tracks. They reach the train before it enters the tunnel not far ahead.*

*On the street the boys run toward the right, pulling the* 97
*wagons. Two cars are following them. As soon as the boys have crossed the square and gone off screen to right, the cars stop and let out several policemen with dogs.*

*The boys by the tracks run in the same direction as the* 98
*train. Barking of dogs is heard.*

*(Railroad yards, MS)* 99

*Some boys race out of the railroad freight sheds, followed at a short distance by the police.*

*(The same shot from somewhat farther away, ELS)* 100
*Some of the boys are already quite far from the station.*

*In the railroad yards the police have caught the slowest* 101
*boys.*

*(Street, TQ)* 102

*Edmund and Christel run on screen from left, then stop*

*behind a small bush to hide. They look around to see if anyone is still following them.*

EDMUND: But where did Joe go?

CHRISTEL: Come on! I know where to find him.

*She starts off, followed by Edmund; they go off screen to right.*

*(Dissolve to . . .*

*(Street, MS)*                                                                    103

*Joe, whistling, pulls his wagon along. Edmund and Christel follow. They all stop (in WF) to have a look at a man sitting by an open fire (camera tracks and pans right). After a few moments they return to where they were (camera pans left).*

EDMUND: Hey, Joe!

*Joe stops (TQ), and Edmund and Christel come up to him.*

JOE: What do you want?

EDMUND: Will you sell me that cake of soap?

*Music begins.*

JOE: You got any money?

EDMUND: How much do you want?

JOE: For you, forty.

EDMUND: Forty? *He takes out the ten marks Enning gave him.* But I've only got ten. Will you give me credit? I'll bring you the rest tomorrow or the day after, all right?

JOE: Yes, all right.

EDMUND: Give it to me!

*The boys trade.*

JOE: All right—hide it, don't let anybody see it!

EDMUND: Wait—first I want to have a look at it.

*He unwraps the package and sees that inside there is only a block of wood. He throws it angrily away as Joe laughs.*

EDMUND: So you tricked me too! Get out of here, you son of a bitch!

JOE, *laughing*: Good night and sweet dreams!

*Joe pulls his wagon off screen to left (camera tracks out in front of him). Then he reappears and gets ready to leave (camera pans and tracks slightly left with him). Edmund starts to follow him. (TQ)*

EDMUND: But where are you going?

JOE: Sorry, I've got a date tonight.

EDMUND: But where are we? I don't know where we are.

JOE: Get going, you can figure it out for yourself.

EDMUND: But I live in Alex, how can I get home at this hour?

JOE: Why do you have to go home?

EDMUND: But, Joe, where'll I sleep? I don't know anyone around here.

JOE: Just look around and choose. It's all free around here.

EDMUND: By myself?

JOE: Why not with her? Isn't she your type?

*Christel, amused, smiles.*

EDMUND: But look, Joe, I—

JOE: You're scared of women, I see.

EDMUND: No, but I want—

JOE: She's not bad-looking, is she? Get to work! *He goes over to Christel.* And you take good care of him, he's a friend of mine.

CHRISTEL: You dope!

JOE: Don't be stupid. Figure something out for yourself.

*Joe takes the wagon and goes off screen to left. Edmund runs after him.*

EDMUND: Wait, Joe, the potatoes! I've got a right to my share, haven't I?

*Joe comes back on screen from left, takes some potatoes from the wagon, and, evidently annoyed, hands them to Edmund.*

EDMUND: Here, in my bag. But why're you giving me so little? Let's divide it evenly.

JOE: You can't get any more in your bag.

EDMUND: It doesn't matter, give them to me. I'll take care of carrying them.

JOE: All right, I'll give you the rest tomorrow.

EDMUND: For sure?

JOE: For sure, for sure. So long, kids, Get happy and sweet dreams. *He pulls their heads together.* And treat him nice, he's just a beginner.

*Joe again takes his wagon and goes off screen to left.*

CHRISTEL: Come on with me.

*She takes Edmund by the arm and tries to lead him away, but Edmund continues to call after Joe. They go off screen to left.*

EDMUND: Joe, wait! Joe, just a minute! Joe!

CHRISTEL: Let him go! Come on, come on!

*Music fades.*

*(Dissolve to . . .*

*(Street at dawn, LS)*  104

*Edmund walks along by himself. There is a factory in the background. Music starts.*

*(Dissolve to . . .*

*(Entranceway of Edmund's apartment, HF)*  105

*The door opens and Edmund walks in, followed by another tenant, Tilgher. They walk toward the Koelers' rooms (MCU; camera pans left and tracks with them).*

TILGHER *(off screen)*: You're in for it now, *(on screen)* my boy! You're really going to catch it!

EDMUND: Why?

TILGHER: A kid of your age out all night long.

EDMUND: And now what am I supposed to do?

TILGHER: Take your medicine and keep quiet.

*(RA; HF)* 106

EDMUND: You see, Herr Tilgher, on the way home I met—

*They cross a central room together (camera pans left and tracks with them, then pans again to left).*

TILGHER: Don't try to pawn your stories off on me! Save them for your sister.

*Edmund has stopped a few steps behind. (TQ)*

TILGHER, *opening the door for him (TQ)*: In you go!

*(Eva and Thilde's room, HS; resume on movement of the* 107 *door, as Tilgher opens it.)*

*Edmund starts to enter, then hesitates and stops. Tilgher encourages him with a nod. Edmund comes in with lowered head (camera tracks with him). He goes over to his sister's bed.*

EDMUND: Eva!

*Eva immediately jumps out of bed, pulls on her dressing gown, and runs toward Edmund. (HF)*

EVA: Edmund! You're back! I thought something'd happened to you. You gave us such a scare! What a bad boy you are!

THILDE *(off screen)*: Fräulein Koeler, what is it?

*Eva goes toward Thilde, who has sat up in bed (camera*

*tracks and pans right, cutting off Edmund).*

EVA: Nothing. Edmund's back.

THILDE: Thank goodness.

EVA: You can stay in bed.

*Eva goes toward the door, forcing her brother to follow her (camera pans to left). They reach the door and open it almost simultaneously. (WF)*

EVA: Go on, quick!

*Music ends.*

*(The corridor, TQ; resume on door opening.)* 108

*Eva and Edmund come out into the corridor. Edmund goes off screen to right. Eva closes the door behind her and, as she finishes fastening her dressing gown, catches up with him (camera pans and tracks right with her). She heads for her father's room but then hesitates and stops. She speaks distractedly, with one ear tuned to the next room, then comes back toward Edmund.*

EVA: Where were you all night? What were you up to?

*She returns to the father's door to make sure he is still asleep. Then she returns to Edmund (camera tracks right, in front of and along with her).*

EDMUND, *pleading*: I didn't do anything wrong, Eva, believe me!

*(Resume on Eva's turn)* 109

*She takes her brother's arm. Worried that they may be overheard, she leads him away from the father's door (TQ; camera tracks out and pans right).*

EVA: I want to know where you were!

EDMUND: To get some potatoes. . . . *He sits down and slips his bag off his shoulder.*

EVA: You were out till now for a couple of potatoes?

EDMUND: Look here! And tomorrow I'll have the rest.

*Sound of coughing from the father's room. Without accepting Edmund's explanation, Eva goes back to the father's door.*

EDMUND: Look, Eva!

EVA, *turning*: Sssh!

*(Resume on Edmund standing up, MCU)*      110

*He joins Eva, who is leaning against the doorpost (MCU; camera pulls back).*

EVA: Papa's awake. Listen to him coughing! He was sick all night long.

EDMUND: Did you tell him?

EVA: Yes.

KOELER *(off screen)*: Eva! Eva!

*Eva opens the door.*

*(Koeler's room, wide MCU; resume on Eva opening the*      111
*door.)*

*She enters briskly and steps aside, going off screen to left, to let the shamefaced Edmund in. She closes the door behind him (camera precedes her).*

EVA: Yes, Papa. *(off screen)* Edmund's back.

*Music begins. Edmund stops. In the background is Karl Heinz, who is awake.*

KOELER *(off screen)*: Come here!

*Edmund takes a step forward (camera pans left, wide MCU).*

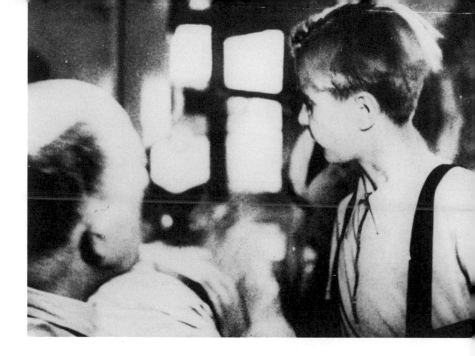

*(Herr Koeler, sitting up in bed, wide MCU)*  112

KOELER: Come over here!

*Edmund (MCU) comes to his father's bedside (camera*  113
*pans left and pulls back). As soon as he is within reach*
*the father smacks him violently. Edmund instinctively*
*raises his arm to shield his face.*

*(RA; resume on Edmund's gesture of defense, HF)*  114

*Edmund, weeping, throws himself on his sister's shoulder*
*and tries to defend himself.*

EDMUND: It wasn't my fault. The other kids took me!

KOELER: That's enough! Don't you lie to me! I'm tired
of hearing lies! You should be ashamed of yourself,
you brazen-faced kid, at your age!

*Still weeping, Edmund moves away from Eva (MCU;*

*camera pulls back). Eva takes his arm and brings him back to the father's bedside.*

EVA: He didn't mean to do anything wrong, Papa. He was just trying to get us something to eat.

KOELER: I won't have any of it!

*(RA; Karl Heinz lying on his cot, WF)* 115

KARL HEINZ: Me either. I prefer to die of hunger.

*(Edmund weeping on his sister's shoulder, HF)* 116

EVA, *to Karl Heinz*: It's easy for you to talk!

KOELER: I can't stay in this bed any more. I can't stand it! *He coughs.*

EVA: Take it easy, Papa. Edmund won't do it again. *To Edmund*: Show him how many potatoes you brought home!

*Edmund opens the bag. Eva sees the can of meat and takes it out to show the father.*

EVA: Look! He's got some canned meat too!

EDMUND: No! The meat's not for us.

EVA: Who's it for?

EDMUND: For Herr Rademaker.

*Music ends.*

*(Apartment entranceway, MS)* 117

*Tilgher (CU) is up on a ladder tampering with the electric meter. Rademaker comes in from the rear and stops by the ladder. (HF)*

RADEMAKER: Well, you've managed it, eh?

TILGHER, *turning a screw*: But it's not so simple, Herr

Rademaker.

RADEMAKER: The main cable passes through here?

TILGHER: Sure, but they'll see it's been tampered with. Let's hope we don't both go to jail for stealing electricity!

*He comes down the ladder, puts his tools in his pocket, and goes off with Rademaker (camera pulls back in front of them, HF).*

RADEMAKER: That's stupid! Don't worry, they're five families in here—how'll they find out who did it?

*Edmund comes on screen from left, carrying the two cans of meat.*

EDMUND: Here, Herr Rademaker.

RADEMAKER: What do you want?

EDMUND: I've brought you some canned meat.

RADEMAKER: Who asked you to?

EDMUND: I sold the scale.

RADEMAKER: So where are my three hundred marks?

EDMUND: This was all they'd give me.

RADEMAKER, *angrily taking the cans*: What?! You have the nerve to bring me this garbage in exchange for my scale! You want to poison us with these cans?

TILGHER: I don't think they're so bad.

RADEMAKER: Then you take them.

TILGHER: Thanks a lot, Herr Rademaker.

*Tilgher leaves immediately. He is about to enter his own room when Rademaker stops him.*

RADEMAKER: And bring them right in to my wife, hear?

*Tilgher changes direction and goes down the hall toward the Rademakers' room. Rademaker and Edmund go toward the room at the end of the corridor (camera pans left). His hand firmly gripping Edmund's shoulder, Rademaker questions him.*

RADEMAKER: Now let's have the truth. What did you do with the money?

EDMUND: What money?!

RADEMAKER: The money you got for the scale—who'd you give it to? Your father?

EDMUND: No, I swear it isn't true!

RADEMAKER: Don't think you can cheat me, kid! We know how you people'll stoop to anything to keep going! *Extremely vexed, he crosses in front of Edmund and*

*goes off screen to left. (off screen)* You settle yourselves down in my house—

EDMUND: We were sent here by the Housing Commissioner!

RADEMAKER *(off screen)*: Sure, and I'm supposed to put
up with you! *(on screen)* You're driving me nuts here,
with that pain in the neck of a father of yours who
never stops complaining! When's he going to drop
dead and give us a little peace?

*Music begins. Rademaker goes off screen to right (camera
adjusts slightly to left and tilts down). Edmund is now
alone. (MCU)*

*Edmund (CU) lowers his head, then turns and leaves.*     118
*Music ends.*

*(Koeler's room, HF)*     119

*Koeler throws off the bedclothes and sits on the edge of
the bed (camera pans right).*

EVA *(off screen)*: Where're you going? *She comes on screen
from right to help her father up.*

KOELER: To the bathroom.

EVA: Wait, I'll help you.

KOELER: Thanks, dear girl.

*Eva supports him as they go toward the bedroom door
(HF; camera tracks sideways with them and pans right).
She opens the door just as Edmund is about to come in.
He enters after they have gone out.*

EVA, *to Koeler*: Careful! *To Edmund*: Your soup's on the
stove there.

KARL HEINZ *(off screen)*: Close the door!

*Music begins. Edmund closes the door and goes over to the stove (camera pans right and tracks briefly to left, HF). He takes his bowl of soup and places it on the table beside Karl Heinz's bed, then sits down beside his brother, who is peeling the potatoes.*

EDMUND: You want some, Karl Heinz?

*(Resume on Edmund sitting down, MCU; tilting slightly*    120
*upward)*

KARL HEINZ: No, I don't feel like it. Eva heated it up for you—you eat it.

*(Karl Heinz is on right margin of frame, Edmund on left) Edmund takes a cigarette from his shirt pocket and holds it out to his brother.*

EDMUND: Want a cigarette? It's an American one.

KARL HEINZ: So Eva can scold me about it the rest of the day? No thanks.

EDMUND: But it's not Eva's. *He puts the cigarette on the table near Karl Heinz.*

KARL HEINZ: Tell me, who gives you money to buy cigarettes?

EDMUND: I didn't buy it, somebody gave it to me.

KARL HEINZ: Who? Those punks you go stealing with?

EDMUND: They weren't punks. A girl gave it to me.

*(RA; MCU, tilting slightly down)*    121

*Karl Heinz continues to peel potatoes as Edmund begins to eat.*

KARL HEINZ: You ought to be ashamed of yourself.

EDMUND: Why? Everybody does it!

KARL HEINZ: That's no reason.

EDMUND: Her name's Christel. She's all alone in the world, 122
and she sleeps in a cellar—*he eats a spoonful of soup*—she's a fine girl . . .

*Karl Heinz shakes his head disapprovingly. (CU)* 123

EDMUND *(off screen)*: . . . and I like her a lot. She always gives cigarettes to her friends.

EDMUND, *eating*: You should have a woman to take care 124
of you.

KARL HEINZ *(CU)*: A woman? Hah, that's all I need! As 125
if this dog's life's not bad enough as it is.

EDMUND *(off screen)*: You mustn't feel that way. Be brave!

KARL HEINZ: I've been brave, because a soldier can lose everything except his courage. But am I still a soldier? I'm nothing—just a useless extra mouth to feed. I'd do better to jump out the window.

*Music ends.*

EVA *(off screen)*: Edmund! Come quick!

*Karl Heinz turns toward the door, stands up, and goes off screen to right.*

*The door opens. Eva enters with Koeler, gasping for* 126
*breath, leaning on her. (WF)*

EVA: Help me, Karl Heinz! Papa's had another attack!

*Edmund and Karl Heinz come on screen from left. As Eva leads Koeler to the bed (camera pulls back to include bed), Edmund hurries to pull back the bedclothes. (HF)*

EVA: We have to get the doctor right away! *To Karl Heinz*: You go!

KARL HEINZ: Me?

EDMUND: No, I'll get him! I know where he lives.

*Edmund runs out as Koeler lies down on the bed (camera pans slightly to right).*

*(Dissolve to . . .*

*(A closer shot of the preceding one, HF)* 127

*As the doctor examines Koeler with a stethoscope, Eva, Edmund, and Karl Heinz silently watch. When he finishes, the doctor taps the patient's cheek.*

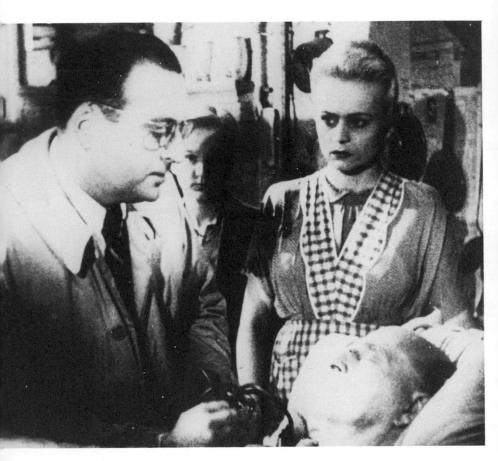

DOCTOR: Heads up, it's nothing serious.

*The doctor leaves the bedside, followed by the three children (camera pans left, to TQ).*

DOCTOR, *softly, to children*: Of course, the heart is weak, very weak, but mainly it's his overall condition, which I find very poor, unfortunately.

EVA: What should we do?

DOCTOR: Well, first of all he needs a good, hearty diet, with fats, vitamins—

EVA: But, doctor, how can we?

EDMUND: They won't give us anything more with our ration card.

DOCTOR: Ah! It's the same story all over! The best thing would be to get him into a hospital, but they're all overflowing.

*Edmund glances worriedly at Eva.*

KARL HEINZ: But, doctor, couldn't we at least try?

*The doctor pushes Karl Heinz slightly aside to get to his bag, into which he puts the stethoscope.*

DOCTOR: Hm, they've turned away even worse cases than this. Mm, I'll see what I can do. I have some good contacts at the Bureau of Health.

*Eva and Edmund run to tell their father the good news (camera pans after them to left).*

EVA: Did you hear, Papa, maybe you can go to the hospital!

KARL HEINZ (*off screen*): Thank you, doctor.

EDMUND: Think of it! You'll have all you want to eat!

EVA: They'll give you three meals a day!

KOELER: Something warm. . . .

*The doctor, coming on screen from left, goes over to Eva to temper their enthusiasm.*

DOCTOR: Just a minute, just a minute, I can't promise anything for sure. I'll try. I just may be able to. Goodbye, I'll let you know.

EVA: Thank you, doctor.

*The doctor starts to leave, followed by Eva and Edmund. Karl Heinz opens the door for him, and Eva accompanies him out. As Karl Heinz closes the door again, Edmund goes toward his father (camera pans right).*

EDMUND: Are you pleased, Papa?

KOELER: Well. . . .

*(Dissolve to . . .*

*(Courtyard of a hospital, LS; several nurses are walking* 128 *in the courtyard.)*

*(Dissolve to . . .*

*(Hospital ward, HF; Eva is seated at Koeler's bedside.)* 129

EVA: So you feel a little better here?

KOELER, *loudly*: Yes, better. I feel much better.

EVA, *looking around to see if anyone has overheard him*: Talk softly, Papa. They'll send you away if they hear you're better.

KOELER, *sitting up in bed, whispering*: Oh, you're right! The doctor told me the same thing. But I have to tell you, it's marvelous here.

EVA: Yes, Papa?

*A nurse comes to take something from the bedside table*

*behind Eva. She fills a glass with water and hands it to the patient next to Koeler.*

KOELER: You know what they give us to eat here? First soup, then a piece of meat with vegetables—fresh vegetables, imagine!—and milk too, this much milk. *He indicates the amount of milk with his fingers.*

EVA: Really?!

KOELER: And every day too!

EVA: I'm glad they're treating you well, Papa.

KOELER: And for supper they give us a bowl of hot soup.

EVA: You'll see, you'll be able to get up soon.

KOELER: Yes, I know. But when I think of you. . . . *He lies down again.*

EVA, *caressing him*: No, you mustn't worry about us. It's enough for us to know you're better, believe me.

KOELER: I won't be a burden for you any more—right, Eva?

EVA: Of course, Papa.

KOELER: You're a good girl.

*(Dissolve to . . .*

*(Koeler's room in the apartment, HF)*    130

*Karl Heinz and Eva's girl friend are sitting near each other.*

FRIEND: You think Eva'll be back soon?

KARL HEINZ: She went to the hospital, but you can wait for her.

FRIEND: Can we smoke in here?

KARL HEINZ: Yes, of course.

*She takes cigarettes from her handbag and offers one to Karl Heinz.*

FRIEND: You want one?

KARL HEINZ: No thanks, I don't feel like it.

*She takes out a lighter, but it does not work.*

KARL HEINZ: Wait, I'll get you a match.

*He turns to look behind him, then gets up to look on a shelf, then goes over to Edmund (camera tracks left with him), who is whittling a stick with a knife (camera tilts up, TQ).*

KARL HEINZ, *whispering*: Hey, have you got a match?

EDMUND: No, there aren't any more.

KARL HEINZ: Then go buy some.

EDMUND: With what money?

KARL HEINZ: Ask Rademaker for some.

*The friend (back to camera) comes on screen from right and steps between the two.*

FRIEND: Don't bother. I'll ask Blanke—I have to see her anyway.

*She turns and starts for the door (camera pans and tracks briefly to left). She stops when she sees Eva returning. Eva comes on screen from left. (MCU)*

FRIEND: Oh, you're back?

EVA: Why, what's up?

FRIEND: There's no hurry. I'll tell you later. I'll wait for you at Blanke's.

EVA: All right.

*Eva goes toward her brothers and past them (camera pans back to right, picking them up on the right and dropping them on the left, with Eva in MCU).*

KARL HEINZ: How's Papa?

*Music begins.*

EVA: He's much better.

KARL HEINZ: And here every day things go *(off screen)* from bad to worse.

*Eva goes toward the table (camera pans after her to right).*

EDMUND *(off screen)*: Eva, they've cut off the electricity.

EVA: The electricity? But why?

KARL HEINZ *(MCU)*: They found out somebody was steal-    131
ing it.

*He moves toward Eva (camera tracks and pans right).*

EVA *(off screen)*: Who was it?

KARL HEINZ: Not us. Somebody else here.

*He comes up to her. Edmund comes on screen from left.*

EDMUND: Rademaker says it was us.

KARL HEINZ: As usual!

EVA: So that's why he was shouting.

*She starts to take off her coat and goes off screen to right. Edmund goes off to left. Karl Heinz (camera moves to him) walks around the room, then sits down on the kitchen counter.*

KARL HEINZ: That black marketer! Someday I'll bust his head in!

*Eva comes back on screen from right and leans against the counter by her brother. (MCU)*

EVA: Sure, you'll bust his head in! You talk big, but when it comes to giving us a hand to keep going here you never do a thing!

KARL HEINZ: Here we go again.

EVA: But are you sure your conscience is clean?

KARL HEINZ: I only did my duty.

EVA: Then you shouldn't be afraid. Everybody says you ought to report in.

KARL HEINZ: The informers say that, to ruin me.

EVA: But an Allied officer said so too!

KARL HEINZ, *scornfully*: That's your morality! Allied officers!

*He goes off screen to left. Eva follows him (camera adjusts to her, pans and tracks, with downward tilt).*

EVA: Of course, you're not interested in our problems. As long as Papa's in the hospital there's one less mouth to feed, but tomorrow they're sending him home and we have nothing here.

*She passes him by and goes over to Edmund, who, still on his feet, has resumed his whittling.*

EDMUND: I'll get us something, now I know how it's done.

*He puts down the knife and goes off screen to left. Eva turns to Karl Heinz, now sitting behind her on the father's bed (camera pans right).*

EVA: Hear that, Karl Heinz? Hear that? Don't you realize Edmund's turning into a thief? You want him to end up in jail?

KARL HEINZ: Eva, let me alone! And go dance with your Americans!

*Exasperated, Karl Heinz gets up and goes off screen to right, leaving Eva alone (camera tilts slightly down and then pans left to Eva).*

*(Street in front of Enning's building, MS)*          132

*Edmund runs, stops (in TQ), then starts forward again (camera pulls back and simultaneously pans left). He stops again and calls.*

EDMUND: Herr Enning! Wait! Herr Enning!

ENNING *(off screen)*: What is it, Edmund?

*(Camera pans rapidly 180° around to pick up Enning and a boy going into the building, wide WF.)*

EDMUND *(off screen)*: Wait a minute! I have to tell you something!

*Enning continues on up the steps (camera tracks forward toward him) as Edmund comes on screen from left.*

ENNING: Then come back later on, or tomorrow morning.

EDMUND: It's important.

ENNING: I've got a lot to do now, I can't waste time.

*(The camera stops tracking.) Edmund has reached Enning and stops (WF), leaning against a column in front of the entrance.*

EDMUND: I'm sorry, but it's about my father.

ENNING: Well, what is it? What do you want?

EDMUND: Could I talk to you alone?

ENNING, *bending over the other boy, and caressing him*: You wait for me—all right, dear? *To Edmund*: What's happened?

EDMUND: Tomorrow they're sending my father home from

the hospital . . .

ENNING: Hm. . . .

*Enning and Edmund walk away from the building's*
*entrance along the sidewalk (camera tracks back out, HF).*
*Enning glances repeatedly at his youthful companion.*

EDMUND: . . . and we haven't got a thing in the house to
eat, see? I haven't got a job, Eva doesn't either, and
my brother still doesn't want to report to the police
so he can get a ration card.

ENNING: I know, I know, but what have I got to do with it?

EDMUND: I'm sorry, but you see, my father needs treat-
ment. Can't you help me? Tell me what I should do.

*Annoyed, Enning moves even farther away from the*
*stairs, passing to Edmund's right. Edmund follows him*
*(camera pans slightly left and tracks backward in front*
*of them).*

ENNING: But there's nothing to be done! Times are tough
for everybody, and worse for the old and weak. *He*
*stops and bends toward Edmund.* You've done what
you could. You can't fight fate.

EDMUND: But if he dies?

ENNING: If he dies, he dies! We all have to die sooner or
later. You all want to drop dead yourselves just to
save a decrepit old man?

*In the background the general is coming down the steps*
*(camera pans slightly upward). He goes over to the other*
*boy and lays a hand on his shoulder. Upon seeing the*
*general, Enning (HF) takes off his hat and makes a little*
*bow.*

ENNING: Herr General!

*(The general and the boy are on the stairs, WF)*   133

GENERAL: Is this another one of your pupils?

ENNING *(off screen)*: No, he's a young friend of mine.

GENERAL: Hm, come with me. I have a nice present for
you.

*The general slaps the boy's shoulder lightly, and they
start up the stairs together.*

*Edmund and Enning (backs to camera) look toward the
entrance. Enning is putting his hat back on as the general
and the boy disappear inside the building. Enning fiddles
nervously with the brim of his hat, looks toward the
windows of his own apartment, then hurries past Edmund
to the corner of the building (camera pans and tracks
with him to right).*   134

ENNING: Well, do you understand? No more senti-
mentality!

*Edmund comes on screen from left, approaching the barred window where Enning has stopped. Slowly he turns away from Enning (MCU). Enning continues to talk nervously, continually glancing around and upward. Then he goes off screen to left, returning on screen immediately after.*

ENNING: That's how life is. We were molded in other times. You're afraid Papa'll die? Learn from Nature: the weak are always eliminated by the strong. We must have the courage to sacrifice the weak. This is a law that not even Man can escape. What counts in a defeat like ours is to survive. *He distractedly fondles Edmund's neck.* Come, Edmund, don't be a goose. You must recognize your responsibilities. Good-bye.

*Enning goes off screen to left, leaving Edmund wondering and saddened, his head hanging (camera adjusts slightly downward).*

*(Dissolve to . . .*

*(Street, HF)* 135

*Edmund walks alone through the city streets (camera tracks left in front of him). As he approaches the hospital he stops for a moment, then resumes his walk, going off screen to left.*

*(Square in front of hospital, MS)* 136

*Edmund comes on screen from right and hurries toward the hospital. A nurse comes out of a small doorway.*

*(Dissolve to . . .*

*(Hospital corridor and ward, MCU)* 137

*Edmund comes down the corridor (camera pulls back in*

*front of him). He turns left into the ward (camera pans right) and hurries toward his father's bed (MS). Koeler is lying down.*

EDMUND: Papa!

*(Hospital ward, HF; resume on Edmund coming toward his father.)* 138

*Koeler is awake. As he sees his son, he sits up happily in bed and motions to the boy to sit down beside him. Edmund sits in a bedside chair (camera pans slightly right). Koeler takes his hand.*

KOELER: Edmund! Come, dear boy, come, sit down . . . closer . . . that's it. Give me a kiss.

*Edmund kisses his father's cheek. Koeler caresses his head, then relaxes against the headboard.*

KOELER: You're good to come see me. These four days have really fixed me up, you know? And it must have been a relief for you kids too.

EDMUND: Papa, you know that without you we. . . .

*A nurse appears to hand Koeler a thermometer (camera pans left and adjusts upward to exclude the man and the boy).*

NURSE: Shall we take your temperature today, Herr Koeler?

*She goes to the foot of the bed to get a medicine chart (camera pans and tracks left), which she brings close to Edmund.*

NURSE: This is your son?

KOELER *(off screen)*: Yes, he's my youngest.

NURSE: What a good-looking boy!

KOELER: Hm.

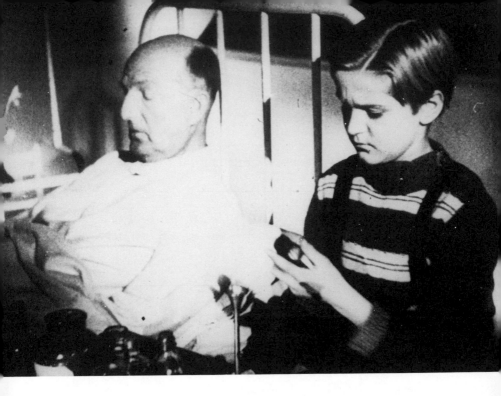

*Edmund has gotten to his feet to let the nurse by. She gestures for him to sit down again.*

NURSE: That's all right, you can sit down.

*She goes off screen to right as Edmund sits down again (camera tilts down and tracks forward; the bottles on the medicine tray are in CU).*

EDMUND: Thank you.

KOELER: Unfortunately, I'm coming back to be a burden to you. I'm no good for anything any more. How much better it'd be if I died! I've even thought of . . .

*Edmund begins to touch the bottles on the tray and picks one up.*

*(Insert: camera subjective from Edmund's viewpoint;* 139

*Edmund's hand clutching a small bottle on whose label is printed the word* GIFT *between two skulls.)*

KOELER *(off screen):* . . . ending it all for good . . .

*(Edmund, CU; the bottles are in the foreground.)* 140

*Edmund stares at the bottle in his hand.*

KOELER *(off screen):* . . . but I don't have the courage to die, I drag along in this life which has become . . .

*Koeler lies back against the headboard, his eyes closed.* 141
*(HF)*

KOELER: . . . a torment for . . . me . . .

*Edmund watches his father, then rapidly conceals the bottle in his hand.*

KOELER: . . . and for you.

*(Dissolve to . . .*

*(Koeler's room in the apartment, MS)* 142

*Karl Heinz is setting the table (CU). Koeler is lying on his bed. Eva is preparing the evening meal. She turns to hand a plate to her father, who pulls himself halfway up in bed. The room is dark because the lights have been cut off.*

EVA: Here, Papa! . . . Boys, sit down!

KARL HEINZ: Shall we move the table over?

EVA: Yes, we can see better over here.

KARL HEINZ: Edmund, help me.

*He lifts one end of the table, dimly lit by a single candle, and moves it toward the center of the room. Edmund comes on screen from right, carrying the other end of the table (camera tracks left). Eva sets a large pot on the table.*

KARL HEINZ: That's it!

EDMUND: A little farther over?

*They move the table closer to the candle over the stove, nearer the father.*

KARL HEINZ: Yes, a little bit—that's it.

*Music ends.*

EVA: Wait, Papa, I'll peel them for you.

*She takes the plate from her father, puts it on the table, and begins to peel his potatoes.*

KOELER: Just potatoes?

EVA: Unfortunately I couldn't make soup.

KOELER: You had enough time to make a little hot soup!

EVA: That's not why. I didn't have any flour or lard.

*(Eva peeling potatoes at right margin of frame; Koeler*    143
*lying in bed, HF)*

KOELER: Do you have a little tea at least?

EVA: No, that's gone too.

*She turns to him, then fills a glass with water and places
it on the table.*

KOELER: Oh, dear God, it would have been a thousand
    times better if I'd stayed in the hospital instead of
    coming back home and starting to torment you all
    again!

KOELER *(CU)*: I have to watch you live in these conditions    144
    without being able to help you. But why am I
    condemned . . .

*Eva stops peeling potatoes and comes over to Koeler's*    145
*bed (camera tilts slightly down).*

KOELER: . . . to live? Lord, why don't You take me?

EVA: No, you mustn't talk like that, Papa!

KOELER: Yes, it would be a way out, for me and for you.

*Eva returns to the table and resumes peeling the potatoes.*

EVA: Be patient, it won't always be like this.

KOELER: If only Karl Heinz had reported . . .

KOELER *(CU)*: . . . I'd hoped that while I was gone he'd    146
    have realized his responsibility. What would you
    have done if I hadn't come back?

*(Camera pans left and upward from Koeler to Eva,
MCU)*

KOELER *(off screen)*: If I'd died? Come on, tell me, Karl
    Heinz, do you want to abandon Eva and Edmund to
    their fate?

*(Camera pans left and downward to Karl Heinz, CU)*

KARL HEINZ: I never said that.

*(Camera pans left to Edmund, MCU)*

KOELER *(off screen)*: If only your mother were alive, but she's been taken away from me too. Everything's been taken from me. My money by the inflation, my children by Hitler.

*Edmund stands up to put a plate down behind him (camera pans back to right to Karl Heinz, CU).*

KOELER *(off screen)*: I should have protested, but I was too weak, like so many in my generation.

*Karl Heinz passes a plate of potatoes to Edmund (camera pans left). Edmund begins to eat, but without appetite. He is obviously upset by his father's words.*

KOELER *(off screen)*: We saw disaster coming, and we didn't stop it, and now we're suffering the consequences. Today we're paying for our mistakes, all of us! You and I both! But we have to recognize our guilt, because just grumbling doesn't solve anything.

*Edmund stands up and passes behind Karl Heinz (camera pans and tracks right and upward).*

KARL HEINZ *(off screen)*: I know, I know, Papa.

*Music begins. Edmund goes to the stove and puts on the tea kettle. Karl Heinz buries his head in his arms, folded on the table (HF; camera pulls back). Edmund returns behind Karl Heinz as Eva comes on screen from right (camera tracks right to include Koeler).*

KOELER *(off screen)*: My days are numbered, but you're still young, you can still do so well. Prove you're a man. Have the courage to report in. You'll see how everything'll be easier for you and for your family. . . .

(*on screen*) Eva and Edmund will be grateful to you for it, and I'll be proud of you.

*Eva is clearing the table. Edmund takes the lighted candle and goes out of the room.*

(*Small storeroom, HF; also shots 149, 151*)  147
*Edmund (back to camera) enters and puts the candle down on a table. He lifts up the cloth covering the table, then takes a tea strainer and fills it with tea he has taken from a shelf. He replaces the package of tea and turns to make sure no one is watching. Then he opens a drawer in the table and searches for something inside (camera pans downward). He takes a box from the drawer.*

KOELER (*off screen*): My son, you can give me new strength to live, you'll find a job, you'll get the Number Two Card. No, don't fight it, you have to stop living like a hunted animal. You have to go back to living among people, you have to go back into the world. There's nothing to be ashamed of in accepting one's fate.

(*Koeler's room; Koeler in CU; also shots 150, 152*)  148

KOELER: I was a soldier too, in the First World War.

*Edmund has taken the bottle of poison out of the box*  149.
*(camera tilts downward). He opens it, looking back toward the other room, and pours several drops into the tea strainer.*

KOELER (*off screen*): According to you all, that was just child's play, but it wasn't so for me. We too went off with our flags flying. We'd occupied half of Europe and . . .

. . . we'd gone into the heart of Russia. It seemed  150 that nothing . . .

*Edmund closes the box and puts it back in the drawer*  151

*(camera tilts upwards). He takes the tea ball, sniffs it, replaces the cloth on the table, and returns to the other room.*

KOELER *(off screen)* . . . in the world could stop us, but suddenly everything changed, first the defeat, then the revolution . . .

. . . I wept too . . .                                                            152

*In Koeler's room (MCU), Karl Heinz shifts his head side-      153
ways on his arms. He is weeping (camera pans upward
and left to include Eva and Edmund, HF, as the boy
comes in). Edmund closes the door behind him and goes
over to the sink (camera pans and tracks right). He puts
the tea strainer into a glass taken from the shelf and
begins to fill it with boiling water from the kettle.*

KOELER *(off screen):* . . . when they tore off my epaulets. No one can say I haven't been a good German, but in spite of that, as I can confess to you only now, during all these difficult years my only hope was that the Third Reich would fall and that we'd be defeated.

*Edmund brings his father the glass of tea (camera tracks
after him to right until he is in MCU). He removes the
tea strainer and, as the father pauses, hands him the glass.*

KOELER *(off screen):* I don't even want to think of how the world would have been if things had ended *(on screen)* differently.

EDMUND: Here, drink this, Papa.

KOELER: Ah, tea!

*Koeler raises himself in bed, takes the glass from Edmund,
and begins to sip the tea.*

EVA *(off screen):* You see? Edmund's found a little!

KOELER, *as he sips the tea:* Good boy! It's a little bitter,

but it's hot. It does me good. You want a little too,
Karl Heinz?

*Edmund prevents his brother from answering by pushing
the glass back to his father's mouth.*

EDMUND: No, no, Papa, I made it just for you!

KOELER, *changing the glass to his other hand in order to
caress Edmund*: You've got a good heart. Thanks!
And to you others too. I'm happy to have children
like you. I have my troubles, but I still have my children.

*Just as Koeler is finishing his tea, someone knocks vio-
lently at the door (camera pans rapidly left, from Edmund and Koeler, in MCU, to the door).*

EVA *(off screen)*: Who is it?

*Eva and Thilde stand near the door (TQ). Karl Heinz,
still sitting at the table, is at the left margin of the frame.*

KARL HEINZ *(off screen)*: Who is it?

THILDE: It's the police! They're searching house-to-house!

EVA: Oh, my God! Why?

THILDE, *to Karl Heinz*: You have to hide!

KARL HEINZ: I've had enough! I don't want to hide any
more.

*He stands up and goes out of the room, followed by Eva
and Thilde, who go off screen to left as Edmund comes on
screen from right.*

EDMUND: Karl Heinz!

*Edmund (TQ) remains alone in the middle of the room,
looking at his father. Eva comes on screen from left.
Music ends.*

*Karl Heinz rapidly makes his way through a small room*    154
*over to the window. (WF)*

*(Street in front of the building, MS from above; camera*    155
*subjective from Karl Heinz's viewpoint.)*

*A motorcycle crosses the frame as a number of policemen*
*run up.*

*Music begins. Karl Heinz draws away from the window*    156
*and begins to take off his army shirt.*

*On the street (MS) a motorcycle driven by a policeman,*    157
*with two others on the sidecar, pulls up in front of the*
*building. A police car follows. The policemen get out*
*and hurry toward the entrance.*

*(Stairway, MS)*    158
*A light is turned on, illuminating the bottom of the stairs.*
*A shadowy figure crosses the entryway on the way to the*
*door, going off screen to right.*

FIRST POLICEMAN *(off screen)*: Open up! Police! Open up!
   Police!!

TILGHER *(off screen)*: All right, all right, just a minute!
   What do you want?

*Karl Heinz runs out of the apartment and looks cau-*    159
*tiously over the stairs. (WF)*

FIRST POLICEMAN *(off screen)*: We have to search the building.

TILGHER *(off screen)*: But everything's in order here . . .

*(Stairway, looking downward from the first landing)*    160

TILGHER: . . . believe me, you're wasting your time.

FIRST POLICEMAN: Check every floor!

*Several policemen start up the stairs (camera pans left*
*after them). At the first landing they find Karl Heinz,*

*who comes on screen from right (HF). Music ends.*

KARL HEINZ: Look, I don't have any papers.

FIRST POLICEMAN, *to the one following him*: See what this is about.

SECOND POLICEMAN: You haven't got any papers?

KARL HEINZ: No.

*The first policeman, followed by a woman in uniform, goes on ahead and off screen to right.*

SECOND POLICEMAN: What did you do with them?

KARL HEINZ: I burned them.

SECOND POLICEMAN: Then come to the station with us. Let's go!

KARL HEINZ: Yes. But can I tell my family?

SECOND POLICEMAN: Yes, but hurry up, we haven't got any time to waste.

KARL HEINZ: Thanks.

*Accompanied by the policeman, Karl Heinz goes up the next flight of stairs (camera pans right and then upward, WF). They knock at the door of Rademaker's apartment.*

WOMAN *(off screen)*: Who is it?

*(The corridor in the apartment, WF)*                                161

SECOND POLICEMAN *(off screen)*: Police!

*Karl Heinz and the policeman walk in as the Rademakers come forward from the back of the room.*

SECOND POLICEMAN, *to Karl Heinz*: Your family lives here?

KARL HEINZ: No, they live in the kitchen.

SECOND POLICEMAN: Go on, hurry up! Turn on the lights!

*Karl Heinz comes toward the camera and goes off screen to left. The policeman moves into the room, followed by the Rademakers.*

FRAU RADEMAKER: They've cut off our lights.

SECOND POLICEMAN: Really?

FRAU RADEMAKER: But it wasn't our fault, you know.

SECOND POLICEMAN: Whose apartment is this?

*Blanke comes on screen from left. As the policeman talks, he follows Karl Heinz, and is followed in turn by the Rademakers.*

RADEMAKER: Mine.

SECOND POLICEMAN: Who else lives here?

RADEMAKER: All women, my dear sergeant.

SECOND POLICEMAN, *to Blanke (HF)*: Profession?

BLANKE: Dancer.

FRAU RADEMAKER: Sure, she's a belly-dancer!

*The policeman goes off screen to left as Rademaker comes forward (into HF) and points out the various rooms (camera tracks along with him and pans left).*

RADEMAKER: Here we have a former expatriate with her daughter, and here there's a pregnant woman—

FRAU RADEMAKER: Her husband's been a prisoner for three years!

*Rademaker turns and goes off screen as his wife comes on from the right. Karl Heinz appears from the door in the rear to the left. Edmund runs after him. (WF)*

KARL HEINZ: Here I am. I'm ready.

EDMUND: No, Karl Heinz, stay with us. *To the policeman*:

He hasn't done anything wrong.

*The policeman comes on screen from left (camera pans slightly to right to center on all three).*

SECOND POLICEMAN: Then he has nothing to be afraid of. Come on!

*He goes off screen to right, followed by Karl Heinz (camera pans right to Edmund).*

EDMUND: Karl Heinz!

KARL HEINZ: Don't worry, it'll be all right, you'll see.

*(Camera pans downward and to left, centering on Edmund.) Music begins. Edmund turns and goes slowly back toward his room. He hesitates for a moment before entering (camera pans left with him).*

*The motorcycle and the police car go off.*                162

*(Corridor, WF)*                                             163
*Eva rushes out of her father's room and into her own (camera pans and tracks left). Then she comes back (toward the camera) to call the expatriate (camera pans left). Finally she runs back to her father's room.*

EVA: Herr Rademaker! *To expatriate*: Please come!

EXPATRIATE: What is it? What's happened?

WOMEN'S VOICES *(off screen)*: What's happened? Come, did you hear? What happened?

EVA: Help! Come quick!

EXPATRIATE, *coming toward Eva (HF)*: Eva, what is it?    164

THILDE: Eva, what is it?

WOMEN'S VOICES *(off screen)*: Eva, what is it? Would somebody tell me what's going on here?

EVA, *panting*: Come here! My father. . . .

*Without stopping, Eva hurries toward the Rademakers'
room (camera pans right). Tilgher comes on screen. Rademaker, his daughter, and his wife, who lights their way
with a candle, come forward from the end of the corridor.*

EVA: Come quick! My father's not moving! I'm afraid—
    I'm afraid he's dead.

*(Dissolve to . . .*

*(Koeler's room)*                                                      165

*Eva and all the other women living in the apartment*     166
*stand around Koeler's bed (HF). He gives no sign of life.
Tilgher is bending over him. He straightens up and turns
to Eva (camera tracks out).*

TILGHER: The old man's dead. There's nothing to be done
    for him.

BLANKE: Take it easy, Eva.

THILDE: He couldn't last, in that state.

EVA: And Karl Heinz isn't here!

EXPATRIATE: Come with me, it's better if you don't stay
    here.

*She puts her arm around Eva and leads her out of the
room. They go off screen to left, followed by Thilde. The
Rademakers move forward.*

BLANKE: But we should at least call a doctor.

TILGHER: A waste of money. No need for a doctor now.

RADEMAKER: There's only one thing to do—hurry up with
    the funeral.

TILGHER: The coffin'll cost an arm and a leg.

RADEMAKER: If worse comes to worst, we can use a paper sack.

FRÄULEIN RADEMAKER: But that's awful! When I die I don't want to be buried in a sack!

FRAU RADEMAKER: Don't say such silly things!

RADEMAKER: What are you still doing here? Get back to your room!

*The daughter goes off screen to left.*

TILGHER: Well, what shall we do? Coffin or no coffin?

RADEMAKER: Forget the coffin. Let's just have him taken away as soon as possible.

BLANKE: Wouldn't it be better to put him out on the terrace?

FRAU RADEMAKER: Don't touch him! What if he had a contagious disease?

TILGHER: What d'you mean disease? He's dead of hunger, not disease. Come on, let's carry him out! *Tilgher begins to remove the bedclothes.*

*Edmund in the corridor. (TQ)* 167

TILGHER *(off screen)*: Come on, give me a hand, Herr Rademaker!

RADEMAKER *(off screen)*: Here I come—come on! *To his wife*: You go ahead with the candle so we can see.

FRAU RADEMAKER *(off screen)*: All right, all right.

*Edmund listens outside the room. He paces nervously up and down, leans against a wall, then turns (TQ) and comes toward the camera. Then he returns toward the wall, hesitates, turns again, and goes toward the room (camera tracks and pans left). At the door (in HF) he is forced to step back as Frau Rademaker comes out of the room, carrying the candle. Tilgher and Rademaker follow her, carrying the corpse (camera tracks right as they pass by Edmund).*

TILGHER: And I thought he was heavier.

FRAU RADEMAKER *(off screen)*: Fine chance, with what we eat!

*Blanke leaves the group and approaches Edmund to comfort him, but he slips away and goes down the corridor. (TQ)*

BLANKE: Courage, Edmund!

FRAU RADEMAKER: Blanke, what are you up to? Aren't you coming?

BLANKE: Here I come. *She goes off screen to right.*

*A dark look on his face, the boy fiddles distractedly with a can (HF; camera tilts up at him).*   168

*(Another room, MS)*   169
*The body has been set down. The adults discuss what is to be done.*

FRAU RADEMAKER: What'll they do with the clothes?

TILGHER: The gravedigger'll take care of that.

BLANKE: That old pair of pajamas is no good now anyway.

FRAU RADEMAKER: Yes, but underneath he has an undershirt, and the socks are wool. *She pulls back the lapel of the pajamas, then indicates the socks.*

*Edmund (CU) stands in the corridor (shorter view of shot 168).*   170

BLANKE *(off screen)*: Really?

*(Fade-out)*

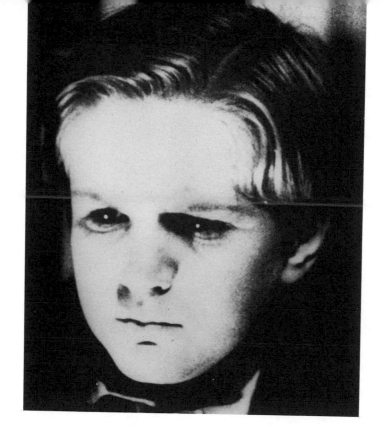

*(Street in front of the building, in the morning, LS)*     171
*A streetcar comes down the street (camera pans right). It
passes in front of the camera and stops. Karl Heinz jumps
out and hurries toward the building (camera pans and
tracks right with him).*

*(Dissolve to . . .*

*(Corridor in the apartment, MS)*     172
*Karl Heinz runs happily into the Koelers' room, closes
the door behind him, comes toward his sister, and embraces her (camera pans left).*

KARL HEINZ: Eva! I'm free!

EVA, *weeping*: Karl Heinz!

*Music begins.*

KARL HEINZ: Eva, what's happened?!

EVA: Karl Heinz, Papa's dead.

KARL HEINZ: Dead!

*He begins to weep and lays his head on his sister's shoulder. Touched, Eva strokes his hair.*

EVA, *weeping*: Yes, dead. Papa, poor Papa!

KARL HEINZ, *weeping*: And I was thinking how happy he'd be to know I was free!

EVA: You've carried out his wish—that should console you. Come see him.

*They go off to their left (camera pans and tracks left).*

*(The room where the dead Koeler is lying, MCU; camera*    173
*pans and tracks left.)*

*Karl Heinz comes toward the table, stops, and lifts up the blanket that covers the corpse. Eva follows him, coming on screen from right. All the women of the apartment gather round. Edmund comes up beside Karl Heinz, on the opposite side from Eva. Karl Heinz replaces the blanket and puts out his hand to caress Edmund, but the boy pulls back.*

KARL HEINZ: Poor Edmund!

EDMUND: They let you go?

KARL HEINZ: Yes, I'm free now.

*Tilgher comes on screen from left to stand beside Edmund.*

TILGHER *(off screen)*: We've already made arrangements for the funeral *(on screen)* and for the coffin.

KARL HEINZ: Thank you. When are they taking him away?

*Karl Heinz moves toward Tilgher, while Eva goes off screen (camera pans 180° to left). They all join at the foot of the table. Eva's girl friend takes Karl Heinz's arm affectionately.*

TILGHER: Who knows? Tomorrow, or next week.

FRIEND: But you can't stay here now.

EVA: Where could we go?

FRIEND: There's room for all of you at my place.

*Edmund is beside Eva's friend, who still holds Karl Heinz's arm (Eva's back is to camera at margin of frame).*

EVA: Edmund, go get your things.

EDMUND: I'm not coming with you.

KARL HEINZ: What? You want to stay all by yourself?

EDMUND: Why not? I've got a place I can go to.

EVA: But, Edmund, who'll take care of you?

EDMUND: That's none of your business.

KARL HEINZ: Who do you think you are anyway? You're still a child.

EDMUND: How come you didn't think of that before, when I had to go out and get food for everybody here?

*As he speaks these last words, Edmund leaves the group and goes off screen to right. Blanke moves into his place. They are all dumbfounded as they watch Edmund go off.*

EVA: Edmund!

*She starts to follow him, but Karl Heinz holds her back.*

KARL HEINZ: No, let him go. He'll come back as soon as he feels lonely.

*(Fade-out)*

*(Street at night, MS)* 174

*Edmund is climbing onto a block of stone (camera pans upward). He steps to the next stone (camera pans slightly right), then returns to the first (camera returns left). He hops to the ground, and then up the steps of a completely wrecked fountain (camera tracks forward). He begins to take giant steps along its base (camera tracks left after him, TQ).*

*(Resume on Edmund giant-stepping along the fountain, 175 WF; camera tracks left first after him, then in front of him, MS)*

*As he reaches a broken spot in the base of the fountain, he climbs up onto the edge, balancing as he walks along*

*it. Then he jumps down and continues his game, first
outside, then inside the fountain. Finally he comes down
again, distractedly kicks some stones, looks around, and
climbs out of the fountain (camera follows his movements
with one tracking shot combined with various pans and
shifts).*

*(Fade-out)*

*(Wipe to right reveals bridge, MCU; nighttime)*  176

*Edmund walks slowly over a bridge, dragging his right
hand along the rail. He stops for a moment, then begins
walking again.*

*(Wipe to left)*

*(Street, CU)*  177
*Edmund comes on screen from right, raising his head to
look at something ahead of him.*

*A pile of rubble blocks the doorway of a building (MS).*  178
*A woman climbs over the obstacle and helps a man up.*

WOMAN: But I told you to be careful. Come on, I'll give
you a hand.

MAN: Thanks. Good night!

WOMAN: Good night!

*They separate.*

*Edmund stops to blow his nose, then walks off screen to*  179
*left. (CU)*

*Edmund heads for the doorway from which the man and*  180
*woman had appeared. He passes by the woman without
a word, climbs over the rubble, and enters the building as
the woman goes off screen to left. (LS)*

*(Corridor of building, LS; a row of rooms full of rubble;*  181

*also shots 183, 186)*

*Edmund runs toward the rear, climbs atop a heap of rubble, and looks around (TQ) as if to discover from where some boys' voices are coming.*

BOY *(off screen)*: . . . then, when the husband found out that Rita was two-timing him, he swore like a sailor.

BOY *(off screen)*: I believe it, I believe it!

*(A room, MS; also shots 185, 187)* 182

*A group of youngsters, about seventeen years old, including Joe and Christel, are talking in an improvised bedroom.*

BOY: But he sure took his time finding out about it.

*Edmund climbs down from the rubble and walks along* 183
*the wall (WF; camera pans left to HF).*

BOY *(off screen)*: No, he knew all about it for a long time, but it was a good thing for him.

BOY *(off screen)*: Of course he knew! He's been out of work for three months . . .

*Edmund stops to listen. (HF)* 184

BOY *(off screen)*: . . . but they manage to eat all the same.

*Music fades out.*

CHRISTEL *(off screen)*: Oh, will you get your hands out of here!

BOY: What's the matter, you ticklish? 185

*One of the boys gets up to pester Christel.*

BOY: The little virgin! You forget . . .

*Edmund moves away from the wall and enters the room.* 186

*(MCU)*

BOY *(off screen)*: . . . you were the one who came to me    187
those nights behind the shanties?

*Edmund enters the room, calling Christel. He clutches her arm and tries to pull her out, but she resists, and is also held back by the other boys, who push the intruder (HF) out again.*

EDMUND: Christel!

CHRISTEL: Why'd you come here? Go away!

EDMUND: Come on, let's go!

BOY: We don't want any babies around here!

EDMUND: Come with me!

BOYS: Get out of here! Go on, scat! What d'you want? Out!

EDMUND: Let me in! Let me in! Make her come, let me in!

*The boys resist Edmund's efforts. Christel comes forward (HF) to have a better look.*

BOY: Come on, get out of here!

BOY, *to Christel*: Aren't you going to defend your boy friend?

CHRISTEL: I don't have anything to do with little kids.

*The boys laugh, surrounding Christel. (HF)*

*(Wipe to right)*

*(Street in front of Edmund's building, CU)*    188

*Music begins. Edmund walks along (camera shoots slightly downward, tracks and pans right). He crosses the street after a few moments' hesitation, then enters his building. (MS)*

*(Stairway of Edmund's building, LS)* 189

*After a few moments, Edmund succeeds in turning on the light in the entranceway, then begins to run up the stairs (camera pans and tracks left and downward with him). He slows down at the first landing (camera tracks out and pans right). He continues on up, slowly and cautiously. At the doorway of the apartment he starts to ring the bell, then changes his mind and sits down on the top step.*

*Frowning, Edmund (CU) covers his eyes with his hand. The light suddenly goes out. Edmund is startled, then realizes that it has been turned off by the automatic timer. He stands up to turn the hallway switch.* 190

*(Resume on Edmund standing up, MS)* 191

*He turns on the switch near the doorway to the apartment, then slowly starts back down the stairs, looking repeatedly backward toward the landing (camera tracks and pans left). He gradually takes courage and takes the last flight of stairs at a run (camera pans right and tracks). Still running, he goes out the front door as if sloughing off a burden.*

*(Street, MS)* 192

*Edmund runs out of the doorway and into the street (camera is rather high, pointing down; it adjusts slightly downward). Edmund turns to gaze at the windows of his building. He stops (HF), stares straight ahead, then goes off to the right.*

*(Fade-out)*

*(Street on which Enning lives, the next day, LS)* 193

*Edmund runs along the sidewalk in front of Enning's building, then crosses into the street and stops (in front of*

*the camera). He looks up toward Enning's balcony (camera pans upward and to right).*

EDMUND: Herr Enning! Herr Enning!

*Seeing no one, Edmund moves to his right, to the side of the building (camera pans right and tracks with him).*

EDMUND: Herr Enning!

*Edmund returns to the front of the building as Enning appears on the balcony.*

ENNING: Oh, it's you? What is it?

EDMUND: Can I talk to you?

ENNING: Of course, come on up!

*Edmund runs toward the doorway (camera pans down-*

*ward and to right, and tracks).*

*(Wipe to right)*

*(Enning's room, HF)*                                                    194

*Enning is seated in the armchair, reading. He turns as
he hears knocking at the door.*

ENNING: Come in!

*Edmund enters, closes the door behind him, and comes
slowly over to Enning, who motions for him to sit down.*

EDMUND, *seriously*: Excuse me, Herr Enning, I have to
talk to you.

ENNING: What is it? Why are you so pale? Come, dear
boy, sit down over here by me.

*(RA; resume on Edmund sitting down, facing Enning,*     195
*who is on left margin of frame, MCU)*

ENNING: That's a boy! Now tell me, what's up?

EDMUND: Herr Enning, it's done.

ENNING: It's done?

EDMUND: I've killed my father.

*(RA)*                                                                   196
*Staggered, Enning jumps up, dropping the book he has
been holding.*

ENNING: You? How could you?

EDMUND: But you ordered me to do it.                             197

ENNING: Me? I never told you that!                               198

*Enning violently cuffs Edmund, who in turn bites*      199
*Enning's hand. (MCU)*

ENNING: You're mad! You're a monster! *Edmund bites*

*him.* Oww!

*(RA)* 200
*Edmund breaks free of Enning and, suddenly conscious
of the meaning of his act, flees to the center of the
room (camera pans right). Overwhelmed, he covers his
face with his arm, then moves toward the window (camera
pans right) and goes off screen to right. (HF)*

ENNING: Edmund! Edmund!

*Edmund comes on screen from left and flings himself* 201
*down on the balcony step, weeping. Enning follows and
tries to remove the boy's arms from his face and to lift
him to his feet. (MS)*

ENNING: Edmund, get up! Please, say something! How
could you do such a thing? Have you gone crazy?
Look, if anyone finds out, I—I never said a word to
you, understand, I never said a thing! Come on,
get up!

*(Resume on Enning standing up, TQ)* 202

*He has managed to lift Edmund to his feet, but the boy
struggles wildly to pull away and finally escapes off screen
to left. Enning, still thunderstruck, tries to stop the boy,
then runs to the balcony to call down to him. (TQ)*

ENNING: Edmund, take it easy! Don't act like that! Don't
act like that! Listen to me! We'll think about what
to do. Believe me, I'm fond of you, dear boy! Don't
be this way! Edmund! Edmund! Edmund!

*Music ends.*

*(Street, LS; camera subjective from Enning's viewpoint,* 203
*showing Edmund running out of the building.)*

*Edmund hurries across the street (camera pans upward
and then left) and goes off down the far sidewalk until
he disappears. (ELS)*

*(Wipe to left)*

*(Street, HF)*

*Edmund walks along (camera pans right and then tracks forward in front of him).*

*He watches some children playing farther ahead of him (at the end of the tracking shot, camera pans right to include, in LS, a deserted, completely destroyed street). Some younger children are playing ball (CU). Edmund makes his way among them (to WF). Their ball passes between Edmund's feet. The temptation is irresistible. Edmund chases the ball (HF) and kicks it toward the other children. They miss it and chase after it (camera pans left).*

EDMUND: Can I play with you?

CHILDREN: No, get out of here! No! We want to play by
ourselves!

EDMUND: I'll show you how to do it.

*The children kick the ball. Edmund chases after them
from the other side of the street (camera pans right). He
runs after the ball, but a girl swifter than he reaches it
first and goes off screen to right with the other youngsters.*

CHILDREN: No, no! Leave us alone! No! Give me the ball!
Come on, let's go! Yes, yes, let's go! Come on!

*Alone, Edmund starts walking again down the middle of
the street (camera pans left).*

*(RA)*                                                       205
*Music begins. Edmund continues walking (LS), then stops
(TQ) and turns to watch the children, who have resumed
their game. He watches for a moment, then resumes his
own aimless wandering (camera pans right, tracks beside
him, then pans right again). He goes off down a rubble-
filled alley. Music ends.*

*(Dissolve to . . .*

*(Street, MCU)*                                              206

*Edmund walks along at an increasingly rapid pace (the
camera, tilting upward, pulls back in front of him). His
face is in shadow. Suddenly the sun comes out, and
simultaneously the music of an organ peels out. Surprised,
Edmund stops to identify the source of the sound. Then
he goes farther on to have a better view of the steeple
of a ruined, roofless church (camera pans right and
upward with Edmund until the entire church structure
is included in the shot).*

*(Church, MS)*                                               207

*In the ruins of the church, atop a pile of rubble in the
roofless apse, a priest is sounding the organ.*

*(The avenue flanking the church, with the ruins of the* 208
*city in the background and on the margins, LS; camera*
*pans right and, upon reaching the church, upward.)*

*Passersby stop to listen to the organ.*

*Edmund hurries away, followed by the sound of the* 209
*organ (HF; camera tracks in front of him). Organ music*
*dissolves into music of next shot.*

*(Wipe to right)*

*(Street, MCU)* 210

*Edmund hurries along. His attention is caught by some*
*marks and spots on the pavement. He begins to play at*
*setting his feet in special patterns, then improvises a game*
*of hopscotch (camera pulls back in front of him, follows*
*after him, tracks after and in front of him, and circles*
*around him). For a moment, evidently overcome by emo-*
*tion, he sits down on the sidewalk (camera tilts down on*

*him) and passes a hand across his forehead. Then, getting hold of himself, he stands up again (camera tilts up) and resumes his meandering.*

*(Dissolve to . . .*

*(Edmund's street, LS)* 211

*Edmund (moving toward the camera) continues his game of hopscotch (camera tracks out in front of him, then pans right, tracks beside him, and pans right after him). He stops at last in front of his building. Traffic moves along the busy street; there are other pedestrians on the sidewalk.*

*(Edmund's building, LS)* 212

*Edmund enters the building across the street. (TQ)* 213

*(Entranceway of building, MS; resume on Edmund enter-* 214
*ing the building, TQ)*

*He makes his way among piles of rubble, stumbles, and leans against the wall. He notices a piece of scrap iron that vaguely resembles a pistol (camera pans right, tracks laterally with him, and pans right again). Edmund (MCU) picks up the iron scrap and twists it free from a piece of wire. He leans against the wall and contemplates his new toy, pretending to pull the trigger, then points it at his head and pretends to shoot again. He goes off screen to right.*

EDMUND: Bang, bang, bang!

*(Stairway, MS; the building seems to be under construc-* 215
*tion rather than bombed-out—the steps have not yet been laid on the cement stairway.)*

*Edmund runs on screen from left and with effort makes his way up the first flight of stairs (camera pans upward*

*to left). He continues rapidly up the second flight, then
goes off screen to right.*

*(Resume on Edmund's appearance farther up the stair-
way, MS)*     216

*(Resume on Edmund leaning against the wall, MS)*     217

*He uses his hands to pull himself up to the top of the
flight of stairs.*

*(Apartment under construction, MS)*     218

*Edmund runs up the last few steps and decides to stop,
although the stairway continues up another flight. He
walks along the railing (camera pans right and tracks
with him) toward the vast empty area, which has not
yet been subdivided into rooms. A line of bare concrete
pillars stretches down the floor, onto which the empty
windows project rectangles of sunlight. Edmund turns
back for a moment, kicks at a brick, then decides to enter
the apartment. He goes off screen to right.*

*Edmund comes on screen from left and passes in front of
a window. The sight of his shadow on the floor gives him
an idea, and after a moment's hesitation he pretends to
shoot at it with his imaginary pistol. (MS)*     219

EDMUND: Bang, bang, bang!

*He hops over the band of light shining on the floor and
goes off screen to right.*

*Edmund comes on screen from left and leans over the
sill of a window on the dark side of the building. He
pretends to shoot out toward the windows of the building
across the street. (TQ)*     220

EDMUND: Bang, bang, bang!

*He lays the toy pistol down on the windowsill, picks up
a stone, and throws it against the wall of the building*

*opposite. He picks up his toy pistol and goes off screen
to right.*

*Edmund's wanderings have taken him into another room.*  221
*He stops beside a large hole in the floor, leans down to
look through it, and spits through it almost as if to check
the depth. Then he begins walking about again, playing
with the imaginary pistol. (WF)*

*Hearing a truck on the street outside, Edmund goes over*  222
*to the window. (TQ)*

*Edmund looks out the window, standing on tiptoe to see*  223
*better. The wall is on the left margin of frame. (MCU)*

*(Street in front of Edmund's building, LS)*  224
*A truck loaded with coffins comes down the street below
(camera pans left, and stops in front of Edmund's building). There are few pedestrians on the street. The truck
driver gets out, enters the building, and immediately*

*comes out again with Tilgher, who, after a few words with the driver, steps a little away from the building, cups his hands, and calls upward.*

TILGHER: Herr Rademaker . . .

*Rademaker's daughter looks out from a window. (LS)* 225

TILGHER *(off screen):* . . . the truck's here!

FRÄULEIN RADEMAKER: Better go call . . .

*Edmund watches from the building opposite. (MCU)* 226

FRÄULEIN RADEMAKER *(off screen):* . . . his kids.

TILGHER *(off screen):* I'll go right away!

*(Street in front of Edmund's building, LS)* 227

*Two men start to carry one of the coffins into the building. A tractor passes by the truck just as Tilgher runs to call the Koelers (camera subjective from Edmund's viewpoint).*

*(Resume on tractor passing, LS from below)* 228

*The men have just entered the building with the coffin; Tilgher has gone off toward Eva's friend's home (camera pans slightly to right with him).*

*Edmund continues to watch the action below. (MCU)* 229

*The two men come out of the building carrying the coffin toward the truck. (LS)* 230

*Edmund watches. (MCU)* 231

*(Street in front of Edmund's building, LS)* 232

*The two men have loaded the coffin onto the truck; they rapidly get back in and drive off in a cloud of dust raised by the passing of a number of tractors. Tilgher, Eva, and Karl Heinz run down the street, coming on screen from right (camera follows them with slight pan to left).*

*(Street, MS)* 233

*Realizing that the truck is now out of range, Karl Heinz stops (TQ). Tilgher stops too, behind him. After a moment, Eva and her two girl friends, dressed in black, join them.*

TILGHER *(to girls)*: Too late!

KARL HEINZ *(to Eva)*: But where's Edmund!

*He moves toward Eva (camera adjusts downward).*

EVA: Where's he gone?

*She looks up at the windows of her building, from which the Rademakers are observing the scene. She holds her hat to prevent it from falling off.*

EVA: Have you seen Edmund?

*She turns toward the street and shouts.*

EVA: Edmund!!

*Tilgher goes back into the building, going off screen to left.*

*Edmund (TQ) quickly steps away from the window as he*     234
*hears his name being called. As Eva's cries continue,*
*Edmund draws further and further back into the room,*
*as if frightened of being discovered.*

EVA *(off screen)*: Edmund! Edmund!!

*Edmund crosses to the other side of the room (camera*
*pans right after him) and looks out the window at the*
*rear. (TQ)*

EVA *(off screen)*: Edmund! Edmund!!

*Edmund moves further to his right and leans against the*
*next window (WF; camera pans right). He is facing half-*
*way toward the window and nervously taps the sill with*
*a piece of brick. Eva continues to call him, but Edmund*
*does not move.*

EVA *(off screen)*: Edmund! Edmund!!

*(Street in front of Edmund's building, MS)*     235

*The small group goes off. Comforted by one of her*
*friends, Eva continues to call her brother, repeatedly*
*turning to look back, almost in tears.*

EVA: Edmund! *(weeping)* Edmund!!

*Karl Heinz follows her with the other friend on his arm;*
*they are heading back down the street (camera pans right,*
*accompanying them down the street into LS).*

*Edmund (HF) moves through the empty rooms of the*     236
*building, now and again looking out of the windows as if*
*to watch the departure of his brother and sister (camera*
*pans right with him, and pans right again). He notices a*
*beam projecting through a hole in the floor. He circles*
*around it, puts his imaginary pistol in his pocket, and*
*sits down on the edge of the hole—his legs dangling in*

*the air (camera tracks forward). With a mechanical gesture he brushes off his jacket, which has gotten dusty. Then he stands up again, slips off the jacket, and hangs it on the end of the beam (camera pans upward and to left). He sits down again on the edge of the hole (camera pans back down and right, with accompanying track right). After a few moments, he pushes off and slides down the iron beam to the floor beneath, disappearing from the bottom edge of the frame.*

*Edmund appears at the top edge of the frame (camera pans right and downward as he slows down), holding the edges of the beam, and comes to a stop. He looks around.*    237

*(The upper facade of Edmund's building, LS)*    238

*Edmund slowly climbs off his improvised slide and goes to look out one of the windows (camera tracks along with him in CU, then tracks and pans to right after him). He gazes (HF) at the half-destroyed building opposite.*    239

*(The lower facade of Edmund's building, LS)*    240

*Edmund gazes stonily at his old building (MCU). His emotion gets the better of him, and he covers his face with his hand, squeezing his eyes shut. The screeching sound of a streetcar lacerates his eardrums.*    241

*(Street in front of Edmund's building, LS from above) The streetcar brakes with a deafening screech.*    242

*Edmund stares out the window, then closes his eyes and throws himself out.*    243

*(Street in front of Edmund's building, MS; camera stationary)*    244

*Edmund is falling through the air.*

*Edmund continues falling (LS; camera pans downward until he disappears at the bottom edge of frame). The expatriate, watching from the street, screams in horror.*    245

*Edmund crashes to the ground and lies still (MS). He* 246
*has fallen onto an area free of rubble—separated from the*
*sidewalk by a low wall.*

*The expatriate screams again.*

*The expatriate (MS) races across the street and looks over* 247
*the wall. Then she steps back and passes over a gap in*
*the wall into the inner area, climbing over piles of rubble*
*and twisted wire (camera pulls back and pans right,*
*following her movements). She moves around Edmund's*
*body, kneels down beside him (camera pans downward,*
*to HF), and raises his head.*

EXPATRIATE: Edmund! Edmund!!

*Overwhelmed, she gently lays his head back down and*
*leans back against the low wall.*

*Edmund is lying diagonally to the frame (WF), with the* 248
*horrified expatriate beside him. A streetcar passes along*
*the street (camera pans upward with it until the two*
*figures are cut out as it halts in front of a background*
*of ruins).*

*(Fade-out)*

## THE END